Christian Ritualizing
and the Baptismal Process

Princeton Theological Monograph Series

K. C. Hanson, Charles M. Collier, D. Christopher Spinks,
and Robin Parry, Series Editors

Recent volumes in the series:

Sammy Alfaro
Divino Compañero: Toward a Hispanic Pentecostal Christology

David L. Balch
Finding A Woman's Place: Essays in Honor of Carolyn Osiek

Paul W. Chilcote
*Making Disciples in a World Parish:
Global Perspectives on Mission & Evangelism*

Eric G. Flett
*Persons, Powers, and Pluralities:
Toward a Trinitarian Theology of Culture*

Vladimir Kharlamov
Theosis: Deification in Christian Theology, Volume Two

Mitzi J. Smith
*The Literary Construction of the Other in the Acts of the Apostles:
Charismatics, the Jews, and Women*

Jon Paul Sydnor
*Ramanuja and Schleiermacher:
Toward a Constructive Comparative Theology*

Philip D. Wingeier-Rayo
*Where Are the Poor?: A Comparison of the Ecclesial Base Communities
and Pentecostalism—A Case Study in Cuernavaca, Mexico*

Christian Ritualizing and the Baptismal Process

Liturgical Explorations toward a Realized Baptismal Ecclesiology

SUSAN MARIE SMITH

With a Foreword by Louis Weil

☙PICKWICK *Publications* · Eugene, Oregon

CHRISTIAN RITUALIZING AND THE BAPTISMAL PROCESS
Liturgical Explorations toward a Realized Baptismal Ecclesiology

Princeton Theological Monograph Series 174

Copyright © 2012 Susan Marie Smith. All rights reserved. Except for brief quotations in critical publications or reviews, no part of this book may be reproduced in any manner without prior written permission from the publisher. Write: Permissions, Wipf and Stock Publishers, 199 W. 8th Ave., Suite 3, Eugene, OR 97401.

Pickwick Publications
An Imprint of Wipf and Stock Publishers
199 W. 8th Ave., Suite 3
Eugene, OR 97401

www.wipfandstock.com

ISBN 13: 978-1-60899-741-1

Cataloging-in-Publication data:

Smith, Susan Marie.

    Christian ritualizing and the baptismal process : liturgical explorations toward a realized baptismal ecclesiology / Susan Marie Smith ; with a foreword by Louis Weil.

    xiv + 272 pp. ; 23 cm. — Includes bibliographical references and index.

    Princeton Theological Monograph Series 174

    ISBN 13: 978-1-60899-741-1

    1. Baptism. 2. Baptism—History of Doctrines. I. Title. II. Series.

BV811.3 S59 2012

Manufactured in the U.S.A.

Contents

Foreword—Louis Weil / *vii*

Acknowledgments / *xi*

Abbreviations / *xiv*

PART ONE: Inherited Expectations of Baptismal Efficacy in the Ongoing Lives of the Baptized

1. "After the Water the Fire": Experiencing the Spirit of the Baptismal Process after Baptism / 3

2. Augustine on Baptism: Holy Spirit and Heart Conversion are Essential / 14

3. Aquinas on Baptism: It's about the Priest, Not the People; It's about Christ, Not the Spirit. (Or Is It?) / 21

4. Calvin on Baptism: Two Perspectives on Sacramentality and the Church / 35

PART TWO: Further Up and Further In: Historical and Theological Patterns of Progressing into Christ

∼ Turning to Part Two / 57

5. Baptismal Experience in the Early Church: Changing One's Lifestyle / 60

6. The Catechumenal Process: A Conversionary Rhythm Progressed by Ritual / 84

7. Theology of the Baptized as Growing and Responding: Theosis and Response-Giving / 105

8. Stages of Faith Development: Maturing in Christ / 139

PART THREE: Making Rituals for Baptismal Fulfillment and the Enlivening of the Church

    ∽   Turning to Part Three / 175

   9   Ritual Theory and Christian Ritualization: The Design of Ritual Strategies / 178

  10   Praxological Becoming and Ritual Competence: A Call for Baptismal Ingemination / 193

  11   Five Principles for Christian Ritualizing in the Baptismal Process: Making Rites for Life Passage, Healing, and Vocational Change / 214

  12   The One and the Many: Personal Rites for Building the Body / 233

Bibliography / 245

Index / 265

Foreword

THE RECOVERY OF THE CENTRAL ROLE THAT BAPTISM IS UNDERSTOOD to play in the Christian life has been a major development in the church during the past several decades. This recovery affects far more than merely the norms for the celebration of the Christian rites of Initiation. For the average person in the pew, the most obvious change has been the shift from the common practice of scheduling baptism as a quasi-private event concerning only the family and godparents of the child to the establishment of having the rite of baptism take place at the primary Sunday liturgy, with the entire congregation present. This one change alone signaled that baptism is not a private event understood to effect the salvation of the child as one individual, to a context in which the clear implication is that this rite is related to the life of the church as a whole.

Yet this is only one aspect of the developments related to the recovery of a sense of the fundamental role of baptism in the church's life. This recovery is related to our understanding of the Eucharist as well. Our understanding of Sunday as the preeminent day of the Eucharist because of its being the day of our Lord's resurrection, reinforces the link to baptism since it is in baptism that all of the baptized are united with the death and resurrection of Christ. In that sense, the Sunday Eucharist is the weekly renewal of our baptismal identity. The memorial at the heart of all forms of the Eucharistic Prayer is the remembrance of his death and resurrection, which is proclaimed in each form of the prayer and with which the whole body of believers is united in its own self-offering: "Recalling his death, resurrection, and ascension, we offer you these gifts." Our oblation of the bread and wine in the eucharistic action is at the same time the offering of "ourselves, our souls and bodies."

We should note also that the recovery of the centrality of baptism has played an important role in the renewal of the understanding of ministry in the life of the church. For centuries, "ministry" was identified almost entirely with the work of the ordained ministers of the church. A major aspect of the recovery of the significance of baptism has been a growing awareness that all the members of the church are, by virtue of their baptism, called to the work of ministry. This does not devalue the importance of the ministries of the ordained, but it sees them within the larger context of the ministries of all members of the church according to the particular gifts of each member, all these gifts serving to build up the common life of all the baptized. The ministries of the ordained bishops, priests, and deacons relate to a particular aspect of the Christian life linked to the celebration of Word and Sacrament. That is the specific area of responsibility which ordination places upon the candidates when they are ordained.

All of this suggests that baptism is not merely a past event in the life of each Christian but rather it continues to operate in shaping the context of daily living. The past ritual event is thus embodied in a life-long process, so that daily each Christian is called to live into their baptism as their life unfolds. This suggests that baptism begins a process of continual growth which culminates in a Christian's final oblation at the time of their physical death. In this perspective, the entire life of a Christian is lived within the framework which baptism creates.

This renewed understanding of baptism links us to an ancient doctrine that has received long overdue attention in recent decades, a doctrine known among the early Fathers both east and west as *entheosis* or "deification." Without question, this term can cause anxiety, and yet it is a well-established teaching that relates particularly to a renewed understanding of baptism. Irenaeus is thought to have been the first to have expressed it: "God made himself man that man might become God."[1] This teaching is echoed in the writings of Athanasius, Gregory Nazianzus, and Gregory of Nyssa. After them, this teaching is repeated down through the centuries, but with particular vigor in Eastern Christianity. The doctrine is understood to refer to the putting on of Christ by initiating a dynamic unfolding of the work of the Holy Spirit in the life of each of the newly baptized. Although not generally well known among Anglicans, A. M. Allchin has shown the place that this teaching has held in the Anglican tradition, beginning with Richard Hooker, and including Lancelot Andrewes, Charles Wesley, and E. B. Pusey. As Allchin states,

---

1. Irenaeus, *Adversus haereses V*, preface.

> the doctrine of our deification, our becoming partakers of the divine nature by God's grace, is inseparably and necessarily bound up with the other two doctrines which stand at the heart of classical Christian faith and life, the doctrine of God as Trinity, and the doctrine of the incarnation of God the Word. All three doctrines belong together, and it may be our neglect of the one which has made us uncertain about the others . . . God who is utterly beyond his creation yet comes to be present at the heart of his creation comes to identify himself with his creation in order to lift it up into union with himself. This union, established once for all in Christ, is constantly renewed in varying ways in the coming of the Spirit.[2]

Deification is thus the hope of all Christians: it is the fulfillment of God's acts in creation, the incarnation, and in the sending of the Holy Spirit; it is the fulfillment to which baptism points us and which is the fundamental orientation of the Christian's life. It embodies our participation in the divine nature.[3]

It is probably evident to all of us that this is a vision of the meaning of baptism that is profoundly ecclesial, which roots our individual existence in the corporate body of the church. It will be clear as well that this is not a vision of baptism that sees it as an isolated event in the past but rather as the beginning of a life-long baptismal process. It is in that regard that the common baptismal practice for many centuries has failed: when baptism has been understood as an individual salvation-event in the past with a narrow focus on saving the candidate from the fires of hell, it is probably inevitable that its being the beginning of a process of deification will be scarcely perceived.

The critical question is: how is the reality of "putting on Christ" to be embodied in the life of each baptized person? Our response must involve the recognition that baptism does not end with the ritual event, but rather is the beginning of a process for which all the members of the church must fulfill their appropriate roles. It is in this context that the work of Susan Marie Smith in the past several years is so important for the renewal of the life of the church and for a more adequate realization of the recovery of the significance of baptism for the whole of the Christian life. One of the great strengths of her teaching is that it unites theory and practice. The theological foundations of this renewal

---

2. A. M. Allchin, *Participation in God* (Wilton, CN: Morehouse-Barlow, 1988), 5.
3. 2 Pet 1:4.

of baptism have been taught in our seminaries for generations, but the pastoral implications of that teaching have seldom informed our ritual practice at the parish level. *Christian Ritualizing and the Baptismal Process* offers the church an important resource for pastors and teachers to begin the reshaping of our baptismal norms and the recovery of a fully ecclesial sense of our membership in the Body of Christ.

Louis Weil
Hodges-Haynes Professor of Liturgics Emeritus,
Church Divinity School of the Pacific
Berkeley, California

Acknowledgments

It is an inspiring humility as well as a great pleasure to offer my thanks to those whose various maieutic influences enabled the dissertation that underlies this book to be written. My committee inspired, challenged, questioned, prodded, and affirmed me through the doctoral program as a whole and this dissertation in particular: Professor Louis Weil, chair; Professor Michael Aune, Professor Catherine Bell, and Professor Jim Fowler. It has been an honor and a pleasure to work with you, and I am grateful beyond measure. I wish also to thank Professor Don Saliers, Professor Duncan Ferguson, Professor Mary Gerhart, and Professor Mary McGann whose work and friendship have inspired me to begin and to complete this constructive project.

Scholarship requires free time and more material and technology than one would ever imagine. I have been blessed with friends who believed in this project, that it would finally come to fruition, and who supported it (and me) with the means to have bed, board, computers, and community. For these I give deep thanks to Carol and Richard White, Nancy Talbott, Pat Gaines, Judy and Jack Dominic, Karen Hunt, Ed and Cristina Larson, Carol Westpfahl, Katherine Bell, Elizabeth Morrissett, Larry Spannagel, Meg Mealy, Judith Berling and Rhoda Bunnell, Sharon Korwan, Jerry and Randi Walker, Pat and Dennis Sullivan, Wesley and Joyce Veatch, Priscilla Camp, Mary and Malcolm McWilliams, Cheryl and Roy Pettyjohn, and Bill and Catherine Beachy at whose lake cabin the final revisions were made.

I am grateful to the Episcopal Daughters of the King Master's Fund, the Anchorage Soroptimists, and St. Mary's Episcopal Church, Anchorage, for prayer and financial sustenance. Special thanks to the Datatel Angelfire Fund and the Graduate Theological Union financial aid gurus. Spiritual guides kept and keep me in the former: Maisie Ferrari, S. Arlene Boyd, RSM, S. Marguerite Buchanan, RSM, the Rev. Zoila Schoenbrun, S. Mary Jo Polak, OSB, and S. Therese Elias, OSB.

The Episcopal Evangelical Educational Society awarded me a grant to consider baptismal ecclesiology with reference to parishes. Barbara Smith pointed me toward the Russian Orthodox theologians. Lyle Settle offered his computer expertise. Barbara Hazzard, OSB, gave me a quiet room and the means to meditate. Diana Lynch opened her house for meditation and hugs. Betty Newman wrote news and encouragement every week. The Sisters of Order of Saint Benedict in St. Joseph, Minnesota, have prayed for me for ten years, *sine qua non dissertatio*.

The women who conducted rituals for me changed my life and showed me the life-changing power of ritualization, which pressed me to do this research. The Anchorage women sent me off with a Blessing Way: Lucia Roncalli, Suzan Nightingale, Mo Dursi, Jane Oakley, Kristin Hanson, Barbara Flaherty, Julia, and Kate. Later, Judith Lethin, Jan Thurston, and Nancy Talbott gathered the women for a pre-ordination re-birthing ceremony. The Cincinnati Grail women prepared me for priestly ordination with a heavenly feast: my thanks to Judy Dominic, Josy Trageser, Mary Ball, Gayle Reichert, Paula Janson, and Brenda, Sandi, Kay, Audrey, Bobby, Dode, Sue, Christine, Nancy, Valerie, and all the other vestment-makers they represent.

My aunts and uncles, Margot and Leonard Smith and Shirley and Phil Woodworth, and my parents, Ruth and Richard Smith, sustained me over the long haul and on many levels. I am grateful to them for dinner parties and tea, the primary sacrament out of which the others arise. For the hospitable sacraments I also give thanks to Nancy and Tom, Rhoda and Judith, Paul and Bill, Claire Creese, the Green Chair Society, Susan Alison-Hatch and the Berkeley jogging team: Margaret, Sally, Andrea, and Meredyth; my partners in creativity, Claire Creese, Richard Stevens, Lea Durard, and Rosemary Dauenhauer; and my immediate family: Carol, Rich, Warren, Wendy, Christopher, Kelly, Amy, Natalie, and Sylvie. My especial heartfelt thanks I offer to Mary McGann, RSCJ, sister in spirit and partner in writing.

My deepest gratitude I offer to my parents, to whose memory this book is dedicated: Richard J. Smith (d. August 25, 2001) and Ruth Elizabeth Baird Smith (d. April 15, 2007). Both were the children of Army officers, and so grew up comfortable with ritual. My father initiated neighborhood rituals everywhere we lived (game day, Fourth of July parade). My mother was the first "priest" in the family, who taught me how redemption is effected through ritualization. I give thanks to her for life and love, for community and celebration. Her father was a writer; I inherited his writing books, and his motivation to write.

And to friends and family who make up my community, I offer my abundant thanks, for you fill my heart with joy.

> For sixty years I have been forgetful every minute
> But not for a second has this flowing toward me stopped or slowed.
> I deserve nothing.
> Today I recognized that I am the guest the mystics talk about.
> I play this living music for my host.
> Everything today is for the host.
> Every thing today is for the host.
>
> —*Rumi*

—Susan Marie Smith
Season after Pentecost, 2010

Abbreviations

AAR	American Academy of Religion
AH	Irenaeus, *Adversus omnes Haereses*
BCP	*Book of Common Prayer*
BEM	*Baptism, Eucharist, Ministry*
CO	*Calvini Opera*
CR	*Corpus Reformatorum*
NPNF	*Nicene and Post-Nicene Fathers*
PL	*Patrologia Latina*

PART ONE

Inherited Expectations of Baptismal Efficacy in the Ongoing Lives of the Baptized

1

"After the Water the Fire"

Experiencing the Spirit of the Baptismal Process after Baptism

> This bread signifies to you how you ought to love unity. It was made out of many grains of wheat, which were separate, but were united by application of water, by a kind of rubbing together, and baked with fire. So have you been ground together by the fast and the exorcism, wetted in baptism, and baked by the fire of Christ and the mystery of the Holy Spirit . . . Notice how at Pentecost the Holy Spirit comes: He comes in fiery tongues, to inspire the love whereby we are to burn towards God and despise the world, and our chaff be burnt away, and our heart refined like gold. So the Holy Spirit comes—after the water the fire—and you are made bread, which is the Body of Christ: and here is the symbol of unity.[1]

THIS PASSIONATE, ANIMATED SERMON-EXCERPT FROM AUGUSTINE is about the eucharist, but the imagery is deeply baptismal as well. After the water comes the Spirit with "fiery tongues, to inspire the love whereby we are to burn towards God and despise the world, and our chaff be burnt away, and our heart refined like gold." The Christian life sounds like a process, intense, hot, that will change us forever—and turn us into food, into bread, but more—we will be changed into Christ, into the very Body of Christ.

Sparked by Vatican Council II (1962–1965), the late twentieth century brought a revolution in thinking about baptism. The major Western Christian denominations revised their liturgical rites of bap-

---

1. Augustine, from Sermon 227, in Horton Davies, *Bread of Life and Cup of Joy*, 127 (*PL* 38.1100).

tism, a process that required rethinking connections between what we believe, what we pray, and what we enact. Saying and doing are not the same, and doing is likely to have a greater impact. Theology that is not translated into action or is not manifest in rite or prayer, art or symbol, is empty theory.

"—and you are made bread." The fire of Christ and the mystery of the Holy Spirit act. But they do not act theoretically or in general; they act on particular human persons. They act *in* those persons to "inspire" them so that they will come "to burn towards God." They act in local communities so that each and all are transformed. Is this a theological statement about God, or is this inspiring poetry that will change the person who hears it?

For years I have understood that the study of "how it is," though important, is inadequate for drawing a person toward the reality of "it." The named theology of life after death is nameless before a grieving person, where explanations are insults and compassion requires silence or poetry. Our words about God are lovely in their proper context, but they are shallow in those moments when Godself is needed; then, it is not our words but our compassionate witness to God's presence or absence that matters. "Theology" is a term that has been applied to the first, to the words about God. A term that applies to the second, the being there, the presence, action, happening, doing, or working, is "liturgy."

Liturgy is a broad term that, however, has been used with various limits. It has referred only to the eucharist or only to Sunday morning worship. In its broader meaning it has referred to worship and to sacramental enactments, but usually in traditions that hold worship to be authoritative. The study of liturgy as "authorized worship" is evolving. While sacramental theology (= what worship *should mean*) began very early in the church (e.g., Augustine of Hippo, late fourth/ early fifth century), the study in the Western church of the worship act (= what actually *happens* in worship) is more recent. Beginning with instruction to priests as to what to do and say during worship, i.e., a study of *rubrics* ("How do we conduct the rite correctly?"), scholarship moved at the beginning of the twentieth century[2] to *liturgical history* ("What

---

2. Kenan B. Osborne dates the beginning of study of the history of each of the sacraments with the publication of Lea's *A History of Auricular Confession and Indulgences in the Latin Church* in 1896, and the myriad responses it occasioned in the succeeding decade. For a synopsis of historical scholars of the liturgy, see Osborne's *Christian Sacraments in a Postmodern World*, 6–9.

were the texts and sequence of former rites in various provinces?"). In the 1960s,[3] a Russian Orthodox priest-theologian, Alexander Schmemann, linked theology with the poetry of human experience by asserting that liturgy, the praise of God, is a source of theology. His assertion is associated with the birth of *liturgical theology* ("What meaning should a particular rite communicate?"). The development since 1977 of the field of Ritual Studies,[4] which enabled insights from the human sciences to affect the study of liturgy, led Mark Searle in 1983 to name a fourth: *pastoral liturgical studies* ("What meaning *does* a particular rite *communicate to the worshippers*?").[5] This more recent field, incorporating ritual theory, focuses on the empirical study of actual worship enactments (which includes factors beyond the text,[6] such as gesture, music, and space) and on the lived experience of the particular worshippers (which includes an experience of God that may or may not match the words about God carefully prescribed by the liturgist-theologians). It is pastoral liturgical studies that points to the importance of addressing the *pastoral* dimension of worship: its effect upon the worshippers. It is the effect of worship upon the worshippers that allows the personal story of a baptismal life to be told. It is

---

3. Kevin Irwin marks the beginning of liturgical theology as a discipline with a speech given by Russian Orthodox liturgical theologian Alexander Schmemann in the 1960s. *Liturgical Theology: A Primer*.

4. Ritual studies as an interdisciplinary field, from which the examination of liturgy as a phenomenon and of its pastoral effects on participants has a relatively short history. Significant moments in its history include:

- 1971: Founding of Murphy Center for Liturgical Research at Univ. of Notre Dame (becomes Center for Pastoral Liturgy) (Center announced in 1970).
- 1973: December, on 10th anniversary of Vatican II's *Sacrosanctum concilium* (on the liturgy), seminal meeting of liturgists held in Arizona which becomes North American Academy of Liturgy.
- 1977: AAR Ritual Studies Group is started by Ronald Grimes
- 1983: Article by Mark Searle in *Worship* gives a name to the ritual study of liturgy: "Pastoral Liturgical Studies"
- 1986: *Journal of Ritual Studies* founded
- 1995: English translation available of Louis-Marie Chauvet's *Symbol and Sacrament: A Sacramental Reinterpretation of Christian Existence*.
- 2013–14: 40th anniversary of NAAL.

5. Searle, "New Tasks, New Methods: The Emergence of Pastoral Liturgical Studies," 291–308. For a scholarly summation of the development of liturgical studies, see Gilbert Ostdiek, "Ritual and Transformation: Reflections on Liturgy and the Social Sciences," 38–48.

6. See Hoffman, *Beyond the Text: A Holistic Approach to Liturgy*.

the effect upon the worshippers that suggests that baptismal theology ought to take account of the baptized; and it is the effect on the worshippers that leads to the question of the *role of liturgy in the ongoing growth and formation of the baptized.*

Taking account of the baptized brings into serious relief the foundational issue at the heart of liturgical theology: namely, the relationship of the theology of sacrament to the theology of lived Christian experience. The problem arises because the theologies held close to the bone for most of 1,500 years have been concerned with the *church's sacramental mediation* of God's grace, as distinct from the *worshipper's reception of* or *response to* that grace. Among many reasons why this may be so is the elusive and diverse nature of experience and the difficulty of identifying, much less studying, human reception and response. Human experience varies widely; it is often unobservable; and it is always unmeasurable. While we may, from an experiential point of view, affirm that ritual events mediate a variety of meanings,[7] how shall we interpret them or take account of them? Shall the varied meanings of baptism for each individual be considered with the same valence as the church's intent to unite the baptized with Christ in the paschal mystery? This focuses the problem, for the ecclesial body is not prepared to suggest that baptism, for example, means "whatever you want it to mean" as crass relative individualism would have it. As a bishop from my own Anglican tradition, Colin Buchanan, has suggested, the church is not prepared to offer two baptisms, one for infants and another for adults,[8] according to the "experience quotient" of

---

7. Among the myriad attempts to identify loci of meaning is Lawrence Hoffman's four: *official* (or *authorized*: see Kahn and Hoffman, "Contemporary Challenges to Jewish Life-Cycle Ritual," 262–85), *public* (or *commonly held but not authorized*: Kahn and Hoffman, 263), *private* for each individual, and *normative* as the meaning which carries over into every-day life and has an extended (ethical) effect. "How Ritual Means," 79–84. My colleague Mary McGann points out that while "private" might mean "individual," *personal* does not, since in worship or other corporate ritual it is not possible for meanings corporately mediated to finally be considered individual. Donald Allchin likewise points out that "when we speak of the individual we speak of each one in his [sic] separateness in competition with all others, [but] when we speak of the person we speak of each one in . . . relatedness, in communion with all others." Allchin, *Participation in God*, 4. Personal is communal.

8. Buchanan, *The Renewal of Baptismal Vows*, 5: "Baptism is *the* Christian initiatory rite, leading the enquirer into the common life of the Christian church. If it is appropriate to baptize infants, then it can only be done with the same theology as adult baptism. In each case baptism must have the same meaning in the recipient's

the one baptized. Rather, there is *one* Lord, *one* faith, *one* baptism (Eph 4:5). Sacramental theology affirms that God acts in baptism, whether the candidate consciously experiences anything or not.

This tension between what occurs and what is experienced is not only a twenty-first-century issue, not only a Western problem, not only a Christian concern. Anthropologists Sally F. Moore and Barbara G. Myerhoff place the question within the study of human ritual and name the axes of the tension *doctrinal efficacy* and *operational efficacy*.[9] Moore claims that both secular and religious rituals exist within the referential bounds of what they *declare* and what they *demonstrate*,[10] what they *say* and what they *do*. As Myerhoff observes:

> What Moore calls the *doctrinal efficacy* of religious ritual is provided by the explanations a religion itself gives of how and why ritual works. The explanation is within the religious system and is part of its internal logic. The religion postulates by what causal means a ritual, if properly performed, should bring about the desired results. A religious ritual refers to the unseen cosmic order, works through it and operates on it directly through the performance . . . Doctrinal efficacy is a matter of postulation. As the intrinsic explanation, it need merely be affirmed.[11]
>
> Doctrinal efficacy must be distinguished from social/psychological effectiveness, here called *operational efficacy* . . . [O]ut-

---

life, if it is to count as the same baptism at all . . . Because baptism is once for all for life (which it is), the person who receives it not only undergoes the rite at a particular point in time, but also thereafter becomes by that very rite a *baptized person*, and remains so. Baptism is always 'there'—not only in the personal history but in the present personal make-up." In n. 2, he emphasizes: "Obviously any invoking of the significance of a past baptism must not be suspended upon the condition 'it depends upon what sort of baptism you received.'" And in n. 3: "This sense of remaining a 'baptized person' is what lay behind the medieval concept that baptism imprints a 'character' (*i.e.*, the Greek word for a 'seal' . . .) on the soul. This is a metaphysical way of saying that baptism once given cannot be given again; indeed it is obvious, once the concept of 'being a baptized person' has been established . . ." We see that Buchanan is speaking from the doctrinal point of view here, the belief that an "objective" shift happens in the person and they become something (forever) which they were not before: "a baptized person."

9. Moore and Myerhoff, "Secular Ritual: Forms and Meanings," 10–15. See also Michael Aune, Introduction to "The Return of the Worshiper to Liturgical Theology," 3–10.

10. Moore and Myerhoff, "Secular Ritual: Forms and Meanings," 11.

11. Ibid., 12.

come or consequence . . . is attributed to operational efficacy. Results, successes, failures, are part of the operational effects of a ritual. These are the empirical questions in analysis. For example, healing ceremonies may or may not make a patient feel better. Political ceremonies may or may not succeed in rearranging images, may succeed or fail in attaching positive or negative balances to certain ideas or persons. Rites may vary greatly in successfully convincing their participants and communicating their messages. Such questions about communicative, social/psychological effects are operational.[12]

Michael Aune refers to these as two poles on a continuum, doctrinal efficacy on the descriptive end and operational efficacy on the interpretive end.[13] Operational efficacy has to do with the *experience of the worshipper.*[14]

The relationship between the doctrinal and operational efficacies of sacramental liturgy, and the need for a hermeneutic to render them mutually coherent and accountable, were brought into high relief for me as I heard a pastor struggle with this very question. The pastor was preaching at the funeral of a woman we shall call "Margaret." The sermon attempted to make a link between the meaning (or theology) of baptism and its result or working out in the life of the deceased woman, an issue all the more stark because of the character contrast between "Margaret" and her now-widower, "John." Margaret was a deeply spiritual and pastoral person with a profound sense of community and of beauty. Her mourners included many members of the congregation who had been recipients of her hospitality, her casseroles, her encouraging notes, her love of children, and her faithfulness even in times of despair. If the Christian life can be measured in ethics and in such fruits of the Spirit as love, joy, and hope,[15] Margaret stood radiant within her community. In contrast to Margaret's radiance was the thick opacity of her husband John. While John also loved the church, he remained unconverted by the gospel. He loved and accepted two of his children but condemned and rejected the other two. His neglect and disparagement of his wife tainted not only their home life

---

12. Ibid., 12–13.

13. Aune, "The Return of the Worshiper to Liturgical Theology," 4.

14. Ibid., 5.

15. The fruit of the Spirit: "peace, patience, kindness, generosity, faithfulness, gentleness, and self-control" (Gal 5:22–23a).

but extended beyond in his extra-marital affairs. While understandably vulnerable during the last months of Margaret's illness when she was bedridden and helpless, John articulated his hope that she would die soon, refusing certain medical procedures for her. His open affair during this period with a woman in the congregation was excruciating and agonizing to family and friends. Yet both Margaret and John had been baptized. Both were active members and supporters of the church.

In the funeral homily, the pastor appropriately sought to connect Margaret's union with Christ, both in her baptism and now at her death, with the Paschal Mystery of Christ's death and resurrection. "What is it that makes her a saint?" he asked rhetorically. "Is it her death? No: it does not take death to bring us to the communion of saints. And death does not suffice for sainthood. But Christ in his cross and resurrection enfolded us in a cloak of righteousness, so that when God looks upon us, it is not our blemishes that God sees. It was at Margaret's baptism that she was cloaked with the garment of righteousness, enfolded in Christ. And it was at her baptism that her sainthood began. As we celebrate Margaret's life today, we could simply say, 'her baptism took.'"

What does it mean for baptism to "take"? Is this a metaphor of inoculation, as in "the yellow fever vaccination took"? Or of fabric dyeing, as in, "we dipped both nylon and cotton into the purple dye, and the cotton cloth took, but the nylon didn't"? Or is this a metaphor of tree grafting, where a branch from one tree is engrafted into another, and if the fluids flow between them and the engrafted branch bears fruit, then we know the graft "took"?

Whichever metaphor we choose, to say that baptism "took" implies that it is possible that it would not take. In this situation of such sharp family contrasts, would we say that it took for Margaret, but not for John? Or is it only at death that we finally know whether the baptism took? If it had been John's funeral, would the pastor have shaken his head, and moaned, "In the case of this man, even though he had a good sense of humor and came to church week after week, he was nonetheless abusive to his children, controlling and insensitive, unfaithful to his wife, angry at her for living to the point where he had to take care of her. He was childish, a man with no maturity—and we simply have to acknowledge that his baptism didn't take."

The idea of baptism "taking" or "not taking" is at the heart of the tension between the understanding of sacramental action, on the one hand, as an action of God and, on the other, as pastorally effective in the lives of the recipients. From the standpoint of doctrinal efficacy in a wide body of Christian denominations, Holy Baptism is understood to be *God's action*. The doctrine of God's sovereignty prohibits any notion of efficacy as contingent upon human manipulation. God chooses persons as part of a covenantal people. When they respond freely to God's invitation, expressed in Scripture, tradition, and theology, by coming to the baptismal font, God acts. Through God's ministers, God unites the persons with Christ in his death and resurrection, seals them with the Holy Spirit, and makes them part of the eucharistic body of Christ. It is *God* who initiates and *God* who acts. It is *God* who calls people into covenant and *God* who grants grace to the people to keep the covenant. From this perspective, baptism *must* be effective. Any notion that baptism *didn't take* would theologically challenge the notion of God's sovereignty and omnipotence—which is theologically impossible. From the standpoint of doctrinal efficacy, baptism *is* effective. There can be no question of its not "taking."

What, then, of this funeral sermon? Was the pastor unfamiliar with the doctrine of sin and the fact that frail, finite humans will always tend to fall away from the grace and purity granted them in baptism? It seems to me likely that this pastor knew all about sin, and probably all about John's sin. The problem of holding Christians accountable to their covenant with God is a large one, one which has been dealt with by public and private penance,[16] ostracism and excommunication,[17] prayer, corporate confession, counseling, spiritual direction, and the reconciling rite of Holy Eucharist. John's problem is a basic human problem. And sin, while fascinating and fundamental, is not our topic here.

Rather, I think this preacher was proclaiming a celebration of Margaret, a baptismal life well lived. Yet Margaret was a sinner, too. The revealing point which the homilist uncovered with the idea of baptism taking or not taking was the implicit tension between the

---

16. For an account of the Order of Penitents in the patristic church, see Monika K. Hellwig, *Sign of Reconciliation and Conversion*, 27–44.

17. One of the most creative and extreme examples is the ostracism of sinners practiced by some Mennonites. See White, *Protestant Worship,* 84–85, *passim*.

sacramental efficacy claimed by churches' doctrinal theologies and the very real issue of a lived Christian life: between doctrinal and operational efficacy. The contrast between John and Margaret reveals grave differences among the lived totality of Christians' lives, works of art of varying beauty, perceivable as a whole only from their end. Margaret's baptismal life is worth celebration because it's beautiful *and remarkable*—because not all the baptized live lives of grace.

Sin alone is inadequate to account for the discrepancy we witness between doctrinal efficacy of baptism (i.e., "God acts to make this person a new creation, united with Christ forever") and operational efficacy, which varies greatly, even for the Margarets of the world who seek to live lives worthy of the Water and the Fire.

The premise of this book is that the *life of the baptized is a process*, in which developmental stages, or crises, or turning points, afford opportunities to affirm or disaffirm the unity with Christ forged at baptism.

If the baptized life is a continuing process of journeying into Christ, then liturgy and the process of making liturgies, which we shall call *Christian ritualizing*, has a significant role to play in these crises or turning-point moments. And if the role of Christian ritualizing is played well, it can affect the vitality of the church in the world.

A step toward revitalizing the church occurred through the liturgical reform in the Western church of the 1960s–1990s when it was reawakened in its identity as not just the hierarchy or the institution, but as the *ecclesia*, the "ones called out." The *ecclesia* include not just the clergy—whether in institutional and sacramental power as in the medieval church or preaching and charismatic power as in a contemporary evangelical church—but *all the baptized*. The imperative of this *baptismal ecclesiology* implies that the role of cleric as servant-leader of the priestly people of God is conjunctively related to the sacred role of the priestly people themselves. There is an intersubjective covenantal relationship between the pastors who care for and make manifest in worship the identity of the *ecclesia*, and the people who discern, claim, and enact their role as baptized *ecclesia* in the world. Our goal, then, in searching for the role of liturgy in the unfolding life of the baptized, is the full empowerment and enactment of the baptized in the world, which I call *realized baptismal ecclesiology*.

We begin our inquiry by taking a reading from the Tradition on the "doctrinal- operational" continuum. From three historic periods, we shall examine baptismal theology from Augustine (354–430), Bishop of Hippo in North Africa, in his work *Against the Donatists* (patristic period), Thomas Aquinas (1225?–1274), Dominican scholastic priest, in the *Summa Theologiae* (medieval period), and John Calvin (1509–1564), Geneva reformer, in the *Institutes of the Christian Religion,* final edition 1559 (Reformation period). Reading their theological statements about the (doctrinal) efficacy they understand baptism to convey, we shall also be attentive for signs or suggestions from these three fathers as to *whether they expect changes or effects to be experienced by and among the baptized.*

Why is this important? Vatican Council II sparked a liturgical renewal that contributed to a reawakening of theology of the baptized as the priestly people of God, covenanted to Christ to carry out his ministry of healing and reconciliation in the world. Yet in many churches fifty and sixty years later, the pastor still fills all the roles. In many churches, the pastor has "a ministry," but not the people. In many congregations, there is only one "minister"—the priest or pastor. The people are expected to show up on Sunday and pay their tithes, and "help out." But the deep sense that the *people are the ministers,* called out to fulfill Christ's ministry in the world, covenanted to God in Christ by the Holy Spirit to use the gifts God gave them for the building up of the body and mediating God's love for the world—this is not fulfilled. The people do not know themselves in this identity *as ministers.* Many were baptized as infants and do not remember the sacrament. But even those baptized as adults may not feel a kinship to the body of Christ, nor see themselves as vital to Christ's ministry in the world, nor live into their identity as God's covenanted people, priestly people, belonging not to themselves, but to the One who made and redeems them. And often, pastors do not see their people in this way, either.

Not only that, but many people no longer feel committed to one denomination, or even to coming to Sunday worship at all. Mainline churches are losing membership. Some leaders' attempts to reverse this trend have erupted in new ways to worship: different music, different buildings, different "feel." Imitate culture, imitate education, imitate entertainment. More technology, more silence, more art. These leaders recognize that worshippers want an *experience* of God and to feel something authentic. They seek to respond to people's longing, even if it does not quite match baptismal theology. Other leaders resist succumbing to cultural trends or worship fads, relying on tradition for the sake of the long view, riding trendy waves in order to provide stability when the tide changes, even if it does not quite match the particular longings of current worshippers.

Yet it is possible that there is in the tradition, over the span of two millennia, a baptismal theology that bends toward worshippers' longing for an authentic experience of God that would change their lives. It is possible that among these three theologians, touchstones for three eras in Christian history, there is a theology of baptism in which what they believed about baptism's efficacy doctrinally, they also expected to be experienced in the lived lives of the baptized. If this be true, perhaps traditional churches would feel freer to open up to the longings of worshippers for authentic experience of their relationship with God-in-Christ-and-the-Spirit. And perhaps free churches would feel more open to deepen their sense of the baptized as the *ecclesia,* the church, called to belong to the Body of Christ of all times and places. And perhaps all the churches could come closer to claiming, and living, the reality that the church is not just the clergy but all the whole people of God; and that therefore, investing in the spiritual growth of those baptized into Christ, ritually and other ways, is the top priority of the churches today.

2

Augustine on Baptism

Holy Spirit and Heart Conversion are Essential

According to Augustine,[1] baptism is of God and is effective irrespective of the purity of the minister or of the baptizand or other worshippers. Augustine works out his theology of baptism in the context of and in counterpoint to the Donatists, who believed that an impure minister mediated an inadequate baptism. Augustine's primary anti-Donatist writing[2] is the one entitled *On Baptism* (*De Baptismo, Contra Donatistas*) (c. 400). It is a work as much about the church as it is about baptism, since, in Augustine's view, the unity of the church had been severed by the Donatists.

The church in North Africa tended toward religious fervor,[3] especially in the rural areas.[4] During the Great Persecution by the emperor Diocletion in 303–305, Christians were threatened with torture and even death if they did not hand over their sacred books. Many Christians were martyred. Many others did give over Scripture to be burned; having surrendered the tradition, they were called *traditores*

---

1. Augustine, bishop of Hippo Regius 395 CE (according to Brown, *Augustine of Hippo*, 76) or 397 CE (according to Hartranft, in Schaff, ed., *A Select Library of the Nicene and Post-Nicene Fathers of the Christian Church*, 376).

2. Some of Augustine's works which deal predominantly with the Donatist controversy are: *Psalmus contra partem Donati* (c. 393); *Contra Epistolam Donati Hœretici* (not extant); *De Baptismo: Contra Donatistas*, (400); *Breviculus collationis contra Donatistas* (411); and *Post collationem contra Donatistas* (412). See Hartranft's "Analysis of Augustin's Writings Against the Donatists" which follows the controversy chronologically through Augustine's sermons, letters, retractions, and other works. In Philip Schaff, ed. *A Select Library of the Nicene and Post-Nicene Fathers of the Christian Church*, vol. 4: *St. Augustine*, 372–404.

3. Frend, *The Donatist Church*, 79.

4. Ibid., 129f.

("surrenderers").⁵ According to W. H. C. Frend, those who relinquished Scripture were not necessarily cowardly, but had lived through persecutions before and tried to reduce disruption as much as possible.⁶ However, when the persecution was over, the indigenous Christian church, following bishop Donatus (+316), instituted *re*baptism of all who had been *traditores*, before permitting them to enter again into communion with the faithful who had risked a martyr's death rather than succumb to the state.

But Augustine opposed rebaptism, even if one had given in to the persecutors. The issues in the Donatist debate are known mostly from their adversaries, no Donatist literature having survived. As the debates were worked out in Augustine, the controversy fell upon several issues quite central to Christianity, including our question from the funeral homily: Can we say that baptism was effective if we later witness a life lived in sin? Did the *traditores'* baptism "take"? The Donatists, on the one hand, would say, "Having betrayed the faithful, you are no longer a Christian; come, let us (re)baptize you, remitting your sins, and become again a Christian." Baptism, therefore, can "fail" and a second touch be needed. Augustine's position, on the other hand, embodies resistance to the notion that a small North African sect should hold the keys to the whole church of Jesus Christ, because unity and catholicity were in the very nature of the Body of Christ since Christ had died for all humanity. In *De Baptismo, Contra Donatistas*, Augustine speaks staunchly of unity, drawing from the much-beloved bishop Cyprian (bishop of Carthage 248–258) who held together the church as these divisions began to take shape, and himself died a martyr's death in 258. Cyprian, however, also supported rebaptism; thus, Augustine uses his rhetorical skills to support and evoke Cyprian on unity while still pointing out the flaw in rebaptism. First, Augustine "defines" baptism as that which has been given "in any place, from

---

5. Ibid., 10.

6. "Already, during the persecution under Decius and Valerian in AD 249 and 258, Cyprian [Bishop of Carthage, North Africa, 248–58] had advised his colleagues against provoking the authorities, and he himself had retired to a landed estate until the worst was over. The view was held that acts of fanatical zeal which might provoke reprisals were to be discouraged. If the magistrates could be satisfied by the production of medical or heretical treatises, so much the better. The congregation could remain quiet and undivided to resume activity as soon as the persecution ended. But the prudence of the bishops did not by any means win the universal support of the Christian community" (ibid., 6).

any sort of men, provided that it were consecrated in the words of the gospel, and received without deceit on their part with some degree of faith" (VII,102).[7] It is "necessarily holy," and has "inherent sanctity" (III.15). However, baptism is distinct from salvation, is distinct from remission of sins, and does impart the Father, and the Son, and the Holy Ghost, but only to a certain extent (VI.29). Perhaps understanding what baptism is *not* will give us insight into Augustine's thinking.

Baptism is *necessary but not sufficient* for salvation. "For it is one thing to say that every one who shall enter into the kingdom of heaven is first born again of water and the Spirit...another thing to say that every one who is born of water and the Spirit shall enter into the kingdom of heaven, which is assuredly false" (VI.19). Baptism, once given, can never be taken away; it becomes the constant (VI.23). Salvation occurs in the Catholic Church; therefore, if a baptized person leaves the Church, they lose their salvation, but they do not lose their baptism. Should they return to the Church, they can regain salvation without rebaptism (VI.23). But outside the Church, baptism has "no power to work salvation" (VI.14).

In addition to being distinct from salvation, in the sense of necessary but not sufficient, baptism is also necessary but not sufficient for the remission of sins. Even though forgiveness is inherent in the washing of baptism, and "the integrity of the sacrament is everywhere recognized," Augustine insists that baptism "will not avail for the irrevocable remission of sins outside the unity of the Church" (III.22). Very plainly, "there can be baptism in a man although there be in him no remission of his sins" (VII.33). The reason for this is that an inner conversion of heart is necessary as well as the outward sign of baptism (VI.62). A heart with malice can prevent the remission of sins (I.18). Remission of sins, therefore, requires the outward sacrament of baptism, the outward sign of unity with the Catholic Church, and the inner conversion of the heart.

And finally, "all who are baptized with the baptism that is consecrated in the words of the gospel have the Father, and the Son, and the Holy Ghost in the sacrament alone; but that in heart and in life neither do those have them who live an abandoned and accursed life within"

---

7. References are to *A Select Library of the Nicene and Post-Nicene Fathers of the Christian Church*. Vol. IV: *St. Augustine: The Writings against the Manicheans and against the Donatists.* Citations will give the book in Roman numerals followed by the paragraph.

(VI.29). Just as remission of sins can be blocked by a hardened heart, so too can the reception of the Holy Spirit. A person "may be baptized with water, and not born of the Spirit" (VI.19).

Although baptism is (necessary but) not sufficient for salvation, nor for the remission of sins, nor for conversion of heart toward full life in the Spirit, Augustine does understand baptism to have partial effectiveness, even outside the Church, even among the Donatists: for Donatists choosing to enter the Catholic Church were not rebaptized, since even having been baptized by Donatist priests (who originally were baptized by Catholics before the schism), their baptism held. Baptism has its own integrity apart from the ones who administer it. Both ordination and baptism have integrity; "neither sacrament may be wronged" (I.2).

Augustine differed from the Donatists, then, in the relationship between the church and baptism. For the Donatists, the relationship is clear: baptism was a doorway into the Donatist church, the true church. In Donatist self-perception, the boundaries around the Donatist church were distinct. The church is a sociological grouping of the pure Christians who have never betrayed the church, have never been *traditores*, have been faithful to the church of the martyrs. The church is self-defined by their purity standard. Baptism is the door through the boundary; those who defiled themselves were required to be re-baptized in order to enter. The Donatist church defined baptism as the rite that purified, thus enabling one to enter the earthly church, which mirrored the righteousness of the church of the eschaton.

By contrast, Augustine did not define baptism in terms of the church as the Donatists did. Baptism had its own integrity apart from the church. In fact, baptism seems almost a "thing" to be possessed: those separated from the church "possess it [baptism], though the possession be of no avail" (VII.98). Again, "it is one thing not to have, another to have so as to be of no use. He who has not must be baptized that he may have; but he who has to no avail must be corrected, that what he has may profit him" (IV.25). Baptism seems almost like a computer: if not "plugged in" to the church, it does no good. Baptism is not a door to the church, but something powerful that needs the church to be effective.

Thus, Augustine explicates something about the nature of baptism, about the church, about the ministers of baptism, and about the baptized ones. Augustine speaks of baptism as a *thing*, something which is given and then possessed, which has its own integrity and cannot be revoked. What metaphor is he using? What is it like to be a "thing" possessed, that is permanent (which no object is), and has its own integrity irrespective of the context, yet whose effectiveness is dependent upon the context? It cannot be like an apple or a piece of furniture, which are not permanent. Is baptism like a plot of land given to the baptizand? That seems an unfitting analogue since the person can simply walk away from the land, so that though it be owned "on paper," the person would not "possess it" integrally as one possesses one's baptism. Further, we know from Augustine's commentary on the Fourth Gospel that he understands a sacrament to be the Gospel word joined to the element (*Accedit verbum ad elementum et fit sacramentum*).[8] Perhaps two of the metaphors we have suggested already fit Augustine's description: the baptized one as fabric, the minister joining the element of dye to the action (instead of word) of dipping; and the baptized one as person, the minister joining the element of serum to the action of inoculation. In both these analogies, the subject is permanently changed by the action and "possesses" some "thing" which was not present before. The tree-grafting simile is less apt, since the branch does not possess anything, but rather is possessed by, is joined to the tree.

Baptism thus "possessed" is not necessarily effective for salvation, however, without the proper context. Baptism is necessary for the salvation of a person but insufficient of itself without the person's communion in the church. In this, the fabric and the grafting are better analogies: the fabric, though now the right color, may not necessarily be sewn into a beautiful garment without the ecclesial context of designer, pattern, seamstress. The branch, though grafted onto the tree, may not bear fruit without the regular nutrients through the tree from the sun and soil. The inoculated one *is* probably effectively protected from the disease inoculated against, but could be said not to be assured of health except other contextual factors be in place (healthy food, sleep, etc.).

Fitting with all these metaphors is the role of the minister, who basically "services" the event, like the dye-master stirring the cauldron, or the nurse administering the injection, or the tree-grafter cut-

---

8. Augustine, *On the Gospel of John*, 80, on John 15.3 (PL 35: 1840).

ting the wedges and tying on the branch. They must be professional, designated by the "church" to do this job. But Augustine is quite clear that the state of the minister's purity is irrelevant to the effectiveness of the baptismal act/event. Baptism can be given "in any place, from any sort of men" provided the proper Gospel words be spoken with the proper application. The minister's integrity (or lack thereof) is not a contingency for the holiness, inherent sanctity, or effectiveness of baptism, which imparts the Trinity to the one baptized.

However, when it comes to the baptizand, Augustine says two different things. On the one hand, as in the case of the minister, the possession and sacredness of baptism are not contingent upon the baptizand, for "there can be baptism in a man although there be in him no remission of his sins" (VII.33). The church, Augustine goes on to say, is a *corpus permixtum*, containing those who are baptized and pure, and those who are baptized and defiled.[9] Baptism exists with its own integrity, and retains its sanctity, though the minister and the baptized be unrighteous.

But, on the other hand, baptism is *not* effective if baptizands be deceitful or faithless; i.e., if their hearts be unconverted. The basic (doctrinal) efficacy itself, though not contingent on the minister's inner state, does require those baptized to receive baptism "without deceit on their part and with some degree of faith" (VII.102). The inner state of the baptizand *is a factor* at the sacramental event. And beyond the event, that which baptism makes possible, salvation, requires yet more from the one baptized. Here, we who read Augustine with a twenty-first-century hermeneutic can see expectations of operational efficacy; salvation is not assured by the end of the baptismal event.

In addition to the outward sign of baptism, the baptized one must experience a conversion of heart (VI.62), freedom from malice (I.18), "the grace of Christ" (VI.87), and amendment of life (IV.31). Fundamentally, charity is essential (I.16). Augustine associates these

---

9. Augustine points out that there are "envious ones also who are of the party of the devil, though placed within the church, as Cyprian tells us, and who were well known to the Apostle Paul, had baptism, but did not belong to the members of that dove which is safely sheltered on the rock" (VI.80). The idea of the visible church, all the baptized, and the invisible church, the righteous and charitable, is suggested here: All who "have not charity . . . cannot attain to eternal salvation, even with all those good things which profit them not" (I.12). Thus Augustine contrasts sharply with the Donatists who considered the visible and invisible church to be coextensive: the pure, who are saved, are those in the church, who must therefore be pure (and not sinners).

with the communion of the church. Augustine understands the church to be the soil of charity that makes effective the remission of sin. And the church, he suggests, will nurture the conversion of heart that, along with baptism, is necessary for salvation. The softening of a hardened heart makes an opening for the Spirit of charity and grace. In an implied high pneumatology, Augustine suggests that in addition to baptism, which can be possessed, conversion of life is needed for life in the Holy Spirit, which cannot be possessed; for one "may be baptized with water, and not born of the Spirit" (VI.19).

Thus, in tandem with the doctrine of efficacy of the event of baptism by whatever minister, Augustine holds the need for an efficacy which works in the life of the baptized person. This operational efficacy, which requires conversion of heart, occurs in communion in the unity of the church, the one, holy, catholic, orthodox church, the nature of which Augustine helped define. Here the tree-graft is closer to Augustine's metaphor of the church as the "soil of charity." How the church should nurture those planted in it, Augustine does not say in *De Baptismo, Contra Donatistas*. Not all parts of the garden have equally fertile soil, for he acknowledges that the weeds and the wheat are both in the church (VII.49).[10] But he is clear in expecting that the church will nurture the baptized toward conversion of heart, essential for life in the Spirit. If not baptism, then surely the church, takes part in ongoing nurture of those called Christian. The church, according to Augustine, has an obligation and a responsibility to cultivate the ongoing conversion of heart of the baptized.

---

10. "[W]e hold that the wicked in no way hurt the good in Catholic unity, until at the last the chaff be separated from the wheat. But our opponents . . . maintain that the good perish as by a kind of infection from communion with the wicked" (VII.49).

3

Aquinas on Baptism

*It's about the Priest, Not the People;
It's about Christ, Not the Spirit (Or is it?)*

LET US LOOK NOW AT THOMAS AQUINAS (1225?–1274) WHO FOLlowed the dialectic argument form of the Greeks to work out a brilliant synthesis of Aristotle's philosophy with Christian theology. We select Thomas for two reasons. First, his mammoth work (here we draw specifically upon Part III of the *Summa Theologiae*) has had tremendous influence on centuries of Christian theology, both in its affirmation (e.g., the Council of Trent) and in its refutation (e.g., Reformers, Chauvet) up to the present day. And second, his doctrine of sacramental efficacy through instrumental efficient causality—a view of sacramental action as "producing" a "quantity" of grace—has had the side effect of contributing to the supereminence of clergy over laity (i.e., "clericalism"), the submission of baptism ("passive") to ordination ("active"),[1] and the diminishment of the free-blowing Holy Spirit to the predictability of instrumental causality. The theology of Thomas stands as an ideological bulwark against baptismal ecclesiology.[2] If

---

1. There are in Thomas three unrepeatable sacraments (baptism, confirmation, ordination) that impart an indelible character on the soul. According to Thomas, baptism imparts a *passive* character, and ordination an *active* character: "[P]ower is either active or passive; active power is bestowed in the sacrament of orders, passive or receptive power through the sacrament of baptism" (III.72.5). *Potentia autem non est nisi activa vel passiva. Potentia autem activa in sacramentis confertur per sacramentum ordinis: potentia autem passiva sive receptiva per sacramentum baptismi.*

2. See Louis-Marie Chauvet, *Symbol and Sacrament*, for a systematic and thorough refutation of Thomas's productionist view, in favor of a theology which accounts for believer's Christian experience, a fuller pneumatology, and an incorporation of the human body as a factor in Christian existence.

we can see in Thomas expectations that baptism will operate effectively in the baptized, we shall be able to understand our twenty-first-century hermeneutic as an evolutionary contribution to the totality of the Christian tradition of baptismal theology. Thus, we will follow Thomas's logic to learn how he understands baptism, as a sacrament, to be effective. We will remain attuned to inferences about its working or operation in the lives of the baptized.

Our entrée into Thomas's view of the doctrinal efficacy of baptism and the role of the minister will be through his two-fold understanding of how sacraments function: by *signifying* and by *causing*. First, Thomas considers that sacraments *function by being signs*. By this, Thomas does not mean what a twenty-first-century person would understand as the meaning-making richness of multivalent symbols-as-revelatory.[3] Rather, standing in the scholastic tradition, Thomas's theological reasoning sought to understand the function or operation of sacrament: what they do, and how they do it. Predominant in medieval theological currency was the understanding that *sacrament operates as a sign of a sacred reality*. Thomas would have been familiar with this concept in the writings of Augustine, Lanfranc, Hugh of St. Victor, and Peter Lombard, among others.[4] To clarify the meaning of sign (and in preparation for his argument that sacrament is "more" than sign), Thomas gives the example

> of one who on offering a leaden denarius receives a hundred pounds by order of the king. This is done not because the denarius he offers is in any way the cause of him receiving so great a sum of money. Rather this effect is produced solely by

---

3. Susanne K. Langer, in *Philosophy in a New Key*, identified the study of symbols as "a new generative idea" that "has dawned" in epistemology (*Philosophy in a New Key*, 21), quite distinct from the Scholastic idea of sign which is concerned with "the existence, reality, or efficacy of *things*" (ibid., 19). This generative idea places philosophy in a "new key" such that "the edifice of human knowledge stands before us, not as a vast collection of sense reports, but as a structure of *facts that are symbols* and *laws that are their meanings*" (ibid., 21).

4. A sacrament is defined as a sign of a sacred reality in Lanfranc, *De Corpore et Sanguine Domini* 12 (*PL* 150.422); Hugh of St. Victor, *De Sacramentis* I.9.2 (*PL* 176.317); and Peter Lombard, *Sentences* IV.1.2. In *Summa Theologiae* III.60.2.*sed contra* and footnote by David Bourke, Aquinas cites Augustine and refers to sacrament as "a visible sign of a sacred thing," or "a visible form of an invisible grace" in *De catechizandis rudibus* xxvi.50 (PL 40.344; tr. ACW [*Ancient Christian Writers*] II.82).

the king's will. Hence Bernard too states in a sermon, [*De Cena Domini*. PL 183.272] *Just as a book is used in the investiture of a canon, a staff in that of an abbot, and a ring in that of a bishop, so too the different categories of grace are conferred by the sacraments.*[5]

Aquinas' example suggests the possibility that the promise to pay one hundred pounds in exchange for the denarius might be revoked at the will of the one in whose name the denarius was issued. That is, the denarius is a sign of a prospective reality, but one that is not sure and certain until the 100 pounds is forthcoming. The sign does not in itself *produce* what it promises. Thus, Thomas looks for a second function of sacrament, in addition to *sign*, that will enable certainty in the desired result—which, in the case of sacraments, is *grace* (cf. III.62) and *justification* (cf. III.64.1). Aquinas' certainty of God's grace is attached to the *conferring* of the sacraments. This occurs not through sacraments' function as sign but through what Thomas refers to as sacraments' function as *cause*.

Second, then, Thomas asserts that sacraments *function by causing*. Thomas's example of the denarius provides the counterpoint needed to make his case of the certainty of grace. Analogically, grace could be assured if the "denarius" went the next step beyond referring to grace in order to *cause* grace. But it is obvious that an object (like a denarius, or bread, or water) cannot "cause" an action or response. The sign alone is insufficient to express Thomas's certainty of God's action and of the fulfilled result of that action in the gift of God's grace. Thomas thereby borrows from Aristotle a masterful distinction in kinds of causes to show how the sacraments are related to the certain conferring of God's grace.

Based upon Aristotle, Aquinas explicates the notion of causes in *On the Principles of Nature*:[6] "It is clear . . . that there are four causes, namely material, efficient, formal, and final . . . Aristotle in his book the *Physics*[7] writes that there are four causes and three principles. He takes the causes to be both extrinsic and intrinsic. Matter and form are

---

5. III.62.1.Reply.

6. I am following the translation of Joseph Bobik, *Aquinas on Matter and Form and the Elements* here. *De Principiis Naturae* was an early work of Thomas, c. 1252–53 (Bobik, *Aquinas on Matter and Form*, xvi).

7. I.6.189a 16–18; I.7.191a 20–21; II.3.195a 15. Bobik, *Aquinas on Matter and Form*, 39 n. 7.

> ### Aristotle's Influence on Scholasticism
>
> As is commonly known, the writings of Aristotle were made available to the Western world in the twelfth and thirteenth centuries, having been felicitously held in the Arab libraries and carried by Jews to the West. The Schools of the eleventh to thirteenth centuries sought to apply the Greek dialectic method of logical reason to contemporary theological issues, scholarly work that offered fresh intellectual contributions to the world of learning. The Schoolmen, or Scholastics, the Father of whom is considered to be Anselm (c.1033–1109, Archbishop of Canterbury 1093), began with "scanty translations of portions of Aristotle's writings and of Porphyry's *Isagoge*, both the work of Boethius (480?–524)" (Walker, *A History of the Christian Church*, 238). By the time of Thomas Aquinas, more of Aristotle was available, and Thomas worked to synthesize Aristotle's "scientific" approach with Christian theology. Thomas adopted Aristotle's moderate realism in which universal realities exist but only in conjunction with their particular manifestation in individual objects:
>
>> The extreme "realists," following Platonic influences, . . . asserted that universals existed apart from and antecedent to the individual objects—*ante rem*, i.e., the genus man was anterior to and determinative of the individual man. ["Humanity" exists for God to enter into.] The moderate "realists," under the guidance of Aristotle, . . . taught that universals existed only in connection with individual objects—*in re*. The "nominalists," following Stoic precedent, held that universals were only abstract names for the resemblances of individuals, and had no other existence than in thought—*post rem*. The only real existence for them was the individual object. This quarrel between "realism" and "nominalism" continued throughout the scholastic period and profoundly influenced its theological conclusions (Walker, *A History of the Christian Church*, 238).

said to be intrinsic to a thing, because they are parts constituting the thing. The efficient and the final are said to be extrinsic, because they are outside the thing."[8]

The extrinsic causes enable the operation or production of something that did not exist before to be brought into existence.[9] The agent or *efficient cause* makes or does something, or intends to produce

---

8. *De Prin. Nat.* 3.17. *Materia et forma dicuntur intrinsecae rei, eo quod sunt partes constituentes rem; efficiens et finalis dicuntur extrinsecae, quia sunt extra rem.* Bobik's translation was made from the critical text of John J. Pauson, *Saint Thomas Aquinas, De Principiis Naturae*, Textus Philosophici Friburgenses, 2 (Fribourg: Société Philosophique, 1950). This passage: Bobik, *Aquinas on Matter and Form*, 39.

9. Bobik, *Aquinas on Matter and Form*, 40.

something (e.g., a sculptor). The *final cause*, that which the agent intends to produce, is the *telos* or goal or purpose or result of the effort (e.g., the statue).

Matter and form are "causes" intrinsic to the process. Once the agent has an intention (final cause), s/he must use some material (e.g., marble), and must shape it into some form (e.g., Michelangelo's *David*). The *material cause* is the raw material or matter; the *formal cause* is the form or shape into which the agent works it.

With this background from his work *On the Principles of Nature*, we turn to the *Summa Theologiae* in which Thomas uses the "causes" heuristically. The *Summa Theologiae* is divided into four parts. The *first part* gives theologies of the cosmos, the Trinity, and humanity. The *first second part* includes questions on human emotions, virtues, sin, and grace. The *second second part* explicates aspects of the Christian life: faith, hope, love, and other virtues. The *third part* addresses Christology and sacraments. Sacraments arise, logically and in the sequence of his exposition, directly from Christ. Thomas explains that sacramental theology begins with Christ, the Incarnate Word (III.1–6). The extrinsic "causes" are quite clear. It is Christ in his divinity who is the efficient cause. And what it is that Christ intends, the final cause, is grace,[10] or justification,[11] in the worshipper.

In Question 62 of the *Summa*, demonstrating "The Chief Effect of the Sacraments, which is Grace," Thomas speaks of the efficacious conferring of grace as if it were a mechanistic process of production and transfer.[12] The metaphor of grace Thomas uses is an object which has

---

10. "The next point which we have to consider is the effects of the sacraments, first their chief effect, which is grace [Question 62], and then their secondary effect, which is character [Question 63]" (III.62.Introduction). The note in the Blackfriars edition by Thomas scholar David Bourke gives this interpretive explanation: "Grace is the principal effect because it is grace alone which sanctifies. Sacramental character is secondary because it does not, of itself, *confer personal sanctification*, but rather deputes *the recipient* to participate in the priesthood of Christ as expressed in the worship of the Church" (vol. 56, Question 62 note b, p. 51, emphasis added).

11. "[T]he interior effect of all the sacraments is justification" (III.64.1, *Sed contra* [*On the other hand*]). "[I]nterior justification . . . is the *reality only*, i.e., it is signified but is not itself the sign" (III.66.1.Reply, on baptism). "Heavenly glory" is "the end of all the sacraments" [*caelestem gloriam, auae est universalis finis sadcramentorum*] (III.66.1.*ad*1).

12. Chauvet calls Thomas's approach "productionist." Louis-Marie Chauvet, *Symbol and Sacrament*, 7, 21–22, and throughout, esp. chapters 1, 10, and 12. Thomas himself says, "It is necessary to say that the sacraments of the New Law do cause grace

quantity, like beads or coins. He defines its sources and shows that the grace that the sacraments convey is in addition to "standard" grace.[13] Sacraments even produce "more" grace than that which accrues from the Gifts of the Holy Spirit and the four cardinal and three theological virtues.[14] In addition to all this grace from the Spirit and the virtues is the grace effected by the sacraments:

> [I]f sacramental grace does not add anything over and above the grace of the Gifts and the virtues it would be futile for those possessing both Gifts and virtues to have sacraments conferred upon them. Yet nothing is futile in the works of God. [*Sed Contra*] . . . Now the sacraments are designed to achieve certain special effects which are necessary in the Christian life . . . Thus just as the virtues and Gifts add something over and above grace according to its common definition, namely a particular kind of perfection specifically designed to enhance the acts appropriate to the powers of the soul, so too sacramental grace adds something over and above grace as commonly defined, and also over and above the virtues and the Gifts, namely a special kind of divine assistance to help in attaining the end of the sacrament concerned (*divinum auxilium ad consequendum sacramenti finem*). [*Responsio*] (III.62.2)

It is at this point that Thomas gives his example of the denarius, showing how some people think of sacrament. In counterpoint, Thomas now moves toward his own contribution.

> But on any right understanding of the matter this way of interpreting the sacraments does not attribute any further force to them beyond that of a sign. For a leaden denarius is no more than a certain kind of sign of the royal prescription directing that the man presenting it is to receive a sum of money . . . On this interpretation, then, the sacraments of the New

---

in some way. For it is manifest that through the sacraments of the New Law man is incorporated into Christ. This is stated by St. Paul in the case of baptism when he says, [Gal. 3.27] *As many of you as have been baptized in Christ have put on Christ.* Now man is not made a member of Christ except through grace." (III.62.1.Reply).

13. I.e., grace "according to its common definition": namely, "a particular kind of perfection specifically designed to enhance the acts appropriate to the powers of the soul" (III.62.2.Reply).

14. "Does sacramental grace add anything over and above the grace of the virtues and the Gifts?" (III.62.2.) The note by David Bourke explains the virtues as "the four cardinal and three theological virtues, which flow from grace; see Ia2ae, 61 & 62; the Gifts of the Holy Ghost; see Ia2ae, 68." In Blackfriars edition, vol. 56, note a, p. 56.

Law would be nothing more than signs of grace. Yet we have it on the authority of many of the saints that the sacraments of the New Law not merely signify but actually cause grace. Therefore we must adopt a different approach based on the fact that there are *two kinds of efficient causes, principal and instrumental*. (III.62.1.Reply; emphasis added)

Expanding Aristotle's efficient causality to account for God's production and conveyance of the "coins" of grace, Thomas explains that Christ in his divinity, as one with the Father, is the principal efficient cause.[15] From Christ's divinity, grace flows through the conjoined instrumentation of his humanity, as a hand is joined to the arm. Grace then flows through the minister, a separated instrument, like a hammer and chisel in the hand of Christ, and through his words (form[16]) over the elements (matter). Thomas's description of separate instrumental agency refers both to the minister and to the *sacramentum* which is, by Augustine's definition, the *word joined to the element*[17] or *sign*. The principal efficient cause is God-in-Christ. The instrumental efficient causes are three: Christ's humanity (conjoined); the priest, speaking

---

15. "Now the divine power is the power of Christ as God and not as man. Therefore it is not as man but as God that Christ works to produce the interior effect of the sacrament" (III.64.3.*Sed contra*); for "[t]here are two ways in which an agent works actively to produce some effect: first as principal agent, second as an instrument. In the first of these two ways, therefore, it is God alone who works actively to produce the interior effect of the sacrament" (III.64.1, Reply). Christ participates in his divinity.

16. Thomas's use of "cause" language is not an exact parallel to Aristotle's, in that "formal" cause does not appear in this portion of Thomas's argument. Thomas contrasts "form" (by which he means not "shape" but *word* or formula: "I baptize you..." or "This is my body") with "matter" (by which he means *element*: e.g., water, bread). The form + matter compares to Augustine's word + element to become *sacramentum* (Latin). What is conferred by the *sacramentum* (form + matter) is the reality (L. res): grace and justification. The res + *sacramentum* is what produces, in baptism, confirmation, and ordination, the *character* imprinted upon the soul which causes an ontological change in the worshipper.

17. *Accedit verbum ad elementum et fit sacramentum*. On the Gospel of John, 80, on John 15.3 (*PL* 35:1840). Note that Thomas distinguishes between "matter" and "element," following Aristotle. While water is an element, Thomas notes that according to Aristotle, bread or the human body are matter but not elements; for elements are "those out of which the thing's primary composition arises ... [which] are not composed of other bodies. ... Whence Aristotle says in book five of the *Metaphysics* that 'an element is that out of which a thing is primarily composed, which is immanent in the thing and which is indivisible according to form'" (*De Prin.Nat.* 3.19).

the word over the matter (separate); and the word-and-matter (the *sacramentum*; separate):

> [T]he way in which a sacrament functions to cause grace is by acting as an instrument [*sacramentum operatur ad gratiam causandam per modum instrumenti*]. Now there are two kinds of instrument, one a separate instrument such as a staff, the other a united instrument, conjoined to the principal agent such as a hand. And it is by the conjoined instrument that the separate instrument is moved as a staff is moved by the hand. Moreover the principal efficient cause of grace is God himself, and the humanity of Christ stands to him in the relation of a conjoined instrument, whereas a sacrament stands in the relation of a separate one. Thus it is *right that the power to bestow salvation should flow from the divinity of Christ through his humanity into the actual sacraments.* (III.62.5.Reply; emphasis added)

As human, Christ "works to produce the interior effect of the sacraments through merit and by way of efficient causality, but still by a causality that is instrumental" (III.64.3.*Responsio*). However, the instrumental causality extends from Christ's humanity to the "separated instruments which are the ministers of the Church and of the sacraments themselves" (*instrumentorum extrinsecorum, qui sunt ministri Ecclesiae et ipsa sacramenta*),[18] analogically the staff in the hand of Christ: "[M]an can work actively to produce the interior effect of the sacrament inasmuch as he performs the function of the minister [*operatur per modum ministri*]. For a minister has the same significance as an instrument in the sense that the action of both is applied from without yet achieves the interior effect from the power of the principal agent which is God" (III.64.1, Reply).

Thus is the sacramental minister, i.e., the priest, an instrument in adding sacramental grace to the (passive) baptized persons who receive the priest's action. We can see in this at once the distinctive power of the priest, over against the laity; but also the machine-like sense of the priest having no personal human involvement. He is merely an instrument: "Now an instrument derives its power from the principal agent, and with regard to the sacraments the agent is twofold, namely he who institutes the sacrament and he who uses the sacrament once instituted by applying it in order to cause it to take effect [God : priest].

18. III.64.3.Reply.

Furthermore the power of the sacrament cannot derive from him who uses that sacrament. For the only active contribution which he makes is as a minister" (III.64.2.Reply).

The third instrumental cause is the sacramental elements, but they are objects and themselves have no agency. Yet "sacraments act as instruments in producing spiritual effects" (III.64.2.Reply). Thomas explains (III.66.1.Reply), in his discussion of baptism, that "three things should be considered: that which is *sign only [sacramentum tantum]*, that which is *reality and sign [res et sacramentum]*, and that which is *reality only [res tantum]*." Further, the material element in baptism is not the water, as Hugh of St. Victor says,[19] but rather the *washing*.[20] In other words, elaborating Augustine's definition of sacrament as word united with the element, Thomas states that "the perfection of the sacrament is not in the water by itself but in the application of the water to man . . . with the prescribed form of words." It is, then, the agency of the priest as extension of Christ who is a primary instrumental cause of grace in applying the "sacrament," (*sacramentum*, sign), which is the matter (e.g., washing) plus the form (e.g., "I baptize you in the name of the Father, and of the Son, and of the Holy Spirit" or, for Thomas, "This is my Body"), to the person. When the minister does this with the intent of the Church, the *res,* grace, is effectively transmitted to the worshipper. The *sacramentum* and *res* together result in both the primary effect of the sacraments, grace, as well as the secondary effect, character (III.63).[21] Thomas stops short of asserting that the priest is an essential instrument, for since it is God who is the efficient cause, God can use any means God wishes. It is in article 64.7, "Can angels be the ministers of the sacraments?" that Thomas points out that while "it is for men, and not angels, to confer (here, *dispensare*) the sacra-

---

19. *Baptismus est aqua diluendis criminibus sanctificata per verbum Dei*: Baptism is water sanctified by God's word for the washing away of sins. Hugh of St. Victor, *De Sacramentis* II.6.2 (*PL* 176:443). Transl. by James J. Cunningham, in Thomas Aquinas, *Summa Theologiae* (NY: Blackfriars, 1975), Vol. 57, IIIa, Question 66.1, point 2.

20. Thomas quotes Peter Lombard's *Sentences* (Book IV, 3.1): "Magister dicit quod *baptismus est ablutio corporis exterior facta sub forma praescripta verborum*," the external washing of the body with the prescribed form of words (III.66.1.Reply), transl. J. Cunningham, *ibid.*

21. Question 63 is given over to "The other effect of the sacraments, which is character." Later, Thomas explains, "The *reality and sign* is the baptismal character" since the sign is the external washing and the reality is the interior justification (III.66.1, Reply) or grace.

ments and act as ministers in them", nonetheless, "just as God did not cause his power to be restricted to the sacraments in such a way that he could not bestow the effect of the sacraments without the sacraments themselves, so too he did not restrict his power to the ministers of his Church." If God wanted to grant angels the power to administer the sacraments, Thomas says, he could, and such a sacrament "would have to be regarded as valid, because it should be evident that this was done by the will of God" (III.64.7.Reply).

> ### Aquinas on Intention in the Sacramental Minister
>
> "Is the intention of the minister required for the sacrament to achieve its effect?" (*utrum intentio ministri requiratur ad perfectionem sacramenti*). III.64.8. Reply: "Thus the act of washing with water, which takes place in baptism, can be aimed at physical cleanliness or physical health, or be one in play, and there are many other reasons of this kind why this action should be performed. And because of this it is necessary to isolate and define the one purpose for which the action of washing is performed in baptism, and this is done through the intention of the minister. This intention in turn is expressed in the words pronounced in the sacraments, as when the minister says, *I baptize you in the name of the Father*, etc.
>
> "Hence: 1. An inanimate instrument does not have any intention with regard to the effect produced. Instead the motion by which it is impelled by the principal agent takes the place of intention here. An animate instrument, on the other hand, such as a minister is, . . . [wills] his limbs to perform the necessary actions. This is why his intention is required, for it is by this that he subjects himself to the principal agent . . . to do what Christ and the Church do.
>
> "2. . . . [Must an intention] be present in the minister's mind, [so] that if this is lacking the sacrament does not take effect [?] [In such a defect, as] in the case of children, who have no intention of coming to the sacraments, Christ makes good . . . by baptizing them interiorly. . . . In the case of adults, on the other hand, it is their faith and devotion that makes good this defect, since they intend to receive the sacraments.
>
> "Now while this might be said to be adequate so far as the ultimate effect is concerned, namely justification from sins, still, so far as that effect which is *reality and sacrament combined* is concerned—in other words so far as character is concerned—it seems that the defect cannot be made good merely through the devotion of him who approaches the sacraments. The reason is that character is never imprinted except through the sacrament itself.
>
> "For this reason, then, others [Albert, *Sent.* IV.6.12. Perer of Tarentaise, *Sent.* IV.6.1, 2] put forward a better explanation . . . [in] that the minister of the sacrament acts in the person of the Church as a whole whose minister he is. And in the words which are pronounced it is the intention of the Church

> that is expressed. This, then, is adequate for the sacrament to take effect [even without intention] unless there is any outward expression to the contrary on the part of the minister and the recipient of the sacrament.
>
> "3. While it is true that someone whose mind is on something else does not have any actual intention still he does have a habitual one, and this is sufficient for the sacrament to achieve its effect. Thus for instance it is sufficient if when the priest comes to baptize he intends in performing the baptism to do what the Church does. . . .[However,] the minister of the sacrament should take the utmost pains to ensure that he also brings his actual intention to bear."

Thomas's mechanistic view of the minister's instrumental role is heightened by his assertion that neither lack of faith,[22] nor the lack of intention,[23] nor the lack of purity[24] in the minister inhibits the effectiveness of the sacramental action. What God wills, God will do, in spite of insufficiencies on the part of the minister. When the minister uses the proper form and matter, God conveys grace to the "recipient" of the sacrament.

It is interesting that while there is much clarity as to the impersonal nature of the minister's role, there is hardly mention of the people at all. According to Thomas, the people are not participants in, but *recipients of* the sacraments (strengthening his notion of sacrament as object conveyed). As was observed earlier, the laity hold a passive position in Thomas, even after baptism:

---

22. III.64.9: "Is the faith of the minister indispensable to the sacrament?" (*utrum ides ministri sit de necessitate sacramenti).* "On the contrary, Augustine tells us [*Contra litt. Petiliani II*.47; PL 43, 298], *Remember that the conduct of wicked men represents no obstacle to the sacraments of God in such a way as to render then either void or less holy.* Reply: . . . it is not necessary for the minister to be in a state of charity in order that the sacrament may be validly performed. On the contrary, sinners too can confer sacraments [Donatist controversy]. In the same way, therefore, the minister's faith is not a necessary condition either. Rather a person devoid of faith can confer a sacrament so long as the other conditions are fulfilled which are necessary for sacramental validity."

23. III.64.8: see text-box, Aquinas on minister's intention, pp. 30–31.

24. III.64.1.Reply 2: "Hence, it is not the case that the effect of the sacrament is better when it is conferred by a better minister." See also: III.64.5: "Can the sacraments be conferred by evil ministers? . . . Hence the ministers of the Church can confer the sacraments even when they are evil. *Ad* 1. The ministers of the Church do not of their own power either cleanse men from their sins when they approach the sacraments or confer grace upon them. This rather is something which Christ does of his own power, working through them as through instruments of a certain kind. And hence the effect achieved in those who receive the sacraments is not to assimilate them to the ministers, but to bring them into configuration with Christ" (III.64.5.Reply).

[P]ower is either active or passive; active power is bestowed in the sacrament of orders, passive or receptive power through the sacrament of baptism" *(Potentia autem non est nisi activa vel passiva. Potentia autem activa in sacramentis confertur per sacramentum ordinis: potentia autem passiva sive receptiva per sacramentum baptismi).*[25]

The passivity of the laity is partially what enabled Thomas to understand the nature of baptism to be like the making and transferring of coins. It is done by God through the conjoined instrumentality of Christ and the separate instrumentality of the priest who speaks the formula during the administration of the water, and through the word + matter as they are *conferred upon* the baptizand.

It is important to note here, however, that Thomas (like all of us) was a product of his time—and in the medieval church, the laity had indeed come to be quite passive. They did not receive either the cup or the bread, except once a year,[26] but encountered Christ at the elevation of the host by gazing upon it. They did not sing or speak in the mass. Thomas in his theology was (among other things) accounting for his own experience of the church and its worship life.

Is there any suggestion at all in Thomas that the effect of this additional grace will be manifest in the lives of baptized persons, passive recipients though they may be? Is there any hint of grace working through time or in any observable difference in the person? In fact, there are some references suggesting that the internal state of the worshipper does matter. For example, apart from the mechanistic requirements of sacramental validity, there are "rites of human institution which are enacted in the sacraments . . . [not] of necessity. Their purpose is, rather, to impart a certain solemnity to the sacraments so as to excite devotion and reverence in those receiving them" (64.2.1). Why would "devotion and reverence" be of value? Thomas does not say, but this is nonetheless a clear reference to affective evocation among the people. The sub-text is the operational dimension. While the Holy Spirit is not mentioned at all here, still, that the people have an experi-

---

25. *Summa Theologiae*, IIIa. Q 63. Art. 2 (reiterated in III.72.5). Thomas does not say what kind of character the third non-repeatable sacrament, Confirmation, imposes (IIIa. 72.5, 6).

26. Cf. Lateran Council IV (1215), which pronounced that the laity must receive the eucharistic bread at least once per year.

ence of being "aroused" (*ad excitandam devotionem et reverentiam*) is acknowledged in Thomas.

Further, while the minister need not have faith, the "recipients" should: While "it is the merit and power of [Christ's] Passion that operates in the sacraments," still, "it is through faith that the power of the Passion is applied to us" (III.64.3.Reply). The recipients have something to do with what is actually received.

And again, "Christ refrained from communicating the power of his excellence to ministers . . . to help the faithful lest they should put their trust in men, and lest there should be different sacraments leading to divisions in the Church, as in the case of those who said, *I am of Paul, I am of Apollo, and I of Cephas* [I Cor 1:12]" (64.4.1).

And finally, validity aside, sacraments should be fitting *to the people*:

> There are two ways in which a given condition ought to be in a sacrament. First as something the existence of which is necessary for the sacrament to be such at all. And in fact if a condition of this kind is lacking the sacrament is not given effect, as when due form or due matter is lacking. The second way in which something ought to be present in a sacrament is by reason of a certain fitness. And this is the way in which the ministers of the sacrament ought to be good men. (III.64.5.Reply *ad* 3)

Thomas makes oblique allusions to operational efficacy even though his intent is to show how grace is produced and transferred by God through the instruments of Christ's humanity, priest, and *sacramentum* (formula + matter). As hard as it is to find, it is, surprisingly, present in his acknowledgment that baptizands (for example) must have faith, and that their devotional involvement is fitting. Thomas represents for us the extreme position of baptism "taking" in the passive baptizand (through the instrumentality of the active ordained person) through the action of God-Christ-priest and conveyed as a coin is handed to someone. Yet even here, in the receptivity, something must needs be going on in the human subject. The baptized person is not, finally in Thomas, an object to be acted upon, but a subject called to faith and devotion, for whom sacraments should be fitting. While not Thomas's emphasis, if one looks deeply, there is an assumption of effect and a hope of some experience of God in the people who receive the sacraments.

But to find the extent to which a sacrament can be fitting to the worshipper, we look to the Reformation turn toward the worshipper. And in John Calvin, we will see articulated how God accommodated Godself to humankind. In the next chapter, then, we examine the two-perspective approach identified in John Calvin's *Institutes of the Christian Religion*.

4

Calvin on Baptism

Two Perspectives on Sacramentality and the Church

Sacrament: God's Accommodation to Humanity So That Humanity Might Respond to God

Introduction to Calvin's Understanding of Baptism

THE REFORMERS USED THE LANGUAGE OF "PLEDGE," "SEAL," AND "testimony" to understand sacrament and to articulate their purpose. John Calvin (1509–64), for example, following Augustine, asserts that a sacrament is "an outward sign by which the Lord seals on our consciences the promises of his good will toward us in order to sustain the weakness of our faith . . . a testimony of divine grace toward us, confirmed by an outward sign."[1] It will be interesting to compare Calvin's use of the pledge metaphor with Thomas's example of the denarius. Calvin says:

> the seals which are attached to government documents and other public acts are nothing taken by themselves, for they would be attached in vain if the parchment had nothing writ-

---

1. *Institutes* IV.14.1. It must be recognized that Calvin's understanding is not simply "sign" but a particular sign which follows the preaching of the word in which faith is awakened ("You see how the sacrament requires preaching to beget faith" IV.14.4) and the promise is proclaimed. The sacrament follows the promise and "is joined to it as a sort of appendix, with the purpose of confirming and sealing the promise itself, and of making it more evident to us and in a sense ratifying it" (IV.14.3). The word, "when preached, [should] make us understand what the visible sign means" (IV.14.4). Yet it is not so much that the sacraments seal the promise (i.e., covenant) but "it is clear from the promises themselves that each confirms the other" (IV.14.5). The kerygmatic word proclaimed prepares the worshipper to encounter the word made visible in sacrament.

ten on it. Yet, when added to the writing, they do not on that account fail to confirm and seal what is written . . . Paul expressly argues [Rom 4:11] that Abraham's circumcision was not for his justification but for the seal of that covenant by faith in which he had already been justified.

For Calvin, following Augustine, the elements (bread, wine, water) are the seal that, when added to the word, results in sacrament.[2] The word (which in Thomas is merely Aristotle's "form")—the Scriptural formula (e.g., "I baptize you in the name of the [Trinity]")—has a broader meaning in Calvin. Calvin's interpretation of the word is as *kerygma*, the effective proclamatory word that goes forth from the mouth of God and "shall not return to me empty, but it shall accomplish that which I purpose, and succeed in the thing for which I sent it [says the Lord]" (Isa 55:10–11). The kerygmatic word is part of the effective sacramental action. It arouses faith in the hearer, such that the seal is effective. There are, then, for Calvin, three essentials in sacramental efficacy:

- the word (proclaimed)
- the elements, and
- the faith of the hearer.

In his example, the writing on the document can be trusted to effect its purpose, the other two essentials being in place (seal, recipient). The writing, the word, is a vow or promise that is not in doubt. In contrast to Aquinas' example where the sign is a promise ineffective apart from something to cause an effect, in Calvin the word communicates a vow or promise which is irrevocable. Calvin presumes in his example that the promise undergirding the written document will be fulfilled—actually, *has already* been fulfilled in Christ, as seen by the comparison with Abraham's justification which has already happened before the circumcision. Aquinas' example, on the other hand, suggests the possibility that the promise to pay one hundred pounds in exchange for the denarius might be revoked at the will of the one in whose name the denarius was issued. Thus, in Calvin's example, the sign (seal) assures the recipient that the promise articulated in the

---

2. Augustine: "*Accedit verbum ad elementum*," in *Treatise on the Gospel of John*, 80.3, on John 15:3 (c. 416): PL 35:1840. "The word is added to the element, and there results the sacrament, as if itself also a kind of visible word," transl. in *St. Augustine: Homilies on the Gospel of John*, NPNF, 344.

written document is confirmed, is true, and is occurring as a sure and certain reality. In Aquinas' example, by contrast, the sign (denarius) is a token of what might occur, but the reality is not sure and certain until the 100 pounds is forthcoming. And grace is "caused" by sacrament.

Yet none of these theologians accepts the possibility of tenuousness in God's good gifts to humanity. For Calvin, the certainty of God's grace comes from counting upon the word of Scripture which points to Christ, the Incarnate Word. The word is manifest in preaching by which the faithful are aroused to receive the sure and certain gift of God's grace. God's offering is certain. What is uncertain is the ability of the people of God to receive the gift: "Yet it is one thing to be offered, another to be received" (*Institutes*, 4.17.33; cf. 4.17.3).

The completion of God's offering through its reception by the faithful is a locus of Calvin's concern. The distinguishing of God's giving and the people's receiving points to a two-perspective hermeneutic in Calvin's theology of baptism and church. Let us look briefly at this perspectival hermeneutic.

Problems in Understanding Calvin's "Contradictions"

The Council of Trent, in its seventh session (1547), stated: "If anyone saith, that these sacraments were instituted for the sake of nourishing faith alone: let him be anathema."[3] This canon was a direct refutation of John Calvin who specifically stated that sacraments are "aids to our faith and supplements to our doctrine."[4] However, this is not the only description Calvin gives of sacrament.[5] For example, in speaking spe-

---

3. *Si quis dixerit, hæc sacramenta propter solam fidem nutriendam instituta fuisse: anathema sit.* For Latin and English, see Schaff, *The Creeds of Christendom*, 120.

4. In *Inst.*4.14.1, as well as in 4.14.13 (*fidei nostrae adminicula essent, doctrinaeque appendices*). In *Inst.* 4.14.19 he calls sacraments "aids to true piety" where "aids" is *adiumenta* in the 1559 edition: *instrumenta* in previous editions. See Riggs, *The Development of Calvin's Baptismal Theology*, 163–64.

5. In addition to "another aid to our faith," a sacrament is:
- "an outward sign by which the Lord seals on our consciences the promises of his good will toward us" (*Inst.* 4.14.1);
- that which "sustain[s] the weakness of our faith" (ibid.);
- an outward sign by which "we in turn attest our piety toward him in the presence of the Lord and of his angels and before men" (ibid.);
- "a testimony of divine grace toward us, confirmed by an outward sign, with mutual attestation of our piety toward him" (ibid.);

cifically of baptism, Calvin says "the power of the keys . . . depends upon baptism" (*Institutes* 4.15.4); "through baptism Christ makes us sharers in his death, that we may be engrafted in it" (*Inst.* 4.15.5); and that baptism has "enclosed in itself, the promise of forgiveness of sins, mortification of the flesh, spiritual vivification, and participation in Christ" (*Inst.* 4.15.16). These descriptions of baptism sound like much more than aids to our faith: these sound as though something is *effected* at baptism, that something *happens*, is *changed*. Do these statements contradict the idea that sacraments—in this case, baptism—is merely an aid to faith?

There have been divers attempts to "pin down" the sacramental theology of Calvin to a foundational thesis. The difficulty of identifying Calvin's thesis has led many studies to conclude that perhaps there is not one; that Calvin's theology "has in fact no basic principle" but that perhaps it could be understood by interpreting its structural development as a *complexio oppositorum*, i.e., "the capacity to integrate doctrines even though they are opposed from the point of view of logic or metaphysics";[6] or, that Calvin's theology is merely reflective of God who is a *coincidentia oppositorum*;[7] or, that there is a schizophrenia in Calvin[8]. The "problem of the structure of Calvin's theology"[9] has led to the suggestion that there may be no "structure," but instead a dialectic, a juxtaposition of opposites. In logical terms, Calvin seems to reject

---

- a sign "which reverently represent[s] sublime and spiritual things" (*Inst.* 4.14.2);
- "joined to a preceding promise as a sort of appendix, with the purpose of confirming and sealing the promise itself, and of making it more evident to us and in a sense ratifying it" (*Inst.* 4.14.3);
- "not so much needed to confirm his Sacred Word as to establish us in faith in it" (ibid.).

6. The perspective of Hermann Bauke (*Die Probleme der Theologie Calvins*, 1922), in Niesel, *The Theology of Calvin*, 11. For a terse history of commentary on Calvin's theology, see Engel, *John Calvin's Perspectival Anthropology*, x–xi.

7. The perspective of Matthias Simon, 1932: see Niesel, *The Theology of Calvin*, 18f.

8. The perspective of Hermann Weber, 1930: in ibid., 12f.

9. Engel, *John Calvin's Perspectival Anthropology*, x. She states, "It is now common to find theologians and historians arguing that there is neither a thematic core nor a consistent formal structure in Calvin's theology. Representatives attribute the alleged lack of consistency to various causes, but all agree that Calvin's theology is, in some sense or some place, finally contradictory" (x).

the law of the excluded middle[10] in that he claims two apparently opposing things to be true at the same time.

We can see clearly the reason for this tendency of theologians to view Calvin this way; for we see him state that baptism is an aid to faith, yet baptism is the means by which Christ makes us sharers in his death; baptism is an outward sign confirming a testimony of divine grace, yet baptism encloses in itself participation in Christ. Was John Calvin unable to make up his mind, or did he perhaps vacillate in his view, proposing one thought and then "trying on" its opposite?

Or is it possible that there is a method in Calvin's "madness"? The confusion of scholars to comprehend Calvin's anthropology has been interpreted by William Bouwsma, John Riggs, and Mary Potter Engle as Calvin's rhetorical *two-perspective hermeneutic*. What appears to readers of Calvin as contradiction are, rather, *consistent statements spoken from two points of view*. Engel identifies a "dynamic perspectival structure" in Calvin's anthropology and explores the distinction between the absolute, heavenly perspective of God and the relative, earthly perspective of human beings.[11] Riggs demonstrates this approach in Calvin's sacramental theology in which Calvin names both the nature of baptism and the way it should be appropriated by the faithful. Bouwsma calls these two perspectives *eruditio* and *persuasio*. This compelling identification of Calvin's rhetorical hermeneutics[12]

---

10. "If it isn't false, it therefore must be true."

11. For a summary of Engel's thesis in *John Calvin's Perspectival Anthropology*, see the Introduction (ix–xv) and chapter 1, "The Dynamic Perspectival Structure of Calvin's Anthropology" (1–35). Engel demonstrates her thesis not in sacramental theology, which is our concern here, but in Calvin's doctrine of humankind: (a) "the problem of the loss and/or retention of the *imago dei* after the fall"; (b) "the problem of the rejection and/or use of reason in human affairs," (c) "the problem of the denial of human freedom and/or the emphasis on human responsibility," and (d) "the problem of the immortality of the soul and/or the resurrection of the body" (ibid., xii). I am grateful to Professor Don Compier for pointing out Engel's helpful treatment.

12. The history of exploration of Calvin's theology as rhetorical could be dated from Quirinus Breen's article in 1957, "John Calvin and the Rhetorical Tradition." E. David Willis (1974) follows Breen in considering Calvin in the tradition of Ciceronian rhetoric. Ford Lewis Battles (1977) set the stage for subsequent analysis in identifying Calvin's rhetorical method as what he calls "accommodation" (Calvin uses *accommodare* or *attemperare*). In "God Was Accommodating Himself to Human Capacity," Battles relates Calvin's approach to the classical rhetoric particularly in the Alexandrian school of biblical hermeneutics (ibid., 22ff.). Battles' examples show how Calvin resolves Scriptural inconsistencies through accommodation (e.g., Scripture apparently teaches that God has a mouth, ears, hands; but God is really infinite and

from the perspectives of the church's mediation and the person's reception points to Calvin's expectation that grace actually operates, functions, is experienced in the lived life of a baptized person.

We will first establish Bouwsma's and Riggs' theses that Calvin presents propositional theology (*eruditio*) but also persuasive or pastoral theology through the use of *decorum* and figures of speech. Then the meaning of baptism for Calvin will be presented through his use of the metaphor of "engrafting in Christ." We will conclude by suggesting how Calvin's method is particularly suited to the expression of, in Ganoczy's term, Calvin's Christ-centered (baptismal) ecclesiology.[13] While both of Calvin's perspectives make up his theology of baptism's (doctrinal) efficacy, his recognition of the distinct perspective of baptism from the point of view of the experiencing person strengthens a perspectival theology of baptism and renders clearer the necessity of accounting for operational efficacy in any complete baptismal theology.

Making Sense of Calvin on Baptism

In seeking to offer an historical view of Calvin from within his sixteenth-century humanist context, William J. Bouwsma asserts two movements in Calvin's theological discourse: description and persuasion.[14] He calls these two *eruditio* and *persuasio*.[15] He supports his

---

spiritual). As nurses do with infants, God speaks "baby talk" to us to make clear to human finitude what God is like (*Inst.* 1.13.1). Battles does not speak of a two-perspective approach; however, in his conclusion he asserts that Calvin sees sacraments and even the incarnation as God's accommodation to humanity (ibid., 36–38).

13. Ganoczy, *The Young Calvin*, 310.

14. Bouwsma, "Calvinism as *Theologia Rhetorica*." This address was taken from chapter 7 of his subsequent book *John Calvin: A Sixteenth-Century Portrait*, 113–27.

15. In our own day there is not agreement as to whether theology should appropriately include both these aspects, especially since *persuasio* engages the whole person (head and heart). However, inasmuch as conversion requires the assent of the whole person, we might note two modern thinkers who have at least considered these same issues that Calvin apparently did.

John Henry Newman distinguishes between notional assent and real assent, the first tending "to be mere assertions without any personal hold on them on the part of those who make them [the assents]," while the second "is directed towards things, represented by the impressions which they have left on the imagination. These images, when assented to, have an influence both on the individual and on society, which mere notions cannot exert" (*An Essay in Aid of a Grammar of Assent*, 38, 72).

appellation of Calvin's approach as *theologia rhetorica*[16] by quoting from Calvin's sermons on Job. Instead of consoling Job, his "friends" offered propositional statements, *eruditio*: "objective" interpretation as to what must have transpired to put Job in this predicament. Detached theological reflection has a place: but here, Calvin asserts, Job's *experience* should have been included in the response of his "friends" who did not consider "the person whom they addressed, for it is necessary to treat one individual differently from another."[17] This was a particular person in a particular circumstance (context): it is Job in particular they should have addressed, for "afflictions are like sicknesses; if a doctor used the same remedy for every sick person, how would that be? It is necessary in the first place to consider what people are like, and then how to deal with them."[18] What was Job's situation, his need?

Karl Rahner also makes room for theology as both experiential and practical in asserting that theological statements and kerygmatic statements are both faith statements, in "What is a dogmatic statement?" *Theological Investigations*, Vol. 5, 48f. He asserts the relational or rhetorical nature of faith, in words that could have been Calvin's: "faith is always the listening by a concrete human being to the Word of God . . . which is actually present only when it is heard and understood" (ibid., 48). He goes on to point out that "theology cannot take its departure, like geometry, from a finite number of axioms which can be strictly defined in concepts used by them" (ibid., 55). Because of the multivalent, nonlinear nature of theology, Rahner supports the use of analogy in doing theology: "the radical openness of the movement of the spirit in analogy really makes the spirit a spirit" (ibid., 59).

16. Bouwsma points out that the phrase *theologia rhetorica* "was coined by Charles Trinkaus to describe the religious thought of Renaissance humanism in *In Our Image and Likeness: Humanity and Divinity in Italian Humanist Thought* (Chicago, 1970)." *Colloquy*, 14 n. 1. For the pioneering work of Q. Breen on Calvin's rhetorical method, see ref. in n. 26. See also work by Professor David Willis (see n. 28), and John Leith's editorial in *Interpretation*, Vol. 31, #1, January, 1977, which is devoted to Calvin studies.

17. "nous sommes admonnestez, quand nous voudrons consoler nos prochains en leurs tristesses et fascheries, de n'y point aller à la volee: comme il y en aura beaucoup qui n'auront iamais qu'une chanson, et ils ne regardent point à la personne à laquelle ils s'addressent, car il faut manier l'un autrement que l'autre." Sermon #62 on Job 16:1-9, Vol. 34, col. 5, in *Ioannis Calvini Opera*, in *Corpus Reformatorum*. Volume numbers will be given according to *Calvini Opera*, abb. CO. (Thus, volume 1 of CO is volume 29 of CR; CO 34 is CR 62, etc.)

18. Sermon #78 on Job 21:1-6, CO Vol. 34, col. 206. "Car les afflictions sont comme maladies: et si un medecin use d'un mesme remede envers tous malades, et que sera-ce? . . . Voila donc comme un medecin meurtrira les malades, quand il n'aura point le regard aux maladies: mesmes il faut avoir cognu les complexions des malades." Bouwsma's translation gives the sense of Calvin's meaning.

What direction should friends have invited him toward? What could be said that would have enabled Job to be united with God, to appropriate God's loving nature (*charis*; grace)? These implicit questions of Calvin's are the questions of rhetoric.

Calvin was not the first Christian theologian to use a rhetorical method. Current work has uncovered this approach in New Testament authors,[19] Tertullian,[20] Gregory of Nazianzus,[21] Augustine,[22] and a variety of Reformation theologians.[23] The concern of rhetoric is concern with the use of language as it affects and moves human beings.

In contrast, however, the medieval scholastic tradition was more concerned with philosophical discourse in a "scientific" methodology. Abelard moved away from philology toward scientific theology,[24] and Thomas Aquinas assumed there was a synthesis of literal and figurative meaning in the Bible:

> Thus in Holy Scripture no confusion results, for all the senses are founded on one—the literal—from which alone can any argument be drawn, and not from those intended in allegory, as Augustine says. Nevertheless, nothing of Holy Scripture perishes on account of this, since nothing necessary to faith is

---

Battles notes that Calvin uses "foundation images for his conviction that in all [God's] ways with man [sic], God is accommodating his infinity to our small measure" (29). These metaphors are God as Father, teacher, and physician, thus comparing humanity to children, students, sick persons. This example from Calvin's sermon on Job would corroborate Battles' observation. "God was Accommodating," 29, 20.

19. See Kennedy, *New Testament Interpretation through Rhetorical Criticism*, and Kinneavy, *Greek Rhetorical Origins of Christian Faith*.

20. See Sider, *Ancient Rhetoric and the Art of Tertullian*.

21. See Ruether, *Gregory of Nazianzus: Rhetor and Philosopher*.

22. See Burke, *The Rhetoric of Religion*, chap. 2, and Burke, *A Rhetoric of Motives*, 49–50. For examples of Augustine's method in his exploration of definition of church and of the meaning of the sacraments, see Douglass, "The Divine Timbre of the Word."

23. The "supposition of a sacral relationship of words to things" is normative for Calvin's time. Elizabeth Clarke points out that the "Renaissance rediscovery of classical rhetoric coincided with a Reformation emphasis on the effectiveness of the written word for salvation. It is not surprising, therefore, to find in the writings of sixteenth-century scholars, both theologians and literary theorists, a concern with the power and status of language that is almost an obsession." "Silent, Performative Words: The Language of God in Valdesso and George Herbert," 355. See, for example, Michael B. Aune's engaging treatment of Philip Melanchthon's use of rhetoric in relationship to Christian ritual in Aune, "*To Move the Heart*."

24. For a summary of medieval hermeneutics, see Jeanrond, *Theological Hermeneutics*, 26f.

contained under the spiritual sense which is not elsewhere put forward by the Scripture in its literal sense.²⁵

Aristotle's categories of analytic and dialectic method may assist us here. Analytic method reasons from accepted first principles, operates in a closed (tautological) system, and provides certainty in its results, making it appropriate for mathematics. Dialectic method, by contrast, is not univocal and cannot claim certainty; but in its ambiguity and openness to new (nontautological) insights, Aristotle considered it a method appropriate to politics, ethics, and poetics.²⁶ Aristotle goes on to state that "rhetoric is the counterpart of dialectic" (*Rhet.* 1354a1) in a practical sense: for example, where dialectic might lead persons to change their opinions, it is rhetoric which would move them to action. Rhetoric is "the faculty of discovering, in the particular case, the available means of persuasion" (*Rhet.* 1355b26).

Bouwsma and Riggs note that Calvin's theological method, like that of his predecessors, indeed includes *eruditio*, analysis, description of the nature of a sacrament. But in addition, they point out that Calvin presents theology "adapted in such a way as to have an effect on those who hear it."²⁷ This is rhetoric, the art of persuading. In par-

---

25. Aquinas, *Summa Theologiae*, Ia. 1,10, 88f. Latin text ed. Thomas Gilby, O.P., *St. Thomas Aquinas SUMMA THEOLOGIAE*, vol. 1, 36f.

26. I am indebted to David S. Cunningham for his helpful summary of the use of rhetoric as theological method. See his "Theology as Rhetoric." See also Breen, "John Calvin and the Rhetorical Tradition," esp. 5, 14 on the distinction between analysis and dialectic. Breen's article, pioneering rhetorical studies of Calvin, notes the use of rhetorical method in Calvin but short of interpreting it, he at least tries to justify Calvin's persuasive ("deliberative") Ciceronian rhetoric, given the "generally accepted assumption" that theology is a science which must be precise and as such must employ syllogistic logic (ibid., 18). He equivocates on the legitimacy of Calvin's method, however, finally pointing out that Calvin wrote for "the common man" (ibid., 19), that moving the heart of a person does not invalidate "the truth of theological statement" (ibid., 18), and that Calvin was "a child of his humanistic age and training. Had he written in syllogistic style his book would not likely have become what it was—a work known everywhere" (ibid., 18).

27. Calvin, Commentary on Lamentations 1:2.

ticular, Bouwsma identifies two means of *persuasio*[28] used by Calvin: *decorum* and figures of speech.[29]

First, as he thinks Job's "friends" should have done, Calvin enlists the rhetorical value of *decorum*,[30] the ability to shape the words to the hearer, in order better to draw the listener into understanding, to persuade or enlighten. Calvin says that a wise teacher "accommodates himself to the understanding of those who must be taught. He begins with first principles in teaching the weak and ignorant and should not rise any higher than they can follow. In short he instills his teaching drop by drop, lest it overflow."[31]

Decorum "dictated attention to the subject and audience of the discourse."[32] God is our example in this, Calvin says, because God "stammers" or "lisps" so that we of limited capacity can understand (*Inst.* 1.13.1). God the Creator had brought writing into existence, and in the same way had compelled "the empty and formless matter of world, called chaos to shine with an admirable fitness [*decore*] and beauty."[33] As Bouwsma paraphrases Calvin, "[t]he creation itself was thus the product of a kind of divine rhetoric, shaped throughout by the decorum of the Master Rhetorician." Christ also spoke to accommodate his teaching to his hearers "to be more easily understood by the simple."[34]

Riggs points out that Calvin "addresses the question of correct appropriation of a sacrament"[35] or the human role in sacramental action. This engaging insight into Calvin's baptismal theology seems, I

---

28. Note that E. David Willis, arguing a different point than Bouwsma, suggests that Calvin had two models of rhetoric open to him, a Ciceronian school and a persuasive school, the latter intending to persuade irrespective of the validity of the position. According to Willis, Calvin follows the Ciceronian school. For his argument, see "Rhetoric and Responsibility in Calvin's Theology," 46.

29. See Bouwsma, "Calvinism as *Theologia Rhetorica*," 2–3.

30. Bouwsma, ibid., 2.

31. Calvin, Commentary on 1 Cor 3:2.

32. Marjorie O'Rourke Boyle, "Rhetorical Theology: Charity seeking Charity," response to Bouwsma, *Colloquy*, 22, in which she contrasts "charity seeking charity" with the traditional approach to theology, "faith seeking understanding." For more on *decorum*, see Boyle, *Erasmus on Language and Method in Theology*, 48–51, and Boyle, *Rhetoric and Reform*, 39–40.

33. Calvin, Commentary on Exodus 31:18.

34. Calvin, Commentary on Matthew 18:16.

35. Riggs, *Development of Calvin's Baptismal Theology*, 10.

suggest, to fall into the arena of *decorum*. Riggs points out that side by side with *eruditio* or propositional description of the nature of a sacrament, Calvin also elucidates its right appropriation in his definition of sacrament. Sacrament is best understood, then, from two sides: its nature, from "God's side," is "the stamp of his promises, or the giving of a testimony by an outward sign"; and its right appropriation, from "the human side, [is] the attesting of our devotion towards God resulting from the promises received or from the testimony heard."[36] Sacraments are not for the gospel, but for us: "not so much needed to confirm [God's] Sacred Word as to establish us in faith in it" (*Inst.* IV.14.3). Again in his description of baptism, Riggs notes that Calvin begins with its right use (human side) and finishes with its nature (God's side):

> [Right use:] Baptism is the sign of initiation by which we are received into the society of the church so that, engrafted in Christ, we may be considered among God's children. Furthermore, it has been given to us by God for this end (which I have taught is common to all sacraments): first, to serve our faith before him, second to serve our confession before people . . . [Nature:] The Lord first says to us that it should be a mark and proof of our cleansing; or (that I might better explain what I mean) it is like a certain sealed document that confirms to us that all our sins are so destroyed, erased and cancelled that at no time can they come to his sight, be remembered, or be charged against us. (*Inst.* 4.15.1; Riggs, 11–12)

Are there two different definitions of baptism which conflict? Some would say so. But the roles of God and human persons are distinct: to speak to each of these in turn would only seem conflictive if one were not aware of the shift in perspective. As Calvin himself says, "Yet it is one thing to be offered, another to be received."[37] Here, God offers; people receive. Calvin uses the language of *decorum* to make his theology fitting for his hearers in order that they might *receive* the message. Something offered but not received is not a gift: the invited relationship does not come to be. Calvin's use of *decorum* appears, on the human side, to be an invitation to the receptivity that is faith, a "coaching" as to how Christians might understand church and receive the sacraments.

36. Ibid., 10. Calvin's description from *Inst.* 4.14.1.
37. *Inst.* IV.17.33 (cf. IV.17.3).

In addition to *decorum* or the accommodating of the words to the audience or readership, Calvin uses another rhetorical device to engage the hearers. Figurative language comes from the Holy Spirit[38] and makes room for the Spirit by opening language to the in-breaking of mystery. Erasmus adjured the theologian to speak metaphorically so that the listener (but also the theologian) might be converted: "This is your first and only goal; perform this vow, this one thing, that you be changed, that you be seized, that you weep at and be transformed into those teachings which you learn."[39]

Scripture uses figurative language to teach and to deepen reverence.[40] Calvin is conscious of using figurative language for this purpose as well as for clarity. He says, for example, that "nothing is more common than metonymy in speaking of sacraments. The name of the thing, therefore, is transferred here to the sign—not as if it were strictly applicable, but figuratively on the ground of that connection which I have mentioned."[41] This connection with the hearer is another kind of accommodation.

And Calvin's writings are rich with metaphor. In his description of baptism, we have already seen Calvin using the image of baptized persons as branches engrafted onto a tree (Christ)[42]: "through baptism Christ makes us sharers in his death, that we may be engrafted in it" (*Inst.*IV.15.5). Also, Calvin describes baptism as a sign and proof of cleansing; baptism is like a promise, a testament in a sealed document (*Inst.* IV.15.1). Baptism is a washing and a purging (IV.15.3), and regeneration (IV.15.6). It provides a protective blanket or garment of Christ's blood (IV.15.9); it is like a letter, sealed by the sender (IV.15.16); it is a confirmation to us of God's promise (IV.15.22). Calvin uses diverse figures of speech, which will speak to diverse persons in a variety of circumstances. Metaphors communicate not just content but affect, and they have the possibility of engaging with the particular experience of the hearer/reader.

---

38. Commentaries on Exod 4:11, 1 Cor. 1:17.
39. Boyle, *Erasmus on Language and Method in Theology*, 73.
40. See Bouwsma, "Calvinism as *Theologia Rhetorica*," 11.
41. Calvin's Commentary on 1 Cor 10:4, CO 49:455.
42. Paul, of course, also uses this image in Rom 11:17–24. Calvin elaborates upon the metaphor in *Inst.* IV.15.5.

Rhetoric, then, enables people to be moved. It is the language of the Holy Spirit. With humanism as well as his profession in law as formative aspects of his thought structure, Calvin's concern, according to Bouwsma, was "to combine responsible and scholarly interpretation—*eruditio*—with a discourse that would move the hearts of his listeners—*persuasio*."[43] Thus, Bouwsma says, Calvin's primary purpose in theological discourse is "to make something happen, rather than to make a careful statement of what he regarded as doctrine."[44] This, then, is the bridge to the operational effectiveness in lived human lives.[45]

To demonstrate Calvin's two-perspective approach, i.e., looking at theological issues from God's perspective, *eruditio*, as well as naming the human perspective or role, *decorum*, we will consider a particular subject *à propos* of baptism: the elect as they relate to the visible-invisible church.

B.A. Gerrish notes that there are two aspects of the hiddenness of God: that which is hidden in the revelation of Jesus Christ and that hiddenness outside revelation which consists of whatever there is of God which is not made manifest in Christ.[46] God for Calvin is hidden,

---

43. Bouwsma, "Calvinism as *Theologia Rhetorica*," 13.

44. Bouwsma, "Minutes of the Colloquy of 28 September 1986," Colloquy 54, September, 1986, 81. Another way of putting this is to claim Calvin's interest in *kerygma* as well as *didache*.

45. Michael B. Aune has demonstrated the rhetorical theology of Calvin's contemporary, Philip Melanchthon (1497–1560), who asserted that the function of dialectic is to teach *(docere)* "but the function of rhetoric is to move *(permovere)* and stimulate minds *(animos)* and thus to affect a person." Aune, "To Move the Heart," 26, quoting Melanchthon's 'Elementorum Rhetorices Libri Duo,' translated by Mary J. LaFontaine (PhD dissertation, Univ. of Michigan, 1968), 85. Aune's study is germane to the two-perspective approach to Christian ritual and is suggestive that the Reformation rhetors may have made available, "visible," for theological reflection the operational dimension which we are only now beginning to appropriate. Elizabeth Clarke points out that the "Renaissance rediscovery of classical rhetoric coincided with a Reformation emphasis on the effectiveness of the written word for salvation. It is not surprising, therefore, to find in the writings of sixteenth-century scholars, both theologians and literary theorists, a concern with the power and status of language that is almost an obsession." Clarke, "Silent, Performative Words," esp. 355.

46. See Gerrish, "To the Unknown God," 134, on the distinction between the two notions of the hiddenness of God, and 141–49 on the relation of Calvin's theology to these two notions. For Calvin, "the profoundest depths of hiddenness are located in the problem of double predestination [to good and to evil], in which the will of God appears divided against itself and the individual is threatened with the possibility of rejection and loss. Here Calvin . . . finds himself on the brink of an 'abyss of sightless darkness.' The revelation of God in Jesus Christ does not mean that God no longer has

and frightening. It is only the revelation of God in Jesus Christ, who was not hidden, which saves us from the terror of the infinite power of the unknown God and enables us to have a relationship with God and be saved from the sin inherent in the human condition. The God behind Christ cannot be penetrated by philosophy or theology, and Calvin seems to suggest we should relate to God in Christ, and rest in the mystery of the God behind Christ, honoring it from a distance. It is only the God manifested in human form which is fitting for human understanding, relationship, and appropriation.

That God is manifest in Christ is indeed good news, since the moral diversity among humans seems unjust and defiant of a loving God. For God to elect some for good and others for destruction is a scandal; our minds reach for an explanation that fits. We cannot help but ask, "why is one person more excellent than another?" (*Inst.* II.11.17). Calvin responds to this human dilemma by calling upon persons to let go of the impossible attempt to "make sense" of this mystery, and cling instead to Christ Jesus in whom we have freedom:[47] "And it would not even be useful for us to know what God himself, to test our moderation of faith, on purpose willed to be hidden . . . let us remember that that invisible God, whose wisdom, power, and righteousness are incomprehensible, sets before us Moses' history as a mirror in which his living likeness glows" (*Inst.* I.14.1).

The doctrine of election, or predestination, is about the diversity experienced by humans in this world: in fact, some have plenty to eat while others go hungry; some are healthy, others racked by tragedy; some, like Margaret in our opening example of the funeral, live lives of blessed goodness, while others, like John, live lives of disgrace. This diversity seems endemic to the human condition, but Calvin finds this, as all else, "inseparable from the notion of grace and its counterpart,

---

secrets he withholds from mankind. *Some* secrets are now open, insofar as this is good for us . . . [But] 'secret' (*arcanum*) remains Calvin's most characteristic description for God's 'design' (his *consilium*), since we cannot always perceive *why* God moves events in just the way he does." Ibid., 141. For further references in Calvin to this question of "Why," see n. 62, p. 341.

47. Calvin states, "We cannot and should not go behind God's act of creation in our speculation" (*Inst.* I.14.1). The philosophic view of God as the mind of the universe "is ephemeral[; thus], it is important for us to know him more intimately, lest we always waver in doubt" (ibid.).

gratitude."[48] But to try to understand this from a human perspective, as we have seen, leads to "an abyss of sightless darkness." As Gerrish puts it, "to move beyond the Word (the revealed will) is to find oneself in terrifying darkness . . . Assurance of our own election is to be found solely in Christ, the mirror of our adoption."[49]

It is, then, freedom from this terrifying abyss which we are given in Jesus Christ. Having named God's perspective, the *eruditio* in which finite humans can only see unfreedom, Calvin then speaks to humans with words of *decorum* in which they *can* find freedom. The secret election by God of some but not all of humanity is incomprehensible "in mind and thought" of "the multitude of the elect, unless we consider the unity of the church as that into which we are convinced we have been truly engrafted. For no hope of future inheritance remains to us unless we have been united with all other members under Christ, our Head" (*Inst.* IV.1.2). "[W]e must believe, therefore, that the former church, invisible to us, is visible to the eyes of God alone, so we are commanded to revere and keep communion with the latter, which is called 'church' in respect to men" (*Inst.*IV.1.7).

All the elect make up the invisible church: the true Body of Christ, which is visible only to God and invisible to humans. The church visible to humanity is the institution, those who gather to worship and study together. Calvin asserts the radical importance of the visible church in spite of the fact that the true body of the elect is "beyond our ken" (*Inst.* IV.1.3). While the role of the mysterious God is to know and to judge the sheep and the wolves, the human role is not to fear for our status *vis-à-vis* predestination, but "to *establish with certainty in our hearts* that all those who, by the kindness of God the Father, through the working of the Holy Spirit, have entered into fellowship with Christ, are set apart as God's property and personal possession; and that when we are of their number we share that great grace" (*Inst.* IV.1.3; emphasis added).

In fellowship with Christ, we find our identity, our freedom: "[B]ecause he foresaw it to be of some value for us to know who were to be counted as his children, he has in this regard accommodated

---

48. Gerrish, "To the Unknown God," 144. "But although God's will is ultimate and hidden, we are certain it cannot be either capricious or unjust as the scholastic doctrines of *voluntas* (or *potentia*) *absoluta* and *deus exlex* wrongly implied" (n. 78); cf. *Inst.* I.17.2; III.23.2, 5, 9.

49. Ibid., 144.

himself to our capacity. And, since assurance of faith was not necessary, he substituted for it a certain charitable judgment whereby we recognize as members of the church those who, by confession of faith, by example of life, and by partaking of the sacraments, profess the same God and Christ with us" (*Inst.* IV.1.8).

God has revealed Godself in Christ, which we appropriate through faith; and from the human perspective "the secret plan of God, which lay hidden, is brought to light, provided you understand by this language merely that what was unknown is now verified—sealed, as it were, with a seal. But it is false to say that election takes effect only after we have embraced the gospel, and takes its validity from this. We should indeed seek assurance of it from this; for if we try to penetrate to God's eternal ordination, that deep abyss will swallow us up. But when God has made plain his ordination to us, we must climb higher, lest the effect overwhelm the cause" (*Inst.* III.24.3). Our salvation is a mystery, and "comes about solely from God's mere generosity" (*Inst.* III.21.1)—we cannot cause or effect our salvation by our faith. Faith is, on the human side, what makes us receptive. God is sovereign over salvation: we are the recipients of God's grace.

Riggs points out that these two perspectives, the theological (*eruditio*) and the anthropological (*decorum*) imply two types of divine power. In describing the nature of sacrament, from God's perspective, God has power unable to be refused: God is sovereign. God has sealed the document: "Now, it seems to me to be a simple and proper definition if we say that it is an external symbol by which the Lord stamps on our consciences the promises of his kindness towards us in order to sustain the feebleness of our faith" (*Inst.* 4.14.1).

If God stamps, we are like an object which cannot refuse being stamped. But in describing the human role or perspective, how the Christian is to respond or appropriate, the God language is relational, thus emphasizing that the people have freedom to accept or reject[50]: "and we, in turn, attest our devotion towards him, as much before him and the angels as before people. It is certainly acceptable to give another, briefer definition: that it be called a testimony of divine grace towards us, confirmed by an external sign, with a mutual attesting of our devotion towards him" (*Inst.* 4.14.1). A testimony is given by one person to another, and the second can refuse to accept it. Here God's

---

50. Riggs, *Development of Calvin's Baptismal Theology*, 13–14.

power is described differently: God cannot guarantee the results. Obviously, God's power does not change: it is the perspective from which Calvin speaks that changes. When speaking to the faithful as to *their* role or part in the divine scheme, Riggs shows convincingly that Calvin speaks in a way fitting to the exercise of human freedom.

The doctrine of election is an example of *eruditio*: it is an explanation that accounts for the total freedom, infinite power, and absolute sovereignty of God *and* the diversity of human experience, while enabling God's gracious mercy in salvation to reflect God's freedom in offering the wondrous gift of God's grace. The doctrine of election solves the logical problem that if it were a "rule" or "law" that everyone will be saved, God's freedom to choose[51] would be denied. From God's perspective, it is not possible for "fortune" or "happenstance" to cause something which God does not will (*Inst.* I.16.8).

From the human perspective, however, trying to make sense of these mysteries or understand whether or not one is personally elected leads only to the darkness of the abyss. Human curiosity will not lead to understanding in this case; knowledge of the invisible church is hidden to us. The *human role* is to seek God as God is revealed (in Scripture; in Christ; in the word written and incarnate in church and sacrament), attach ourselves to God-in-Christ, and orient our lives (through partnership in the community of the church and openness to hear the word) to receive the grace offered to us by God—grace we dare to believe was actually offered to *us* because we feel assured of this gift through participation in church and sacrament. It is in recognizing Calvin's own distinction and focusing on Calvin's *decorum*, the human role in living out this relationship with God, that has the possibility of empowering and freeing people from existential *angst*.[52]

---

51. Note, however, Catherine Mowry LaCugna's challenge to the notion of God's freedom as consisting in "choices" in *God For Us*. Rather, she suggests that divine freedom means not "having an infinite array of choices," but "conformity to nature" (ibid., 298–99). Thus "freedom of the Spirit of God [for example] means that the Spirit is altogether consistent, dependable, and trustworthy *as God*, that is, as love" (ibid., 299). It is not possible, then, that the free Spirit would choose to be "capricious, erratic, unreliable" (ibid., 299). Freedom is not an attribute of God but part of God's nature, God's being (*cf.* 260–62). While it is not possible to project Calvin into the twenty-first century, it seems clear that LaCugna's assertion of both freedom and relationship as being in the very nature of God would not be inconsistent with Calvin's own theology, albeit expressed out of a very different context.

52. The attempt to appropriate Calvin's doctrine (i.e., *eruditio*) as a way of being in the world (*persuasio*) has in fact alienated generations of Christians who could

Calvin is an "objective" theologian; but he is also a pastor, concerned that his people will be able to appropriate the freedom and love of Christ. God accommodates to our need by giving us the visible church which we can see and know and come to understand. The sacraments and the visible church are gifts, pastoral, fitting (decorous) gifts of God in Christ to God's people.

The Church: Growing up Together in Christ

We have seen that the realm of God is the realm of the hidden, the invisible. Humans cannot know God as God *is*, but only as God is *revealed*. The figures of speech Calvin uses, the *decorum* of the two perspectives in which he expresses his theology, as well as the sacraments which are visible and physical, both reveal and conceal the unknown God. Without them, however, God would remain altogether hidden. Thus, Calvin uses metaphor and metonymy to clarify in finite human terms realities about God as revealed in Christ: "the similitude He brings in takes away all ambiguity, because grafting denotes not only conformity of example, but a secret conjunction, whereby we grow up together with Him."[53]

The locus of "growing up together" in Christ, of course, is the (visible) church. "For as God, regenerating us in Baptism, ingrafts us into the fellowship of the church, and makes us His by adoption, so . . . He performs the office of a provident parent in continually supplying the food by which He may sustain and preserve us in the life to which He has begotten us by His Word" (*Inst.* IV.17.1). Engrafting into the Body of Christ is *member*ship in the church: "God hath saved us by His mercy, the symbol and pledge of which He gave us in Baptism, by admitting us into His Church and engrafting us into the Body of His Son."[54]

The eschatological element is present in Calvin's ecclesiology. Union with Christ is begun in baptism, and continues in the hear-

---

not stand the idea that they were totally corrupted (*Inst.* II.3.1–5). Ironically, no one understood this problem better than Calvin himself.

53. Calvin's Commentary on Romans 6:5, *CO* 49:106. Yet even as Calvin uses linguistic figures to make present to the hearer the reality of Christ, he is always aware of their limits. The mystery by which salvation occurs in Christ through the Holy Spirit is hidden to us. Here he refers to "a secret conjunction," humanly incomprehensible.

54. Calvin's Commentary on Titus 3:5, *CO* 52:430.

ing of the word[55] and the eating of the Supper: but this union is only completed in heaven (*Inst.* IV.17.33). The sacraments are "a pledge of its present yet hidden fullness," a pledge of redemption not only "of our souls but also of our bodies."[56]

Calvin's way of writing theology matches his theological understanding of how God works: it is a mutual, two-way, reciprocal relationship. God and humanity are related in union in Christ, which is a process: grace works over time in the church, which is the body of people growing up in faith together in Christ. The relationship of God and humanity, which occurs in Christ through the Holy Spirit, includes the freedom of both: the free sovereignty of God, yet the free will of humanity. Calvin is able to explain this through *decorum* because *the roles of God and human beings are different*. God offers a gift; it is for the people in covenant relationship with God to receive it: "it is one thing to be offered, another to be received."

Thus, for Calvin, both church and sacrament are visible signs of God's presence in Christ. The church is the Body of Christ; sacraments are the presentation of Christ in a physical way within the church body such that the people can receive and appropriate them, thus being united with Christ. It is in the appropriation of engrafting and continual nourishment in the Body of Christ[57] that salvation for humanity is effected. Jill Raitt puts it thus: "The mind illumined by the Holy Spirit through the gift of faith is stimulated by the word and the analogy presented in sacramental action."[58] The mind is stimulated

---

55. The Word is not the subject of our essay here, but it is very much related. Sacraments, we have seen, are the means by which God's salvific grace is communicated to and appropriated by God's chosen people; but this instrumentality is no less effected by the *kerygma*, the proclamation of the Word, which for Calvin is actually prior in effectiveness, and prior liturgically: neither sacrament occurs except in the gathered community *after* the preaching of the word. Christ, the Word, is first; thus, preaching Christ is first ranked, and sacraments are "ranked in the same place as the Word. So while the Gospel is called the power of God unto salvation to every one that believeth, we hesitate not to transfer the same title to the sacraments." Calvin, *CO* 9:182. Church does not exist except where "the Word of God [is] purely preached and heard, and the sacraments administered according to Christ's institution" (*Inst.* IV.1.9).

56. Wallace, *Calvin's Doctrine of the Word and Sacrament*, 156.

57. Engrafting and continual nourishment in the Body of Christ occurs through preaching and hearing the Word, and through administration and reception of the sacraments, by ministers of the church, in (and only in) the gathered community.

58. Raitt, "Three Inter-Related Principles," 55.

to receive, to appropriate, to be open to the presence of Christ. Both the visible church and the sacraments enable appropriation by human persons. Calvin preached Christ, the Word, to make him accessible to his Genevans; Calvin wrote his theology to make Christ, the gospel, receivable to his readers, because for Calvin, the church is the very Body of Christ: the church, where the word is preached and heard and sacraments are administered and received, is, in Christ, God's very *decorum* to humanity.

PART TWO

Further Up and Further In

*Historical and Theological Patterns
of Progressing into Christ*

∽ Turning to Part Two

HAVING EXAMINED THREE FATHERS OF THE CHURCH, WE SEE THAT while there are significant differences in expectation and emphasis on the baptized person's involvement in experiencing Christ, there is a clear expectation in Augustine and Calvin (but less so in Thomas) that the efficaciousness of a sacrament presumes a participative experience of the worshipper. The ministers of a sacrament—including, in Calvin, the sacrament of proclamation—are part of its effectiveness (and receive a certain sacramental grace through their own participation).

Yet in spite of differences, it is clear that no sacrament can be said to be effective apart from experiential active receptivity on the part of the worshipper. Augustine asserts faith on the part of believers (*On Baptism*, VII.102) and conversion of heart (VI.62); Calvin, receptivity of the worshipper (*Inst.* IV.17.33) and varied efficacy depending upon the "particularity as to what the person is like" (Sermon 378 on Job 21:1–6). Even Thomas—for whom God-in-Christ is the only actor except for a certain instrumental agency on the part of the priest (*Summa*, IIIa.64.2.Reply)—recognizes value in the worshipper's having devotion, reverence (64.2.1), and faith through which "the power of the Passion is applied to us" (64.3.Reply). There are signs of operational efficacy in all three.

For Calvin, the point of word and sacrament is God's accommodation to the Christian so that reception of Christ can occur. He also seems to correlate awareness of the human response and awareness of the action of the Holy Spirit. Calvin recapitulates Augustine's theology in which the Holy Spirit arouses the baptized to active receptivity and agency in the world. He distinguishes between God's action in offering the Gift, and the (free, volitional, faithful) human activity of receiving the gift, an activity that has an operating affect upon lived Christian lives. Calvin clearly accounts for operational efficacy in his baptismal theology. This perspectival theology of Gift offered and received reappears with a slightly different orientation in Louis-Marie Chauvet's theology of response-giving, recounted here in chapter 7; the sign of receiving a gift is the offering of a thanks-gift, and this is what Chauvet calls Christians to consider: that their lives are response-gifts to God.

But Thomas is different. We can account for this difference in part by his context, which is Christendom, a hierarchical society where church and state were one and in which clergy were powerful and laity were not. His theology reflects his context. Thomas develops an onto-theology,[1] a sacramental theology of being that emphasizes change (in the elements and in the baptizand) from one state to another. What the laity *become* is doctrinally explained; what the laity *experience* themselves is not his concern. God initiated it, the priest did it, and that accomplished it.

Yet even Thomas, as we shall see in his discussion of the virtues (chapter 7), understands sacramental action to work in believers toward their *deiformity*, their growing into the shape of God. Thus we find evidence in all three theologians of both the importance and the expectation of a *changed human person* as a result of baptism. To varying extents, the doctrinal efficacy itself expects an operating efficacy in the heart and life of recipients of a sacrament.

In Part Two, then, we look at existing patterns of progressing into the shape of God. Chapter 5 gives a detailed account of how the early church's rhythm of preparing persons for their new life in baptism was effective in changing their lives into Christ. The contrast between the early church and Christendom is stark: Christendom minimized the baptized life as a changed life. The conversionary pattern, therefore, was cut short when Christendom began and "joining the church" became the conventional social thing to do.

But now, as Christendom is waning, this conversionary process is being reclaimed in many denominations in the preparation of adults for baptism (sparked by the liturgical renewal of the 1960s to 1990s). This catechumenal process will be discussed in chapter 6.

Chapter 7 offers two ancient-contemporary theologies that give meaning to the idea that the Christian is not "just a nice person" but is called to become a particular kind of person and lead a radical life. The first is *theosis* or *theopoeisis*, which means "being fashioned toward

---

1. For a critical account of Thomas's onto-theology, see Chauvet, *Symbol and Sacrament*, 7–83; and Osborne, *Christian Sacraments in a Postmodern World*, 48–50, *passim*.

God"—a radical idea that a baptized person is not just supposed to do good deeds but is supposed to live a holy God-like life. The second is a contemporary realization that God's covenanted people are actually called to *be in relationship with God,* which means not only receiving from God, but offering back to God our response, our lives, our thanks—which is a kind of ongoing turning of our selves over to the One who made and redeems us as part of the community of covenanted (baptized) people.

And then in chapter 8, a theology of holy maturation, "adulting in Christ," is offered through James Fowler's faith development theory, in which the science of psychology is incorporated into the very clear call that to be human is to be constantly in the process of becoming. Living a baptized life just gets going on the day of one's baptism, and it involves a process of changing, growing, deification, and moving deeper and deeper into the heart of God. This is called *the baptismal process,* and is a radically different stance than the very Christendom pattern of "getting the baby done," which is, however, still prevalent and operating in many places, in spite of all the leanings away from Christendom.

There are lots of reasons why the current church, in the current age of post-Christendom, would do well to support the baptized in the non-Christendom style familiar to the churches, including the historical and theological patterns named in this section. These patterns are presented here to strengthen the argument that the future of the church is in calling *all the baptized* (not just the ordained) to live a Christ-like life in the Spirit; or, as C. S. Lewis put it in the *Chronicles of Narnia,* to go "further up and further in" (cf. *The Last Battle*), into the very life of the Holy Trinity.

5

Baptismal Experience in the Early Church
Changing One's Lifestyle

IN HER BOOK *THE GREAT EMERGENCE*, PHYLLIS TICKLE QUOTES A colleague as saying that every 500 years, the church holds a giant rummage sale:[1] that "the empowered structures of institutionalized Christianity, whatever they may be at that time, become an intolerable carapace that must be shattered in order that renewal and new growth may occur."[2] The popularity of her book attests to the current sense of upheaval and the urgent desire to make meaning of the shifting ground beneath our feet. The current quake seems to be marking the end of Christendom and the emergence of a post-Christendom era. What a hopeful shift in metaphor to reinterpret what feels like tectonic shifts as the normal 500-year "attic-cleaning" for a giant rummage sale!

Tickle gives yet more hope by asserting that the church's liberating emergence from reified, encrusted structures has historically led to new life: a new and "vital form of Christianity," a refurbishment of the older form, and a wider spread of Christianity.[3] I want to argue that

---

1. Tickle cites a colleague, but the source of this idea seems to be Ralph Adams Cram, *The Great Thousand Years* (Boston: Marshall Jones Company, 1919). Cram sees history unfolding in "a deep throbbing in five-hundred-year epochs" (ibid., 3) in which there is a great surge of accomplishment and then, at the end of the 500 years, a great decline. My thanks to Linda Kulzer, O.S.B., who presented Cram's idea in *Oblate News: Newsletter for the Oblates of St. Benedict's Monastery* (St. Joseph, Minnesota), December, 2010, p. 2. Most of Cram's monograph can be found online at http://www.amazon.com (search for "ralph adams cram + great thousand years"): accessed August 24, 2011. Kee puts it differently: "in some ages the rate of change seems to speed up . . . Life seems to be open at both ends; the past seems to be crumbling, and the shape of the future has not yet become clear." *Understanding the New Testament*, 17.

2. Tickle, *Great Emergence*, 16.

3. Tickle, *Great Emergence*, 17, 121.

the realization of baptismal ecclesiology through a process of ongoing conversion would at least refurbish the existing churches and result in the spread of Christ's ministry to far reaches and small corners of the earth, wherever the baptized are. The current 500-year shift is (among others) a transition from Christendom to post-Christendom.

Because it is now generally accepted that we are moving toward (as well as living in) the post-Christendom era, we are in a position to look back on where we have been, and to get a clearer sense of what the current transition or emergence looks like. But this chapter will use a telescope to look back even further, to the beginning of the road, in order to get a good view of the early process of making Christians, which was a "complete make-over" of a person in their new adoptive Christian family (*belonging*), their new life-style (*behavior*), and their worldview (*beliefs*).

In the first three centuries, Christianity was illegal. Christians were persecuted, and the risk was too great for anyone to become Christian casually. Therefore, candidates for baptism were guided and supported, for three to five years, in a vibrant experience of the Christian community in which their lives were held up to the priorities, commitments, and worldview of the Christians. Changed minds and changed hearts were the result. In fact, operational efficacy—the experiences of baptismal candidates through practices and stories—was primary over doctrinal efficacy or belief system for three centuries. The nature of Christian experience during this time was rich and intense.

Then came Constantine. On the eve of a battle in 312 CE, Constantine saw in a dream the symbol *chi rho*, the first two letters of Christ's name in Greek (*Christos*, ΧΡΙΣΤΟΣ). He had standards made and rode into battle under the sign of Christ—and won. When he then became the Roman Emperor, he honored the One who had given victory by stopping persecutions and legalizing Christianity.

This Peace of Constantine (313) lifted the fear of torture and provided great relief (*peace*) to the Christians. From illegal and marginal, Christians now began a legitimate relationship with state and society, even as emperors sought to unify the realm under the banner of Christ. This comfortable relationship between church and state, spilling over into culture, is called *Christendom*.[4]

---

4. Kreider, *The Change of Conversion*, 91–92.

But in the course of cultural change, the church also changed, in size and thus in structure and character: in polity, symbolization, theology, and behavior. The Christianity of the state, Christendom, has a history through the Roman Empire, the Holy Roman Empire, and various established churches in Europe. It continued into the twentieth century until the end of colonialism, when the peoples marginalized by Christendom found new voices, and until the cross-fertilization of the world's peoples and cultures through war, study, communication, and travel, began to crack the shell of Christendom. The term "post-Christendom"[5] refers to changes, struggles, and new growth popping out of established attitudes and behaviors that marked Christendom.

But before the current end of Christendom came the beginning of Christendom, usually given as 313, the year of the Peace of Constantine. Release from persecution eased the early church's sense of urgency for thorough conversion, which became impracticable anyway with hundreds of persons seeking out the religion favored by the emperor. Historian Alan Kreider argues that the change in conversion, from three to five years of total life-style change to conversion "lite" which took less time and required less change, is what resulted in the marriage of church, state, and culture called "Christendom." And Christendom has been the predominant practice of Christianity for 1500 years.

We will want to learn both from the way in which the early church made Christians, and from the way it changed as Christendom began from 313. This chapter will offer a lens into what changes early Christians were called to make before Constantine, and what changes were no longer invited after Constantine. Then the next chapter will show how the early process of making Christians was structured, a process called the catechumenate (*catechumen* = hearer). The early catechumenate was a tidal rhythm of lived experience and Christian story, punctuated by three baptismal rituals: admission, enrollment, and washing (= baptism). I argue that this pre-Christendom rhythm, this vibrant conversionary process with periodic rituals, would be an animating rhythm now for the post-Christendom church, even for those already baptized, for their post-baptismal ongoing conversion deeper into Christ.

---

5. Or, sometimes, the shorthand "post-Christian" (applied to a society) is used.

Conversion as a Process of Personal Transformation Before Committing to Christ in Baptism

Alan Kreider has chronicled the early evolution of conversion in his study of the making of Christians from the second to the sixth centuries in his book *The Change of Conversion and the Origin of Christendom*. Kreider has identified a correlation between the way Christians were formed and the way Christendom was formed. His analysis is worth noting.

Kreider found that making Christians always involved *change*. The various words used to describe what would happen to a person as they undertook their new religion include *epistrepho*, *metanoia*, and *conversio*, all connoting change.[6] In his thorough study of what early bishops and catechists taught the catechumens and newly-baptized, Kreider noticed that the locus of change—while it varied according to circumstances, location, and context—always included change in *behavior, belonging,* and *belief*; and change very often was related to an *experience*[7] of the person in relationship to the numinous self-revelation of God. At the same time, the proportion of instruction on belonging, belief, and behavior, varied considerably. In the early days of persecution, *behavior and belonging* were of utmost importance. Would-be Christians were taught belief, but the bulk of catechetical material was focused upon helping catechumens turn from typical Roman cultural patterns and change their life rhythms to conform rather to the new community, which would become their primary identity.[8] Later, after the Peace of Constantine when the cultural context itself began to be

---

6. Kreider, *The Change in Conversion*, xiv.

7. "[C]onversion to Christianity involved a change of a person's belief, belonging, and behavior, in the course of which there might be a strong religious experience" (Kreider, *The Change in Conversion*, 34). For a contemporary treatment of the phenomenon of conversion, see Rambo, *Understanding Religious Conversion*.

8. We shall see evidence of this in the *Apostolic Tradition* c.215, in Cyprian [d.258], and in Chrysostom. John Chrysostom's preaching in Antioch, for example, came after his period as a hermit following the Pachomian Rule (c.373–c.381) and before he was made Patriarch of Constantinople in 398. While these seventeen years were in late-fourth century after the Peace of Constantine, Kreider points out that in Antioch there were several viable religions with compelling claims upon the populace. Christianity, therefore, continued there as a minority religion. Chrysostom's catecheses reflected this church-cultural relationship. It is probable that Chrysostom's mystagogical sermons were given while he was a priest in Antioch up to 397CE before he became Patriarch (cf. Yarnold, *Awe-Inspiring*, 150).

Christian, the balance shifted. By the end of the fourth century, Cyril (313–387 CE),[9] for example, shows the major emphasis to be no longer on behavioral change or even belonging, but on right belief. We will follow Kreider's evidence through this change.

Change in Behavior

Christians of the first three centuries were starkly distinguishable from other members of Roman society by their peculiar behaviors, both public and private. They were, for example, expected to renounce extravagant living in favor of simplicity and generosity; engage in hospitality to the stranger, the sick, and imprisoned; curb the desire for power over others in order to live in peace with the other; and be pure in thought and word, repudiating superstition and misuse of the Lord's name. We can find insights into this behavior from Cyprian of North Africa, both from his own experience of conversion to Christianity and from his oversight of catechesis as Bishop of Carthage (c.249–258). Cyprian's teaching of others included the necessity of letting go of wealth—a problem close to the core of Cyprian's own upper-class experience.

Evidence of what Cyprian considered important to teach catechumens is found in his three books compiled in response to a request from Quirinius, possibly a catechist. While Book I of *Ad Quirinum* covers salvation history, and Book II, Christology, Book III (twice the size of the others together) includes Cyprian's curriculum for Christian formation. Most of the precepts in Book III teach the *behavior* befitting a Christian, both to one another and to all others: support one another (III.9), eat simply (III.60), detach from possessiveness (III.61), live simply (III.36); pay just wages (III.81), charge no interest for loans (III.48), and do not retaliate if injured (III.23).[10]

Underlying the behaviors in Cyprian's catechesis is his own experience as a catechumen and a new Christian, working to change life patterns that had been foundational to his pre-Christian life.

---

9. There are two sets of Cyril's sermons extant. The first set, preached c. 348, includes *Procatechesis* for catechumens and eighteen *Catecheses* delivered to candidates during the Lent immediately prior to their baptism. The second set, the *Mystagogic Catecheses*, were preached to the newly-baptized in Easter week some decades later, closer to the end of Cyril's life. See Yarnold, *Awe-Inspiring*, 69.

10. Cyprian, *Ad Quirinum*; in Kreider, *The Change in Conversion*, 29–31.

Struggling to let go of his attachment or addiction to elegant clothing and extravagant food, he managed to curb his appetites and increase his generosity. Cyprian's story of his conversionary process, recounted in his *Ad Donatum (To Donatus)*, begins both with dissatisfaction in his upper-class life and with his encounter with the Christian community which deeply attracted him. The simple communal lives of the Christians stood in stark contrast to his aristocratic life-style as a pagan rhetorician in which he was "used to liberal banquets and sumptuous feasts," and to "glittering in gold and purple, . . . [being] celebrated for . . . costly attire" and "[being] dignified by . . . an officious train." Torn between enjoying such privilege and yet finding it oppressive, ("gilded torment," a life of "darkness and gloomy night,") Cyprian found himself a slave to "luxury and wealth rather than their master."[11]

Caecilianus, a Christian presbyter, was Cyprian's guide through the catechumenate, a process in which Cyprian worked bit by bit to be free of his extravagant habits and to change his life patterns to be more in keeping with the Christian way. Pontius' *Life of Cyprian* gives insight into this difficult, turbulent journey, a path toward freedom from addiction to wealth and power. In comradeship with fellow journeyers, Cyprian developed new, Christian behaviors, including selling some of his lands and estates, and caring for the poor.[12] It was at baptism that he experienced the Breath of freedom: what had been an impossible burden became, through the Holy Spirit, a wondrous achievable possibility. Kreider concludes: "As a bishop he is reported to have lived simply and hospitably, with his home open to the poor. His clothing, which had been so important to him before his conversion, was 'subdued to a fitting mean' (*Vita Cypriani* 3, 6). When in 258 he came to be executed, he was wearing an outer cloak and a dalmatic, but no purple (*Acta Cypriani* 5)! For he had been converted, and his behavior, like his beliefs and his sense of belonging, had been conformed to those of the Christian community."[13]

A second example of typical and normative Christian behavior comes from a remarkable essay by Tertullian (c.160–c.225), also of

---

11. Cyprian, *Ad Donatum*, 3, 3, and 12; in Kreider, *The Change in Conversion*, 7–8. I draw what follows from ibid., 7–9.

12. Pontius, *Vita Cypriani (Life of Cyprian)*, 6; in Kreider, *The Change in Conversion*, 7–9.

13. Kreider, *The Change in Conversion*, 9.

North Africa. In *To His Wife*, Tertullian gives a perspicuous window into the activities Christians were normally expected to follow, activities which by societal standards were peculiar. Here, Tertullian advises Christian widows not to remarry, and especially not to remarry pagans. His exhortation is strong because the pattern of activities normative for every Christian were so encompassing that they defined a lifestyle:

> For who would suffer his wife, for the sake of visiting the brethren, to go round from street to street to other men's, and indeed to all the poorer, cottages? Who will willingly bear her being taken from his side by nocturnal convocations, if need so be? Who, finally, will without anxiety endure her absence all the night long at the paschal solemnities? Who will, without some suspicion of his own, dismiss her to attend the Lord's Supper, which they defame? Who will suffer her to creep into prison to kiss a martyr's bonds? nay, truly, to meet any of the brethren to exchange the kiss? to offer water for the saints' feet? to snatch [somewhat for them] from her food, from her cup? to yearn [after them]? to have [them] in her mind? If a pilgrim brother arrive, what hospitality for him in an alien home?[14]

The enactment of compassion and hospitality, the tangible manifestation of *diaconea*, along with Christian cultic (worship) patterns were endemic to Christian every-day life, patterns in stark contrast to behaviors normative for Roman culture.

The specific expectation that all Christians will visit the imprisoned is borne out in the experience of Pachomius (c.290–346) who, tradition holds, was a recipient of these compassionate ministrations. Confined in prison in Thebes (Egypt) along with others abducted for conscription into the Roman legions, Pachomius was purportedly fed and attended by people "merciful to everyone, including strangers." When he asked who they were, he was told they were people "who bear the name of Christ, the only begotten Son of God, and they do good to everyone, putting their hope in Him who made the heaven and earth and us humans."[15] The story is told that Pachomius prayed

---

14. Tertullian, *To His Wife* 1.4; in Kreider, *The Change in Conversion*, 12.

15. *First Greek Life of Pachomius* 4–5; in Kreider, *The Change in Conversion*, 19. Many lives of Pachomius leave unclear what is fact and what legend. For Greek lives, see Halkin, *Subsidia Hagiographica*, xix; for French translation of *Vita Prima*, see Festugière, *Les Moines d'Orient*, iv.2.

to the God of these people, asking for release and promising in return to serve this God with his life.

Pachomius was released in 313 and, as is well known, founded cœnobitic Christian monasticism, establishing a first monastery in 320. By the time of his death, he was serving as abbot-general over nine monasteries for men and two for women.[16] What was normal behavior from the point of view of the Christians was experienced as astonishing life-changing care from the point of view of Pachomius, the vulnerable one, the recipient. His conversion was a direct result. From his then-outsider's perspective, the behavior of Christians was attractive, even beautiful.[17]

These three stories exemplify some basic Christian behaviors: for Cyprian, freedom from addiction to wealth; for Tertullian, regular worship and hospitality, and visiting the sick and imprisoned; and also for Pachomius, visiting the sick and imprisoned. Freedom from addiction included not only money, but also sex, power, and other impurities. Stories about these attachments are poignant and relevant.

The *desire for money* and wealth can indeed be an addiction. We have seen Cyprian's own struggle with the help of his catechists to break the strangling compulsion of wealth and possessiveness. The admonishments about addiction to wealth were persistent and strong in his catechesis.

But Cyprian was not the only catechist to exhort those preparing for baptism about the dangers of money. John Chrysostom (c.347–407, Antioch and Constantinople) warned catechumens that money "often takes those who have a passion for it and surrounds them with

---

16. "Pachomius," *The Oxford Dictionary of the Christian Church*.

17. The "beauty of life encourages . . . strangers to join the ranks . . . We do not preach great things, but we live them" (*Octavius* 31.7; 38.6) (Kreider, *The Change in Conversion*, 17–18). It's the integrity of living what they claim to believe that is so compelling. Justin (martyred 165 CE) wrote, "those who are found not living as [Christ] taught should know that they are not really Christians, even if his teachings are on their lips" (I *Apology* 14). Kreider points out that while the behavioral change which is conversion was universally required in the early church, this did not include proselytizing, or speaking publicly about one's faith, or calling others overtly or verbally to change. In contrast to some contemporary evangelism, early Christians lived an attractive life that impelled others to seek and to join those in change. Worship, likewise, was not "seeker-sensitive" but was only for Christians (with catechumens permitted to attend the first part of worship through the sermon). Kreider, *The Change in Conversion*, 13–14.

dangers they cannot resist."[18] Christians, rather, are called to a life of "self-control and simplicity" and freedom through almsgiving.[19] Justin (c.100–c.165, Ephesus and Rome) also asserts, "we who once took most pleasure in the means of increasing our wealth and property now bring what we have into a common fund and share with everyone in need."[20]

The best-known *struggle for sexual continence* is Augustine's battle with "the filth of concupiscence."[21] Among others, Justin also warns Christians against sexual compulsion: "we who once rejoiced in fornication now delight in continence alone."[22]

The surrender of *power-lust* was a third release toward freedom in Christ. Justin writes: "[W]e who hated and killed one another and would not associate with men of different tribes because of [their different] customs, now after the manifestation of Christ live together and pray for our enemies."[23] And in the *Apostolic Tradition* (Rome, c.215): "One who is a gladiator or teaches gladiators to fight, or one who fights with beasts in the games, or a public official employed on gladiatorial business, let him cease or be rejected . . . He who has the power of the sword, or is a magistrate of a city who wears the purple, let him cease or be rejected. Catechumens or believers who want to become soldiers should be rejected, because they have despised God."[24]

Related to power-lust was the fourth habit or addiction inconsistent with the freedom and purity of life in Christ: *occult activity or swearing oaths*. According to Justin, "we who made use of magic arts have dedicated ourselves to the good and unbegotten God."[25] The *Apostolic Tradition* asserts: "If anyone is a sculptor or a painter, let them be instructed not to make idols; let them cease or be rejected . . . If anyone is a priest, or keeper of idols, let him cease or be rejected . . . A charmer, an astrologer, a diviner, an interpreter of dreams, a

---

18. Chrysostom, *Baptismal Instructions*, 8.12; in Kreider, *The Change in Conversion*, 50, *passim*.

19. Chrysostom, *Baptismal Instructions*, 4.13 and 7.27; in Kreider, *The Change in Conversion*, 50, *passim*.

20. Justin, I *Apology* 14, in Kreider, *The Change in Conversion*, 5, 50.

21. *The Confessions of St. Augustine*, Book 3.1.1. See especially Books 2 and 3.

22. Justin, I *Apology* 14, in Kreider, *The Change in Conversion*, 5, 50.

23. Justin, I *Apology* 14, in Kreider, *The Change in Conversion*, 5.

24. *Apostolic Tradition*, also called *Hippolytus*, ed. by G. Cuming, § 16.

25. I *Apology* 14, in Kreider, *The Change in Conversion*, 5, 50.

mountebank [quack, charlatan] . . . let them be rejected."[26] "If anyone is possessed by a demon, he shall not hear the word of teaching until he is pure."[27]

Likewise, John Chrysostom (c.347–407), a presbyter in Antioch where in the 380s he wrote his *Baptismal Instructions*, sermonized against charms, incantations, and omens.[28] Even worse was the loose-mouthed invocation of the Name of the God of all for trivial or unwarranted purposes: "Whether we are buying vegetables and arguing over two obols [coins][29] or are threatening our servants in our anger, we always call on God as our witness . . . When you are talking about goods for sale and money and insignificant things, you drag in the King of heaven and Lord of angels to be your witness."[30] This habitual oath taking, falsely or truly, was for Chrysostom an addiction as dangerous as the others. It was "a destructive drug, a bane and a danger, a hidden wound, a sore unseen, an obscure ulcer."[31]

So there was an intensity of teaching and a commonality of expectation that Christians would behave with purity and simplicity, renouncing extravagant living in favor of sharing and generosity, caring for the stranger, the sick, and imprisoned, curbing the passion to fight or exert power over others, and repudiating superstition and misuse of the Lord's name. And just as surely as the behavior was expected was the certainty that such behavior was not the cultural norm nor the starting-point of would-be Christians. To live this way required *change*.

Christian catechetical history also includes some very *practical teachings*, such as how to stand firm when questioned by authorities or facing persecution, how to "be alert to the needs of poor people," and non-defensive "gentleness and love" even to those who persecute.[32] It was not always obvious how to change one's profession or one's household or one's own bent. A quite remarkable piece in the early baptismal

26. Cuming, *Hippolytus*, §16.
27. Cuming, *Hippolytus*, §15.
28. *Baptismal Instructions* 12.53, in Kreider, *The Change in Conversion*, 50.
29. An *obol* [L. *obolus*, from Greek *obolos*] is "an ancient Greek coin or weight equal to 1/6 drachma." *Webster's Ninth New Collegiate Dictionary* (Springfield, MA: Merriam-Webster Inc., 1987).
30. *Baptismal Instructions* 9.45, in Kreider, *The Change in Conversion*, 51.
31. *Baptismal Instructions* 10.18, in Kreider, *The Change in Conversion*, 51.
32. Kreider, *The Change in Conversion*, 28–29.

literature is a template for change offered by John Chrysostom to his catechumens to help them break an unwanted habit. Change is difficult, especially those ingrained behaviors (like swearing) that we do without consciousness. To be a Christian, even these must be changed, converted, rooted out, replaced. In one of his sermons, he exhorted the change of the swear-habit. That this change be done both by the individual and also in and by the community is apparent in this six-step procedure:

- ask others to remind you
- be attentive to the power of habit even contrary to your will
- make a conscious, willful decision to change the behavior
- reproach others when they engage this behavior
- set a time-frame within which to eradicate the habit
- fine yourself whenever you falter after the time-limit is past.[33]

For those becoming Christian, changing life-behaviors, both major patterns and minor habits, was expected. Such change represented and enabled the foundational self-opening to transformation and newness of life in Christ-and-the-Spirit needed by those preparing for baptism. Changing their lives as catechumens was the first sign of God's working in their lives and that they belonged no longer to themselves, but to a new and holy community.

Change in Belonging

The second major emphasis in catechesis before the shift to Christendom was complete was an emphasis upon *belonging*. A person is identified not only by how they act themselves, but also by the legacy they extend and by the company they keep. Early Christians were not just individuals, but were persons-in-community; the behaviors they adopted matched those of their new community or siblinghood. One's primary identity was no longer as Roman citizen, but was that of sharing the Name of the Lord: Christian. The shared behaviors themselves were the mark and the means of belonging, for the community of belonging was the community of those who shared common worship, ministries, hospitality, and other ethical practices. But in addi-

---

33. Chrysostom, *Baptismal Instructions*, 9.42–46, in Kreider, *The Change in Conversion*, 52.

tion to the behaviors, Kreider noticed that there are specific teachings among early catechists that describe the attitude and action by which Christians should treat each other.[34]

Not unlike Judaism, where the ethical behaviors are understood to be moral imperatives of the community in covenant with the Holy One, Christians, too, understand themselves as the Body of Christ, covenanted with God through Christ's blood. Thus, particular care of the other covenanted ones is mandatory. For example, Chrysostom uses several metaphors to describe the neophyte's new belonging at baptism: a "spiritual marriage" with Christ resulting in purity and beauty; a new family; a new citizenship.[35] For the sake of Christ, one another, and the world, which in seeing the church sees Christ, Christians must hold each other accountable to their covenantal standards, and "take up the task of your brother's salvation" by correcting and encouraging one another.[36] Cyprian insisted that "[B]rethren ought to support one another" and settle disputes among themselves instead of before a "Gentile judge."[37] As in Scripture, catechesis involved exhortations to treat each other in a way worthy of the Name borne by each and all, for love's sake, and for the sake of the gospel: "For when they hear from us that God says, 'It is no credit to you if you love those who love you, but it is a credit to you if you love your enemies and those who hate you' [cf. Luke 6:32, 35], when they hear these things, they marvel at such extraordinary goodness. But when they see that we not only do not love those who hate us, but do not even love those who love us, they scornfully laugh at us and the Name is blasphemed."[38]

---

34. The first three centuries include the period of oral tradition, scriptural writing, and canonization. Behaviors appropriate within the Christian community are thus also attested to in Scripture: e.g., "They devoted themselves to the apostles' teaching and fellowship, to the breaking of bread and the prayers" (Acts 2:42); "encourage one another" (I Thes. 5:11); "stir up one another to love and good works" (Heb 10:24); "Do not speak evil [nor grumble] against one another" (Jas 4:11 [5:9]); "practice hospitality" to one another (1 Pet 4:9); "Confess your sins to one another, and pray for one another" (Jas 5:16); "love one another" (1 John 3:23; 4:11), etc.

35. Chrysostom, *Baptismal Instructions*, 1.11; 3.5; in Kreider, *The Change in Conversion*, 49–52 passim.

36. Chrysostom, *Baptismal Instructions*, 6.18; in Kreider, *The Change in Conversion*, 49.

37. Cyprian, *Ad Quirinum (To Quirinius)* 3.9, 3.44; in Kreider, *The Change in Conversion*, 30.

38. 2 Clement 13.4: "An Ancient Christian Sermon, commonly known as Second Clement," in *The Apostolic Fathers*, 2nd edn., 74–75.

Change in Belief, and Changing Only Belief

The third source of change for a person becoming Christian is *belief*. In pre-Christendom, belief—although not emphasized like behavior and belonging—was always a part of catechesis. In addition to practical instruction about how to behave as a Christian, Kreider notes that the academic content of instruction swirls around three eddies of knowledge: the teachings of Jesus, the narrative background of the faith (including the Hebrew Scriptures), and primary or controlling metaphors, such as the three young men in the fiery furnace (Dan 3) and beating swords into plowshares (Isa 2:2–4 and Mic 4:1–4).[39] All the catecheses teach belief, including the Apostles' Creed. But in his study of pre-Christendom texts, Kreider finds the material on belief to be significantly less than that of behavior and belonging. What finally made a Christian was *change in action*, and *change of identity* to a community who shared in that action. It was the experience of God-through-Christ-in-the-Spirit through the ministry and integrity of Christians that attracted persons to the community of those who understood themselves on a journey together, becoming "other christs."

With the advent of Christendom in 313, however, change began both in the church's cultural context and in the type of Christian the church sent into that culture. Conversion itself was changing. With the Peace of Constantine came new motivations for becoming Christian. While some continued to be attracted to such a strong, countercultural community of lavish compassion and mysterious cult, it also became possible for those with less committed motives to approach. Worship no longer had to be conducted in secret. One could attend worship services to be with one's friends or to curry favor with the emperor or other government officials. As Christianity spread and eventually became the official state religion,[40] the government encouraged these other motivations by offering official inducements to become Christian, as we shall shortly see.

The new relationship between church and state engendered foundational changes in each. Two identifiable threads of ecclesial change teased out of this new relationship contributed to new patterns of con-

---

39. Kreider, *The Change in Conversion*, 26–28.

40. Christianity became legal under Constantine in 313, but it later became the official state religion in 380 under Theodosius I, emperor 379–95. See *Oxford Dictionary of the Christian Church*, "Theodosius."

version and catechesis that marked a path to clericalism. The first is the "liminal," borderline, "more-or-less" Christian—a model begun in the person of Constantine who refrained from baptism until shortly before his death. The other, related, is the beginning of a hierarchy not marked by servanthood: a Christian aristocracy exempted from the expectation of actual behavioral change.

The first thread becomes apparent in the question, "Was Constantine a Christian?" On the one hand, some say so, pointing to the vision Constantine experienced on the eve of his victory at the Milvian Bridge as his conversion.[41] He outlawed the flesh-burning branding of the face of convicted criminals "which has been made in the likeness of celestial beauty."[42] He was favorable to Christianity and was instrumental in erecting many great buildings for the church's worship, influenced by his mother Helena, who was involved in the dedication of the churches at Bethlehem and on the Mount of Olives.[43] Constantine spared the church from persecution, made it legal, and restored confiscated properties.[44] He summoned the Council of Nicea; he referred to the bishops as "beloved brethren" and himself as "your fellow servant."[45]

On the other hand, since he did not choose to become a catechumen until just before his deathbed baptism, he was never able to worship with the community on Sunday, even the first part through the sermon. He never belonged to the community. Although we can identify several behavioral changes that would suggest his identity with the ecclesia, there were other behaviors that suggest a different primary identity. Constantine ordered the killing of his wife and son in 326; in his reign torture increased; and the number of crimes designated as capital increased to over 600.[46] In belief, Constantine (having never become a catechumen) was self-taught. He was not instructed system-

---

41. Kreider, *The Change in Conversion*, 34.

42. *Codex Theodosianus* 9.40.2; Pharr, ed., *The Theodosian Code*; in Kreider, *The Change in Conversion*, 35.

43. Wilkinson, "Introduction: The Orient in the Fourth Century," *Egeria's Travels*, 12–13.

44. Kreider, *The Change in Conversion*, 33.

45. Coleman-Norton, ed., *Roman State and Christian church*, 59–61; Eusebius, *Vita Constantini* 3.12; in Kreider, *The Change in Conversion*, 34.

46. MacMullen, "Judicial Savagery in the Roman Empire," 213. In Kreider, *The Change in Conversion*, 35.

atically in a community, with a bishop-mentor. He did not visit the sick and imprisoned; he did not (that we know of) offer hospitality to the poor. He did not submit to examination and exorcism.

Was Constantine converted or not? Was he a Christian or not? Kreider shows Constantine as the first of a series of liminal Christians, "sort-of" Christians, "of two minds," a foot each in two worlds.[47] As he was favorable to the church, so the church was to him. But the bishops did not alter the catechumenal structure to accommodate Constantine; and it was not until the end of his life in 337 that he was made a catechumen, and baptized.

So throughout two decades of his reign, Constantine offered the world a new possibility of an unbaptized, uncatechized person who nevertheless somehow was a Christian—a Christian lord who had not bowed his knees to the Lord of the Christians.[48]

There came to be, then, a third category of person: (1) non-Christians, (2) Christians, and (3) what we may refer to as "half-Christians." How should the church treat such a liminal Christian, catechized but unconverted, supportive but unbaptized? This leads us to the second thread. After Constantine, we can find other leaders and aristocrats in a "half" relationship with the church, which accepted and eventually encouraged such liminality.

An interesting example of this shift is the story of the Roman patrician Volusian who was sent in the early fifth century (411–12) to Carthage as proconsul.[49] His female relatives made contacts with North African Christians to befriend him, and religious discussions ensued. But it was not concern about Christian behavior that was at stake. Rather, Volusian's questions were around *belief*. Christian beliefs were illogical. How could the virgin birth have happened? How could such an almighty God be concerned with such small things as healing individual illnesses? Wasn't it absurd to consider that any ruler or aristocrat should espouse such strange behaviors as giving also away one's coat when one's tunic was taken, or responding to evil with good? Volusian's relatives, Melania the elder and the younger, put him in

---

47. Eusebius, *Life of Constantine* 4.62; in Kreider, *The Change in Conversion*, 35.

48. Kreider, *The Change in Conversion*, 36.

49. Kreider, 65–70. He cites Chastagnol, "Le Sénateur Volusien," 241–53, and *Les Fastes de la Préfecture de Rome*; also Elizabeth Clark, ed. *The Life of Melania the Younger*, 129–33. Melania the Elder and the Younger were Christian relatives of Volusian.

touch with a Christian aristocrat in Carthage called Marcellinus, who saw Volusian daily.

When the questions became deeper and Volusian found himself doubting but intrigued, he wrote to Augustine, Bishop 395–430 in Hippo. Augustine responded to him, and their letters have survived. Augustine addressed him with the respect appropriate to an aristocrat: "noble lord, justly distinguished and excellent son."[50] Carefully responding about the reasonableness of Christian beliefs, Augustine encouraged Volusian to join the growing number of Christian aristocrats like himself: "Though few in number [the Christians] are spread over the world; with marvelous ease they convert whole peoples; they grow in the midst of enemies; they increase under persecution; and by the pressure of affliction they are scattered to the ends of the earth. Though once the most ignorant, the most lowly, the fewest in number, they become learned, they are ennobled, their numbers are multiplied."[51]

It is not absurd to imagine Christians running the state, Augustine explained, because the behaviors mentioned in Scripture are not intended to be lived literally, but rather as "interior dispositions of the heart." The behavior of someone as "distinguished and excellent" as Volusian would not have to change should he become Christian.[52]

This one example illustrates what by the fifth century had become what Peter Brown called "a respectable, aristocratic Christianity"[53] in which the earlier Christian demands to share property, give alms, and welcome the poor, were attenuated by the clergy for the sensibilities of the wealthier citizenry. What a contrast to 150 years earlier when Cyprian had required Christians to change their lives according to the "example of living in Christ"![54] We begin to see warping through Christianity a single, stronger twine of christianesque persons whose behaviors do not match the purity and charity of converted life: both liminal Christians like Constantine, in relationship but not marked even as a catechumen, and aristocratic exceptions, those accepted in

---

50. Augustine, *Letters* 137–38; in Kreider, *The Change in Conversion*, 66.

51. Augustine, *Letter* 137; in Kreider, *The Change in Conversion*, 66.

52. Augustine, *Letters* 137, 138; in Kreider, *The Change in Conversion*, 67.

53. Peter Brown, "Aspects of the Christianization of the Roman Aristocracy," in Kreider, *The Change in Conversion*, 69.

54. Cyprian, *Ad Quirinum* 3.39; in Kreider *The Change in Conversion*, 69.

baptism *without having converted their behavior*. It is perhaps from this phenomenon that Augustine describes the church not as pure or holy, but as a mixed body, a *corpus permixtum*.[55]

We then notice this new twine shuttling into a pattern of collaborative inducement by church and state for persons to become these very same (liminal) Christians—inducements that were often tightened into compulsion.[56] From Constantine through the Code of Theodosius II (ordered in 435; effective from 439) and the Code of Justinian (529), imperial inducements became coercion to join not the distinctive-behaving marginal community of the first three centuries, but a culturally-behaving mainstream community of the new category of favorable-though-not-committed. For the church's part, the new category of Christian began with a foot in the margin and a foot in the mainstream; but as these Christians became more and more common, *they began to define the mainstream*. Later aristocrats were no longer expected to follow the standard pattern as Constantine had been. Rather, they were admitted as they were, merely following acknowledgment of *correct belief* (which came to be the meaning of "orthodox"). Further, the church leadership, too, in correlation with the state, compelled and coerced persons to "become Christian." But at the point of compulsion, to "become Christian" meant something different than it had before.

We have an example in the continuing story of our aristocrat Volusian. Volusian did not present himself as a catechumen, even after Augustine's persuasive letters to him. Later in his life, his relative Melania the Younger, head of a monastery near Jerusalem, sought again his baptism, this time referring to the Code of Theodosius (16.5.42; 16.19.21) requiring conversion, and threatening "to take the matter to

---

55. According to Robert Markus, Augustine took the notion of the church as bipartite, a *corpus permixtum* to be separated by God in the eschaton, from Tyconius, a fourth-century North African lay theologian (Markus, *Saeculum*, 122). For Augustine on the church as *corpus permixtum*, see *The City of God* (117–22), and also his *De Baptismo* in which he understands the church to include both the just and the unjust, both the wheat and the tares (VI.48; from Matt 13:24–30). Later in *De Baptismo* Augustine writes, "As therefore there is in the Catholic Church something which is not Catholic, so there may be something which is Catholic outside the Catholic church" (VII.77).

56. Kreider borrows the terms "inducements and compulsions" from Butterfield, *Christianity and History*; in Kreider, *The Change in Conversion*, 39; xvi–xvii.

the emperors."[57] He was baptized at last when his health declined, and to Melania's joy he was able to receive communion three times before he died. Such threats as Melania posed to him were introduced quite early after Constantine. The marginal community of attraction was changing into a mainstream community of compulsion.

What were some inducements and compulsions? We have noted that Constantine was favorable to Christianity; but more than that, he offered strong incentives for persons to become Christian. Beyond the relief from horrible persecution, which had been so hard on Christians at various periods for 300 years, incentives included relief from civic duties for church leaders and career advancement for civic workers who were Christian. Inducements turned to stronger persuasions as the tables were turned, and around 340 CE, pagans were now treated as Christians had been before, as dangerous counter-cultural outcasts.[58] By 380 under emperor Theodosius I,[59] when Christianity became not merely tolerated or favored, but the established state religion, unorthodox "heretical" Christians were denied public worship; by 392, even pagans were denied public worship. Ironically, after Hippolytus' stipulation that those in the Roman army must desist or be rejected from the catechumenate, in 416 "an imperial edict specified that only professing Christians could be hired by the imperial armies and civil service";[60] the Code of Theodosius II (435) outlawed paganism and penalized heresy; the Code of Justinian (529) compelled baptism of all infants. The church and state, coming to provide strong and dependable mutual support unifying society through uniformity of religion, set a context within which both the church and the state could compel "conversion."

Free choice for Christianity was certainly preferred. Augustine expressed the same claim for freedom of religious conversion (*Retractions* 2.31) that he did about learning Latin; namely, that "free curiosity has greater power to stimulate learning than rigorous coercion" (*Confessions* 1.14.23). But even Augustine employed the army

57. Gerontius, *Life of Melania* 52–55; in Kreider, *The Change in Conversion*, 68–69.

58. Kreider, *The Change in Conversion*, 39.

59. Theodosius was Emperor 379–395. Note that Constantine (emp. 311–37) was succeeded by Constantius II (emp. 337–61), whose successor was Julian called the Apostate, nephew of Constantine and cousin of Constantius (emp. 361–63). Julian promoted paganism. He was very unpopular and died of an arrow wound.

60. Kreider, *The Change in Conversion*, 39.

as a police force "in applying the policy of suppression against the Donatists."⁶¹ In order to build an orthodox, faithful, united church, discipline must be applied. Attraction was the preferred option. But without the universally-distinguishing behaviors of minority Christianity, attraction was not as strong. In fact, the disjuncture of Christian preaching from the lived practice of so-called Christians was *un*attractive. The inducements and compulsions to orthodox belief and to baptism, however, resulted in many coming to the catechumenate not out of commitment to a distinctive and compassionate way of life, but rather out of threat or fear, or the desire to ingratiate oneself with civil authorities. Augustine's approach to the unattracted (not unlike that of the eighteenth century American preacher Jonathan Edwards) was to get their attention by arousing such a dread of God's displeasure that one would leap to faith.⁶²

A hundred years after Augustine, in Gaul, Caesarius, bishop of Arles (502–42), attempted at first to elicit conversion by attraction: "You ought to think that every man is your neighbor, even before he is a Christian . . . Perhaps . . . through the mercy of the Lord he will be converted to God in such a way that he will deserve to hold the first place among the saints" (*Sermon* 180.1). But when that did not work, coercion was the next choice. Here, he exhorted landlords to "convince" their workers to give up their pagan ways: "Chastize those whom you know to be [guilty]; warn them very harshly; scold them very severely. And if they are not corrected, beat them if you have the power; and if they are not improved by this, cut off their hair too. And if they still persevere, bind them in iron shackles, so that those whom the grace of Christ does not hold, a chain may hold."⁶³

It is interesting that when the Christians found themselves repressing other religions and compelling "conversion," they did not understand it to be persecution. It was, rather, a way to help people make the right decision to "become Christian."⁶⁴

---

61. Peter Brown, *Augustine of Hippo*, 421.

62. Augustine, *First Catechetical Instruction*, 7.11; in Kreider, *The Change in Conversion*, 55–57.

63. Caesarius of Arles, *Sermon* 53.2; in Kreider, *The Change in Conversion*, 71–73, *passim*.

64. Kreider, *The Change in Conversion*, 71–73.

In other words, in even the beginnings of Christendom, while *change* in belonging disappeared, the *fact* of belonging became compulsory. That is, in the first three centuries, persons becoming Christian had to change their primary community of identity, and to take on the activities and religious dispositions and orientations of *Christian* belonging. But as conversionary requirements were altered and attenuated first for aristocrats and eventually for all, the community of belonging was no longer distinct from the cultural community of the Roman and Holy Roman Empires. The catechumenate was shortened, and eventually, eliminated; years of preparation and re-orientation of one's life ceased to be part of making Christians. Change in community and its distinctive behaviors ceased to be a factor in becoming Christian. At the same time, however, profession of orthodox belief became essential. "Heresy" was punishable, eventually by death; and a single event in the process of making Christians, the specific rite of Holy Baptism, which marked the turning point, became the mark not only of ecclesial but of civil belonging and compliance. Left from the early process were only these two: profession of right belief and submission to baptism; and the stakes around these got higher (and often burned very hot).

The "half" Christian of Constantine and Volusian on the cusp of pre-Christendom became the mainstream Christian of High Christendom. The nature of belonging in the Body of Christ was no longer doing something different, but was simply "fitting in," going with the flow. From a well-defined counter-cultural community, itself liminal and marginal, calling all of its members without exception to behaviorial change and to internal standards of care-full maintenance, the ecclesial community's borders faded into those of civic life and culture, and the locus of liminality shifted from the community itself to certain of its members: namely, clergy and monastics.

The Change in Conversion

Wayne Meeks has identified two directions of conversion in various societies. The first entails a religion calling people from the mainstream to life in the margins, to a change in behavior and belief from that of common life to that of a small, counter-cultural group. The second kind of conversion is the call of people from the margin to the mainstream: "someone who was leading a dissolute, barren, or otherwise deplorable life... turns about, shapes up, and henceforth exhibits deportment approved by all... The deviant has been won over to the norms that society at large upholds."[65]

This seems a helpful description for the shift in direction of conversion to Christianity. In the first centuries, before 313, Christianity engaged in the first type of conversion. The Christians were a small, marginal, counter-cultural, sometimes persecuted minority group. Conversion from mainstream civic life came from a strong attraction to a stabile communal life of worship and daily acts of compassion and hospitality. The change that was enjoined to become part of such a group required practice in new behaviors and a commitment to a new community of belonging. Such change took time; it took free will; it took the support of the community and its leaders. Such change ran deep and was a transformation into the Community of the Beautiful.[66]

Beginning in 313, however, conversion in Christianity itself underwent a change, from Meeks' first direction to the second. Even by Augustine's time in the early fifth century, the mainstream was Christian or became solidly so. Those who were not Christian by belief and baptism began to be seen as "barren" or "deplorable." Conversion was now to win over the deviants to the proper state religion. Kreider's thesis is that this very change in the meaning and intention of conversion is what contributed to the establishment of Christendom.[67]

Kreider has pointed out, then, an ironic contrast. The early church was set apart from the world, drew its identity not from the culture but from its own master story (*mythos*), and served prophetically to minister to and care for the world. But after 313, the church of Christendom *became* the world.

And here is a second irony: In Christendom, where there was no longer a separation between church and world, the separation came to be between the clergy and the laity.[68] When the behaviors of Christians were no longer distinct from common cultural behavior, those persons with deep commitments and longings to live a radically distinct life

---

65. Meeks, *The Origins of Christian Morality*, 21, 26; in Kreider, *The Change in Conversion*, 69–70.

66. Garcia-Rivera, *The Community of the Beautiful: A Theological Aesthetics*.

67. Kreider, *The Change in Conversion*, 69–70.

68. Kreider, *The Change in Conversion*, 95.

became monks, like Pachomius, or clergy. It worked, since the average Christian was not required to make any major changes, except to profess certain orthodox beliefs, since heresy was not tolerated. Thus, any "super-Christian" activity was given a different name and contained under separate structures.[69] This split within the Christian community altered the sense of who was "truly the church." And clericalism was born.

Kreider's summary of the marks of Christendom is helpful:

Christendom

Christendom: "a culture seeking to subject all areas of human experience to the Lordship of Christ." (Kreider, *The Change in Conversion*, 91–92).

Christendom is marked by:

A COMMON BEHAVIOR
1. Behaving "like a Christian": common sense, custom, Scripture
2. Enforcement of behavioral norms (by social pressure, church, state legislation)
3. Exceptionally committed Christians: within Christendom "there are people whose religious commitments are especially intense. It is these people who are likely to have had a life-changing experience, which they may call 'conversion' ... These people are often counseled to become members of the clergy or of religious communities ... Christendom cultures honor committed minorities, provided they do not suggest that their way of life ought to constitute the way of life for 'normal' Christians" (ibid., 97).
4. Coercion: inducements and compulsions; church tax; positions open only to Christians.

A COMMON BELONGING
1. Recruitment—the christening of all infants
2. The church and its constituent parishes are large
3. Church/state symbiosis
4. Lack of choice

---

69. In Christendom, "there are people whose religious commitments are especially intense. It is these people who are likely to have had a life-changing experience, which they may call 'conversion.' ... These people are often counseled to become members of the clergy or of religious communities ... Christendom cultures honor committed minorities, provided they do not suggest that their way of life ought to constitute the way of life for 'normal' Christians" (Kreider, *The Change in Conversion*, 97).

> ### *Christendom* (cont.)
>
> 5. Church and world are understood to be one.
> 6. Clericalism: "Within Christendom the fundamental division is not between church and world but between *clergy* and *laity*" (ibid., 95).
> 7. Localism: identity and loyalty are local (thus, Christian states can war against each other)
> 8. Mission is not emphasized except beyond the borders of Christendom: i.e., to foreigners.
>
> *A COMMON BELIEF: Orthodox Christianity* (ibid., 92ff.)
> 1. Heresy is not tolerated.
> 2. Unofficial alternatives live on.
> 3. Religious instruction is often rudimentary.
> 4. The society's symbols, art, and ritual are Christian.
>
> CONCLUSION
> "What has happened when measures of inducement and compulsion, initially applied in the fourth century, are peeled away?" (ibid., 98). "[M]any Westerners . . . resist Christianity in general, because they associate it with things that authority figures have forced them to say or do. Because of Christendom, when Christianity is mentioned they will experience boredom or revulsion" (ibid., 100).

What implications does this have for us today, as the church moves again toward Meeks' first conversionary direction, away from Christendom, as mainline churches lose members but house churches are growing? What does conversion look like in post-Christendom? For one thing, conversion would change, increase, and become normative again. As it is, the contemporary church still stands closer to Christendom than pre-Christendom in that most of the baptized in the liturgical churches are baptized as infants, and many have been neither catechized nor converted. For another, a renewal in conversion of the baptized would invert church structure from clericalism to realized baptismal ecclesiology, with clergy again serving and enabling the baptized in their process toward Christ and their priestly ministry in the world. To mediate these changes, it will be essential to identify ways in which those living the processual baptismal life can come to conversion and to catechesis, and to be supported in their growth and maturity by the Spirit.

Kreider's research on the rise in Christendom and the minimizing of conversion raises some questions: *If Christendom is indeed marked by a change in conversion then in this post-Christendom era is it not necessary to attend to another change in conversion?* Inasmuch as the post-Christendom church has some significant things in common with the pre-Christendom church, we hypothesize that the catechumenal process done before baptism in the early church may have much to commend to us for a post-baptismal process. *What was the process of catechesis in the early church and how might we employ it today, here, now?* To be able to identify what we can claim about the catechumenate, we need to know how it works. This is our next task.

6

The Catechumenal Process
A Conversionary Rhythm Progressed by Ritual

Forming Christians in a State Religion: Mixed Reviews

ALAN KREIDER'S THESIS, WHICH WE FOLLOWED IN THE LAST CHAPter, is that a change in the relationship between the church and the state was effected by a change in the meaning of conversion as the church lived it out. Throughout church history, the relationship between the *ecclesia* and the "world" is one of tension, sometimes creative and sometimes antagonistic. The fourth century was a period when both extremes lived side by side. At one extreme was the apocalyptic tendency of those persecuted to see the Roman Empire as the enemy, the Beast, "an alien and hostile world";[1] at the other was the Eusebian view that the empire is the means by which Christianity will enact its saving work.[2] Eusebius calls the empire and the church "twin roots of blessing."[3] At the first extreme, the zenith of human heroism is martyrdom, the faithful foundation of the church. At the second extreme, the emperor is understood to manifest God's saving work on earth, representing the authority of the sovereign God even as the church manifests Christ's saving words and ministry. In the middle are views of those like Augustine for whom the empire is neither the enemy nor the pseudo-savior, but is theologically neutral. The church is in the

---

1. Markus, *Saeculum*, 55.

2. See Markus, *Saeculum*, 48–54 on these two views. For Augustine's middle position, see ibid., 54–62; for the relationship with the *City of God*, see ibid., 63f.

3. Markus refers his readers to *Laus Const.* XVI, 4 for the "fullest concise sketch of the Eusebian scheme" which Eusebius built on the theology of Origen. *Saeculum*, 50 n. 1.

world, is made up of people who are finite, sinners, even evil, yet is the Body of Christ, chosen of God, drawn toward the eschaton.

At the beginning of the twenty-first century, the whole range of perspectives and realities are manifest at once in different places. Yet in the contemporary movement away from Christendom, we are witnessing a movement away from expectation that civil life will impart Christian values. According to Kreider, in the early church, the "typical pagan entering Christian catechism had a mental mélange of historical data—myths about gods, national exploits, local heroes. To enable the catechumen to become ready to join the Christian community, the catechist needed to replace this mythico-historical mix by an alternative narrative, by the history of salvation as recounted in the books of the Hebrew Scriptures which culminated in the person and work of Jesus Christ and which continued in the life of the transnational church and the sufferings of the martyrs."[4]

In the contemporary church, we can find this same situation repeated. For example, in the 1990s, I had occasion to tutor a ten- or eleven-year old for the God and Country Award for her Girl Scout troop. I was amazed by what she did not know about her faith. The apex for me of the "mental mélange" of various religions mediated through new-age simplism was when I asked her about Easter and she replied, "That was the day Jesus was reincarnated."

To become a Christian is to enter into a world, to cultivate the eyes to see reality in a particular way. In the evolution of conversion, Kreider has shown that this catechumenal cultivation emphasized behavior and belonging at first, moving with Christendom to an emphasis on changed (and orthodox) belief, a focus that endured through the Middle Ages (and the Inquisition). Following the sixth-century requirement that all infants be baptized, within a generation there were virtually no adults needing baptism, and the catechumenate disappeared altogether. A millenium later, at the Reformation, catechisms were created[5] for those (already baptized) preparing for

---

4. Kreider, *Worship and Evangelism in Pre-Christendom*, 24.

5. For example, see Martin Luther's *Short Catechism* (1529), which superseded the Greater Catechism of 1528 and became "the standard book of instruction for Southern Germany" (Bettenson, *Documents*, 201–4). In England, see for example, *A Short Catechism or Plain Instruction containing the sum of Christian Learning, set forth by the King's Majesty's Authority, for all Schoolmasters to Teach* (1553), in *The Two Liturgies*, 485–540.

Confirmation—often in a question-and-answer form to enable the confirmand to memorize right beliefs. Christian behaviors were formed by the culture at large, in fact and in the breach.

The reclaiming of the catechumenate from the early church to its contemporary call to conversion of adults in behavior, belonging, and belief has felicitously occurred at the end of the twentieth century out of the liturgical renewal precipitated by the Vatican Council II. The Roman Catholic Church issued the *Ordo initiationis christianae adultorum* in 1972 (English vernacular version for the United States of America, 1988[6]), which makes use of the scholarship giving us access to the early church's rhythm of instruction and rite. This Rite of Christian Initiation of Adults, R.C.I.A., has also been appropriated for use in other Western Christian churches.[7]

We have seen the contrast between baptism as the culmination of a catechetical conversionary process in the early church, and baptism without catechesis or conversion beginning in the fifth century and, including infants, into the present day. The Christendom model, in which those converted in behavior and belonging become clerics and monastics, represents a clerical ecclesiology and has predominated in Christian history. If the church today is serious about returning to a baptismal ecclesiology, in fact to realizing the church as the priestly people of God, then an examination of the conversionary process as practiced in the early church before Christendom is crucial.

What was the rhythm of preparation for persons seeking to live a Christian life in the early church? How is it reclaimed or adapted in our own day? Is it a rhythm flexible enough to operate whether Christianity be in the mainstream (as it still is in many places) or whether it retreat to its prophetic place at the margins of civil and cultural life (as it was at first, and as it is becoming again)? Would such a rhythm serve a catechetical and conversionary function in our own day, enabling the

---

6. *Editio typica* approved by the National Conference of Catholic Bishops in 1986, by the Congregation for Divine Worship in Rome in 1987, and approved for use July 1, 1988 (and required for use effective September 1, 1988). *Rite of Christian Initiation of Adults*, Copyright page.

7. In the Episcopal Church, for example, see the *Books of Occasional Services*, and the Associated Parishes for Liturgy and Mission (www.associatedparishes.org). For Protestant church involvement (especially Lutheran), see *North American Association for the Catechumenate* (www.naforum.org).

ethical Christian life of pure and charitable behavior called for by the gospel and required of a strong counter-cultural community?

Substantial material has been published translating early baptismal documents and describing catechesis in the early church. Because this material has been fully explored and is readily available, there is no need to repeat it here.[8] However, it will be worth our while to recount the early conversionary tidal rhythm as it has been recapitulated ecumenically in the twentieth- and twenty-first-century church's liturgical renewal. Because this rhythm led persons into foundationally new behaviors, beliefs, and belonging in the early period when Christianity was a minor counter-cultural religion without civil privilege, its pattern may prove valuable for the contemporary post-Christendom church wherever a call for conversion is identified. We examine it for what it may contribute to a different era and a *post-baptismal* process.

Catechumenal Rhythm: Instructional Content

The conversionary pattern of the catechumenate can be described as a rhythm. It is like a wave pulling out into lived-experience in the world, and drawing in to teaching/reflection in the group of catechumens with their teacher: outward, inward. This primary, catechumenal, outward-inward rhythm between the sea of the world and the shore of the catechumenal community is punctuated by coves and caves of rites of liturgical action. Our knowledge of the catechumenal process and especially of the rites used comes predominantly from homilies that have survived from the fourth century, the period right on the cusp of the shift to Christendom. These are collectively referred to as "the mystagogical catecheses" and come from four sources: the *Mystagogic Catecheses* of Cyril, bishop of Jerusalem

---

8. See, for example, Finn, *Early Christian Baptism and the Catechumenate*; Fisher, *Christian Initiation: Baptism in the Medieval West* and Fisher, *Confirmation Then and Now*; Johnson, *The Rites of Christian Initiation*; *Made, Not Born*; Turner, *The Hallelujah Highway*; Whitaker, ed., *Documents of the Baptismal Liturgy*; and Yarnold, *The Awe-Inspiring Rites of Initiation*.

(c.349–86);[9] *De Sacramentis* of Ambrose, bishop of Milan (374–97);[10] *Baptismal Instructions* of John Chrysostom of Antioch, eventually bishop of Constantinople (397–407);[11] and *Baptismal Homilies* of Theodore of Mopsuestia, also priest in Antioch before becoming bishop of Mopsuestia (392–428), a town 100 miles away.[12] We shall use the heuristic of a correlation of the points of conversionary change—behavior, belief, and belonging—with the catechumenal rhythm of experience, teaching/reflection, and rite.

Life experience is the first locus of heart-change. We have seen Pachomius' experience in Egypt of Christians caring for strangers in prison and how that moved him to a life conversion. Teaching which occurs after experience and with reference to it is likely to be more effective, as Cyril says in his first mystagogical instruction, explaining why the instruction about baptism is coming *after* they have

9. Of the twenty-four catechetical sermons, delivered c.348–50 (Cross, *Oxford Dictionary*, 369), Yarnold finds the last five to have a later date. The first set includes a *Procatechesis*, preached to the newly-enrolled who had given in their names for Easter baptism, and the *Catechesis*, eighteen sermons given in Lent during that year, mostly on the Creed. The second set, preached some thirty years later, make up the *Mystagogic Catecheses* preached during Easter week to those baptized on Easter (Yarnold, *Awe-Inspiring*, 69). See Cross, ed., *St. Cyril of Jerusalem's Lectures on the Christian Sacraments*.

10. Ambrose, *On the Sacraments* and *On the Mysteries*.

11. See Harkins, *St. John Chrysostom: Baptismal Instructions* (*Ancient Christian Writers*, vol. 31); in Yarnold, *Awe-Inspiring*, 150 n. 1. For what follows, I am following Yarnold.

12. It is generally held that Theodore's sixteen catechetical sermons were preached in Antioch before he became a bishop. The hermeneutical split between the more literal interpretation of Scripture favored in Antioch and the more allegorical employed in Alexandria had occurred by the late fourth century. The more literal Antiochene approach, apparent in Theodore's teaching, leans toward the fullness of Jesus' human nature, with the accompanying difficulty of explaining the union of divine and human natures in Jesus Christ. "Theodore, for example, preferred to speak of the Word 'assuming a *man*' (cf. B[aptismal] H[omilies] 3.21, 24; 24:5.2, 10) rather than 'becoming *flesh*,' thus preparing the way for the Nestorian heresy that Christ consisted of two persons, a human and a divine, united in moral union and functional collaboration" (Yarnold, *Awe-Inspiring*, 165–66).

The first eleven catechetical sermons were preached in Lent to the enrolled candidates for baptism. The last five, called by Yarnold *Baptismal Homilies*, explain the sacraments. Unlike Cyril and Ambrose (but consistent with Antiochene hermeneutics), Theodore (like John Chrysostom) explained baptism to candidates *before* the rite, but all four of them withheld instruction on the Eucharist until after the initiates' experience. For more on Antiochene hermeneutics, see Jeanrond, *Theological Hermeneutics*, esp. 18–22.

been down in the water: "I well knew that visual testimony is more trustworthy than mere hearsay, and therefore I awaited this chance of finding you more amenable to my words, so that out of your personal experience I could lead you into the brighter and more fragrant meadow of Paradise on earth."[13]

Life experience—in this case, the experiences of nakedness, immersion, anointing, being garbed in white, first Eucharist—is the first locus of heart-change. If the point of Christ's coming is to enable persons and communities to be more fully human, then it is in everyday experience that epiphanies of God-in-Christ-and-the-Spirit will occur. It is in living that God's curing-correcting-caring is effective. Whether the encounter with the Holy One is through deep suffering, or the inadequacy of one's worldview to accommodate to the magnitude of a crisis or a joy, or the selfless outpouring of love of someone, or the sheer Beauty of a sunset, a silent starry night, a friendship, the hatching of a chick, or even the death of a beloved, life itself arouses the human yearning for connecting to the Sacred. Awakening to the Holy may happen in witnessing the beauty and behavior of others (human and non-human), or in one's own stretching toward service or disciplined discipleship. Enacting self-giving love is its own teacher. Human life experience, acting and being acted upon, *behavior*, is the outward rhythm of conversion.

In the catechumenate of the early church, persons inquiring about the Christian faith met together with the bishop to study and make connections between the Christian master narrative and one's own life experience. As we saw in the last chapter, Kreider has unearthed four areas commonly communicated to catechumens in the early church. The first is "the *fund of narratives* of the Christian communities."[14] Converts from Judaism and persons such as the Ethiopian eunuch (Acts 8) knew the Hebrew Scriptures and the Hebrew *mythos*, including, for example, history as the arena of God's salvation, God as redeemer, and the promise of Messiah. But pagans knew none of these. The teaching of foundational stories is essential for the teaching of the faith, to enable the interpretation of life experience in terms of the master narrative of a people.

---

13. Cyril, *Mystagogical Catechesis* 1.1 (in Yarnold, *Awe-Inspiring*, 70).
14. Kreider, *The Change of Conversion*, 26 (emphasis added).

The second curriculum of catechesis was "*controlling images*"[15] or metaphors by which experience is shared and common Christian identity is created. Kreider mentions images repeated in the artistic renderings in the catacombs, such as the three men in the fiery furnace (Dan 3) or Christ's miracles of healing, as well as those recounted in early Christian writings, such as the image of the new Jerusalem in which the people "shall beat their swords into ploughshares, and their spears into pruning-hooks" (Isa 2:2–4/ Mic 4:1–4).[16] The vibrant images are the stuff of *credo*, inspiring one to "set one's heart on" such a compelling vision of life.[17] The metaphoric overlays give, in Paul Ricoeur's words, a surplus of meaning to life experiences in which stories from Hebrew Scriptures (e.g., Jonah or Abraham's three visitors) become *typos* of Christian realities; and in the surplus created in the overlay, there is room for Christians to include their own life experience. For example, a colleague had a child in the congregation come to her after his parents had announced their divorce. After some conversation, she asked him, "How does it feel to you knowing that your parents are getting a divorce?" The boy paused for a moment. Then he said, "It feels like Jonah in the belly of the whale." She realized that the church had given the boy a language to describe his experience, and at once a connection with a people: he was not alone, for Jonah had already experienced this, and all the people who tell this story and call it sacred affirm it as legitimate. And the boy knew the end of the story: Jonah is saved, follows God's call, and the people of Nineveh are also saved. In recounting this metaphor for his feeling, he was also recounting to himself before her the salvific ending to his own current agony.

The third catechetical curriculum in the early church was the *teachings of Jesus*. The parables and Sermon on the Mount, for example, are instruction for what Christians believe, how Christians interpret experience, what priorities Christ calls us to. "You have heard it said, 'You shall do no murder;' but I say to you, everyone who is angry with a brother or a sister has committed murder of the heart" (Matt 5:21–22). The radical spiritual teaching of Christ teaches a radical view of

---

15. Ibid., 27 (emphasis added).

16. Ibid., 27.

17. For a word study on the relationship of "belief" to "faith" and the engagement of the whole person, see Fowler, *Stages of Faith*, 9–16.

neighbor and a radical view of the Realm of God, which is proclaimed as immanent. These teachings form a belief system, the heart of faith.

And the fourth early teachings are quite *practical teachings* for how to live as a Christian. Citing *Apostolic Tradition, Didascalia Apostolorum* 5.6, and Origen's *Contra Celsum* 3.8, Kreider shows teachings leading to behavior change, such as awakening to the needs of the poor, faithfulness when under interrogation, and non-defensive "gentleness and love" even to those who persecute.[18]

While Kreider does not mention it, it is clear from the mystagogical catecheses that a fifth curriculum was the *Creed*, handed down to candidates in the week prior to baptism and rendered back to the bishop just before entering the water; and a sixth, the *sacraments*. These were the symbols of the faith in the *disciplina arcani*, for initiates only. The mysteries (Gk: *mysterion*) or sacraments (L: *sacramentum*), were the mysteries of baptism explained the week after the experience (Ambrose, Cyril) or just before it (Chrysostom, Theodore), and Eucharist explained after the first experience following baptism.

It is now generally accepted that extended catechetical instruction occurred quite soon in the beginning of the church. From the second century, for example, both the *Didache*[19] and Irenaeus' *Apostolic Preaching*[20] appear to be catechetical instruction manuals. Early catechumens, then, brought their living experience to catechesis, and their catechesis began to inform their living. Though the emphasis varied, belief and behavior were worked, received, engaged, tried, and reflected upon in the outward-inward rhythm of living and studying-reflecting together. In the new rites as in the old, this rhythm occurred

---

18. Kreider, *The Change in Conversion*, 28–29.

19. "The first six chapters of *Didache* are generally recognized to be a catechetical manual . . . If, as seems most likely, the manual in *Didache* is based upon a Jewish catechetical method, then we must suppose that some such extended catechesis was already being practiced when *Didache* was produced." Talley, *The Origins of the Liturgical Year*, 164. The *Didache* is dated late first or early second century.

20. Irenaeus (c.130–c.200), Bishop of Lyons, is best known for two works: *Against the Heresies* and *On the Apostolic Preaching* (also translated *Proof of the Apostolic Preaching* and *Demonstration of the Apostolic Preaching*). For discussion of this work as a catechetical manual, see Behr, *St Irenaeus of Lyons*, 7ff.; and Ferguson, "Irenaeus' Proof of the Apostolic Preaching," 119–40.

during periods of formation over several years: at first three (*Apostolic Tradition* 17)[21] or even five (*Canons of Elvira* 11)[22] years.

Catechumenal Rhythm: Stages transitioned by Rites

The periods were divided by what Yarnold calls "steps": ritual actions that celebrate the converting movement of the person, marking changes in status (i.e., passage from one status to the next), and symbolizing (making real) the continuing newness of the person. The RCIA identifies three ritual "steps" that punctuate the conversionary catechumenal process and describe what happened in pre-Christendom:

1. Acceptance into the Order of Catechumens
2. Election or Enrollment
3. Initiation (Immersion, Anointing, Eucharist).[23]

Because of the highly focused nature of liturgy and its resulting power to effect identity, the catechumenal process is more closely identified with these liturgical actions than with the outward-inward rhythm which underlies them. Not all liturgical actions occurred in the same way in all the rites, but the basic periods and ritual steps were common.[24] We shall summarize the periods and the ritual steps that distinguish them.

The first period is variously called the *Precatechumenate* or the period of *Inquiry* or of *Evangelization*. One meets Christians, learns something about the Christ they follow. In the early church, persons in this stage or period, called *inquirers*, did not attend worship. Today, it is not forbidden for inquirers to attend worship, and they might attend with friends. Because Christian worship is primarily intended for the initiated, however, a lone inquirer without familiarity with the master

---

21. Cuming, ed., *Hippolytus*, § 17, p. 16.

22. Early fourth-century Spain. Hamman, "Catechumen, Catechumenate," in *Encyclopedia of the Early Church*, 151–52. In Kreider, *The Change of Conversion*, 24.

23. Yarnold, *Awe-Inspiring*, 1–17ff. See also *RCIA*, "Acceptance into the Order of Catechumens," 17; "Election or Enrollment of Names," 63; "Celebration of the Sacraments of Initiation," 123.

24. For clear and helpful distinctions among rites in different regions, see Fisher, *Christian Initiation: Baptism in the Medieval West* and Fisher, *Confirmation Then and Now*.

narrative or the meaning of the symbols might not be attracted to the faith through the worship.[25]

During this period of instruction, inquirers are likely to become engaged and seek to continue and even deepen their connection to the community. Or they could leave their Christian inquiry for another way. If they desired to deepen, and if the bishop and/or catechist determined that they were serious in their desire and willingness to make the life-changes needed for a life of Christian discipleship, their deepening was effected by a liturgical action in which their status was changed from inquirer to *catechumen*.

The rite that launched them into a deeper level of commitment is called *Acceptance* or *Admission* into the *Order of Catechumens*. In this rite, the person accepted the gospel and may have been given a Bible as a sign of their journey into Christ. The person was given a sponsor (godparent) who assumed particular responsibilities for the new catechumen and symbolized that they no longer belonged only to themselves but to the community of faith. Aspects of the rite were dramatic. Persons were signated with the cross of Christ. Hands were laid upon them, a universal gesture of blessing, healing, ordering, and of passing on the tradition. They received "blessed salt also, to signify that just as all flesh is kept healthy by salt, so the mind which is drenched and weakened by the waves of this world is held steady by the salt of wisdom and of the preaching of the word of God."[26] And they were exorcised of the devil, since: "Before we believed in God the dwelling-place of our heart was corrupt and weak . . . because it was full of idolatry and was the home of demons, since we did everything that was opposed to God."[27]

Admission into the Order of Catechumens was a rite of commitment. It was a commitment, yes, to continuing to learn and grow and purify one's behavior. But it was also a commitment to the community of faith. Catechumens were now permitted to attend the first half of the liturgy, leaving after they were prayed for but before the rest of the

---

25. The contemporary "Seeker Services" are an interesting cultural adaptation in which culturally familiar procedures are conducted at the standard Sunday-morning church service time for the attraction of the uninitiated. For a treatment of this phenomenon, see Ruth, "Lex Agendi, Lex Orandi," 386–405.

26. From a letter to the Roman nobleman Senarius by John the Deacon, c. 500. In Whitaker, *Documents*, 155.

27. *Epistle of Barnabas* 16.7 (second century). In Yarnold, *Awe-Inspiring*, 5.

prayers of the faithful (since they were not yet counted among the baptized faithful), and, of course, before the Lord's Supper. And persons who died as catechumens had the right to Christian burial.

After the rite of Admission came the period of the *catechumenate* which could be as short as the Lenten period or as long as most of a lifetime. In the early church, it was understood that at baptism one was freed from sin, and that sin was inconsistent with the baptismal life. Thus, sin could not happen after baptism. For those who were concerned that they could not live sin-free following baptism, a common solution was to postpone baptism until nearer death when there would be neither time nor occasion to violate their baptismal purity. It was common, as we have seen, to have an extended period of catechumenate. As Yarnold puts it,

> Hippolytus prescribed at least three years of catechumenate, but it became customary to put off baptism for much longer, for it took the Church some time fully to realize her powers to forgive sins committed after baptism; consequently many who were convinced of the truth of Christianity preferred to postpone baptism at least until the passionate time of youth was over. Baptism involved such a radical change in life that one would not receive it until one felt completely ready. St. Ambrose himself, though coming from a devout Christian family, had not yet been baptized when the people chose him to be Bishop of Milan. So too St. Augustine's mother St. Monica decided that he should not be baptized when he was young because of the inevitability of sin.[28]

Thus the period of the catechumenate could be lengthy. One was, in a sense, a partial member of the church; and though not fully initiated, the belonging had begun. The regular instruction and reflection, the changes in behavior, the formation of belief, were intentional within the community of catechumens and under the authority of the bishop. Lives were turned, changed, converted.

When the catechumenate was completed, the catechumens "gave in their names" for the second step: the rite of *election* or *enrollment* in which the person became a *candidate for Baptism*, sometimes called the *elect* (chosen, *electi*), *competentes* (applicants), or *photizomenoi* (destined for illumination). In the first century, any Sunday was considered appropriate for baptism. The association of baptism with the

---

28. Yarnold, *Awe-Inspiring*, 6–7.

symbolism of the church year evolved slowly. Thomas Talley points out that the "earliest definite reference to paschal baptism is the text in Tertullian's *De Baptismo* 19" where any Sunday is still considered proper, but Pascha is the first choice and Pentecost the second as days for solemn baptism. Pascha (Easter) became the principal feast for celebrating baptism during the third century.[29] Tertullian's homily on baptism (c. 200) says:

> The Passover provides the day of most solemnity for baptism, for then was accomplished our Lord's passion, and into it we are baptized . . . After that, Pentecost is a most auspicious period for arranging baptisms, for during it our Lord's resurrection was several times made known among the disciples, and the grace of the Holy Spirit first given . . . for all that, every day is a Lord's day: any hour, any season, is suitable for baptism. If there is a difference of solemnity, it makes no difference to the grace.[30]

In the *Apostolic Tradition* (c. 215), there is evidence of a focused period immediately preceding baptism in which those "chosen" from the catechumens for baptism are "set apart," for fasting and prayer, exorcism and a kind of final purification or sanctification before entering the holy water. How long or when this period of time was is not indicated:

> And when those who are to receive baptism are chosen, let their life be examined [yet again]: have they lived good lives when they were catechumens? Have they honored the widows? Have they visited the sick? Have they done every kind of good work? And when those who brought them bear witness to each: "He has," let them hear the Gospel.
>
> From the time they were set apart, let hands be laid on them daily while they are exorcized. And when the day of their baptism approaches, the bishop shall exorcize each one of them, in order that he may know whether he is pure. And if anyone is not good or not pure, let him be put aside, because he has not heard the word with faith, for it is impossible that the Alien should hide himself for ever.[31]

---

29. Talley, *Origins of the Liturgical Yea*, 34.
30. Tertullian, *On Baptism*, 19; in White, *Documents*, 150.
31. Cuming, trans., *Hippolytus*, § 20.

The Fourth Century Catechumenal Process as Recapitulated in the Twentieth Century

By the fourth century, with the Peace of Constantine and the additional motivations for joining the Christian church, the number of baptisms increased dramatically. It was no longer possible to conduct a three-year catechumenate with the intimate relationship enjoyed in marginal years with the bishop-catechist. Instead, now that baptism had become associated with the Paschal Easter season, the forty-day period preceding Easter (Lent) became a fitting time for the catechumenate. It could be difficult, however, to get catechumens to actually commit to an Easter baptism. By the third century a way of being reconciled with the church following post-baptismal sin had been worked out;[32] but now there was a dual pressure, to live sinlessly, or to endure the public shame and ordeal of being reconciled should sin occur. Postponement was still common. Augustine adapts his methods and his theology to accommodate to the difficulty of getting people to hand in their names and commit to going through with their baptism. He preached every year hortatory sermons to get people to submit their names and present themselves for baptism: "Look, it's Easter time, put your name down for baptism. If the festival doesn't get you excited, at least let curiosity lead you on" (*Sermon* 132.1).

Ambrose, too, experienced a lack of response to his preaching for catechumens to give in their names, a situation he compares to the apostles' failure to catch fish (Luke 5:5).[33] Using a text from Sirach 5:8, Augustine also preached this:

---

32. Gregory the Wonderworker (Thaumaturgus) (c.213–c.270) "testifies to five grades or degrees of penitents, modeled on the existing pattern for the admission of catechumens but slightly more elaborate. There is no doubt that the ceremonies dramatize the readmission of the alienated to the heart of the community of worshippers." The five gradations toward reconciliation were marked by the degree of communion penitents were permitted to have with the worshipping community: *mourners*, wailing outside the church during Eucharist; *hearers*, permitted to stand just inside the door to hear the service of the catechumens (through the sermon); *fallers* or prostrators, permitted to be inside the nave during the synaxis (service of the catechumens); *bystanders*, now permitted to stand inside for the whole of the liturgy, but not to receive communion; and finally, they were reinstated to their status as baptized, cleansed *faithful*. Hellwig, *Sign of Reconciliation*, 36.

33. Ambrose writing on Luke *In Expos. Ev. Luc.* 4.76 (PL 15.1634f.).

You in particular, you bad procrastinator with your bad longing for tomorrow, listen to the Lord speaking, listen to holy scripture preaching . . . "Do not be slow to turn to the Lord, nor put it off from day to day. For suddenly his wrath will come, and at the time for vengeance he will destroy you." Did I write that? Can I cross it out? If I cross it out, I'm afraid of being crossed out myself . . . I'm compelled to preach it. In terror I aim to terrify. Be afraid with me in order to rejoice with me. Do not be slow to turn to the Lord.[34]

The process of "giving in one's name" is, in the contemporary rite, the literal inscribing of one's name in a register during the rite of enrollment. Egeria, the fourth century pilgrim to Jerusalem from (we think) Gaul or Spain, wrote in her journal to her "loving sisters" (24.1) an account of the rite of enrollment, showing the importance of sponsors, the spiritual "fathers" and "mothers":

> I feel I should add something about the way they instruct those who are to be baptized at Easter. Names must be given in before the first day of Lent, which means that a presbyter takes down all the names before the start of the eight weeks for which Lent lasts here, as I have told you. Once the priest has all the names, on the second day of Lent at the start of the eight weeks, the bishop's chair is placed in the middle of the Great Church, the Martyrium [built by Constantine], the presbyters sit in chairs

---

34. Augustine, *Sermon* 40.5. Augustine's pressure for catechumens to enroll at the beginning of Lent for Easter baptism consists with his understanding of church as a mixed body, full of goodness as well as dysfunction, a *corpus permixtum* as we have said. For Augustine, the church is the "threshing floor" holding both the wheat and the chaff (Sermon 80.8; Kreider, *Change*, 64). Baptism is necessary but not sufficient for salvation. "For it is one thing to say that every one who shall enter into the kingdom of heaven is first born again of water and the Spirit . . . another thing to say that every one who is born of water and the Spirit shall enter into the kingdom of heaven, which is assuredly false" (*On Baptism* VI.19). Very plainly, "there can be baptism in a man although there be in him no remission of his sins" (VII.33). The reason for this is that an inner conversion of heart is necessary as well as the outward sign of baptism (VI.62). A heart with malice can prevent the remission of sins (I.18). Remission of sins, therefore, requires the outward sacrament of baptism, the outward sign of unity with the Catholic Church, and the inner conversion of the heart. Thus, "all who are baptized with the baptism that is consecrated in the words of the gospel have the Father, and the Son, and the Holy Ghost in the sacrament alone; but that in heart and in life neither do those have them who live an abandoned and accursed life within" (VI.29). Just as remission of sins can be blocked by a hardened heart, so can the reception of the Holy Spirit. A person "may be baptized with water, and not born of the Spirit" (VI.19). Augustine (Augustinus), *On Baptism*.

on either side of him, and all the clergy stand. Then one by one those seeking baptism are brought up, men coming with their fathers and women with their mothers. As they come in one by one, the bishop asks their neighbors questions about them: "Is this person leading a good life? Does he respect his parents? Is he a drunkard or a boaster?" He asks about all the serious human vices. And if his inquiries show him that someone has not committed any of these misdeeds, he himself puts down his name; but if someone is guilty he is told to go away, and the bishop tells him that he is to amend his ways before he may come to the font. He asks the men and the women the same questions. But it is not too easy for a visitor to come to baptism if he has no witnesses who are acquainted with him.[35]

The contemporary RCIA also emphasizes the role of godparents or sponsors to testify on behalf of the state of formation of the candidates-to-be.[36] RCIA §120 states: "Before the rite of election is celebrated, the catechumens are expected to have undergone a conversion in mind and in action and to have developed a sufficient acquaintance with Christian teaching as well as a spirit of faith and charity. With deliberate will and an enlightened faith they must have the intention to receive the sacraments of the Church, a resolve they will express publicly in the actual celebration of the rite."[37]

The bishop should preside at this rite which "is the focal point of the Church's concern for the catechumens,"[38] or "a priest or a deacon who acts as the bishop's delegate."[39] The rite is as follows: After the homily, the catechumens are presented; the godparents or sponsors affirm that "these candidates [are] worthy to be admitted to the sacraments of Christian initiation" and that they "are sufficiently prepared to be enrolled among the elect"; the community may affirm the sponsors' testimony and pledge to support the candidates "in faith, prayer, and example" or to "include them in your prayer and affection." Following the presentation and testimony, the candidates state their intention and then inscribe their names in the registry. The enrolled are then proclaimed "members of the elect, to be initiated into the sacred mys-

---

35. Egeria, *Egeria's Travels*, section 45:1-4, pp. 143–44.
36. *RCIA*, § 118–19, "Election or Enrollment of Names," 63.
37. *RCIA*, § 120, "Election or Enrollment of Names," 63.
38. *RCIA*, § 121, p. 63.
39. *RCIA*, § 121, p. 63.

teries at the next Easter Vigil." Prayers for the elect ensue. They are then given a solemn blessing and dismissed. The service continues with the Creed (optional) and the Eucharist.[40]

In the Episcopal *Book of Occasional Services 1994*,[41] the rite and rubrics are a bit more simple than in the Roman Catholic RCIA, but still indicate that the candidates-to-be will come forward with their sponsors, publicly state their intentions, and inscribe their names in the book of election. The Episcopal rite places the enrollment *after the Creed*, which breaks with the early church practice of handing over the Creed closer to baptism. It is also ritually confusing since, like the RCIA, the Presentation of the Creed may be done in the Third Sunday in Lent. In the early church, the Creed was part of the discipline of secrecy, and was "handed over" (*traditio*) phrase by phrase, which the candidates memorized. During the following week, their sponsors helped them memorize it, and they gave it back (*redditio*) memorized to the bishop prior to baptism.

The rite of enrollment marks the beginning of the third period, variously called the period of *illumination, enlightenment*, or *purification*. This period includes instruction and other kinds of purification, strikingly marked with ritual action. Exorcistic prayers, called *scrutinies* (Roman Catholic) or *prayers* (Episcopal), are conducted on the 3rd, 4th, and 5th Sundays of Lent (or alternatively in the Episcopal *BOS*, they may be done the 2nd, 3rd, and 4th Sundays of Advent if the baptism is to occur on the feast of the Lord's baptism). These consist of intercessory prayers for the elect while the sponsors stand next to them, their hand on the candidates' shoulders, followed by an exorcistic prayer by the presider, and then their dismissal from the assembly.[42] Yarnold points out that in the early church, the community scrutinized the candidates, while in the contemporary rite, the candidates scrutinize themselves during the silent prayer before the intercessions.[43]

There is a heightening of liturgical action in that this third stage, the shortest, is not only initiated by a rite (i.e., enrollment) but is punctuated with liturgizing which moves the candidates daily toward the

---

40. See the text of this rite in *RCIA*, 67–76.

41. For the material which follows, see ibid., 122–30. This material is available in any edition of *Book of Occasional Services*, published every three years since 1979.

42. The video *This is the Night* demonstrates the solemnity of this rite.

43. Yarnold, *Awe-Inspiring*, 11.

life-changing paschal rite of baptism. The Episcopal *BOS* expects that in addition to the public liturgical prayers for exorcism, "this stage [of purification] involves the private discipline of fasting, examination of conscience, and prayer, in order that the candidates will be spiritually and emotionally ready for baptism. It is appropriate that, in accordance with ancient custom, the sponsors support their candidates by joining them in prayer and fasting" (*BOS*, 116). The "ancient custom" is mentioned in Justin Martyr's *First Apology* 61 in which those who "promise that they can live accordingly, are instructed to pray and beseech God with fasting for the remission of their past sins, while we pray and fast along with them."[44]

The third and final liturgical "step" is the rites of initiation themselves in all their unhurried profound vulnerable dramatic glory. The many accounts of baptism by immersion in living water, with anointings, followed by the first occasion to pray the prayers of the faithful and to share the heavenly banquet at the Lord's Table, convey the initiatory effectiveness of this baptism so long belabored and prepared for by the candidates.

The fourth and final stage was a period (typically fifty days) of post-baptismal catechesis and reflection called *mystagogy* in which the newly-baptized neophytes were led by their bishop-catechist through a reflection upon the sacramental mysteries just experienced.[45] As recounted in the surviving fourth-century catecheses of Bishop Ambrose and Bishop Cyril, mystagogy occurred during the Great Fifty Days of Easter. During the time of Christian persecution, and under the influence of the oriental mystery religions, what was actually going to happen had been kept secret from the unbaptized. This cult of secrecy, later called the *Disciplina Arcani*, was intended to protect the faithful from reports brought against them by those uncommitted and uninitiated. It may be hard for us to imagine, but they did not know ahead of time what would happen to them—that their clothes would be removed, that they would be anointed all over their bodies and led down into the water, to repeat the Creed they had just learned and to be immersed three times as they proclaimed their faith in God the

---

44. In White, *Documents*, 147.

45. The similarity of the mystagogical method to contemporary methods of adult education in which a common experience is reflected upon together has been noted. See Browning and Reed, *The Sacraments in Religious Education and Liturgy*, and Hughes, *Saying Amen: A Mystagogy of Sacrament*.

Father, God the Son, and God the Holy Spirit. They were then dressed in a pure white baptismal garment and led to the waiting community where for the first time they would pray the great priestly intercessions, bless God for creation and salvation in Christ and the animation of the Holy Spirit, and witness and receive the holy meal. The meaning of all these things was interpreted for them in mystagogical reflection. The period of mystagogy was important, and brought to completion the initiatory process.

Looking toward a Catechumenal Process in the Twenty-First Century

Does conversion happen in the periods of inquiry (the catechumenate and enlightenment/purification) before baptism? Or does conversion happen in the rites of baptism? Some would make doctrinal or theological claims about this. The contemporary RCIA expects that conversion will happen before baptism, before enrollment even.[46] Augustine believed the preparation was extremely important, but that it was not complete until baptism. In fact, Augustine recognized that even baptism did not complete the conversion of some, which he noted in sermons: "We can't convert the vast majority to a good life, can we?" For there are only a "few who walk along the narrow road."[47]

From the operational perspective, we cannot know when conversion happens for a person. According to the process of the catechumenate, change can happen during experience in the world, during teaching, in reflecting and integrating experience and learning, in the process of preparing for the various rites, in the rites themselves, in reflecting upon or living the effect of them later. Change can occur for a person in all these loci, and in myriad mental-emotional-social-prayerful connections that can be neither isolated nor named. William Cieslak has suggested that the English translation "Rite" of Christian Initiation of Adults is not as apt as the Latin term *Order* of Christian Initiation of Adults, since it is a process most assuredly involving more than "a rite."

---

46. See the text of paragraph 120 above. *RCIA*, 63.
47. Augustine, *Sermon* 80.8, and *Sermon* 224.1. In Kreider, *Change*, 64. See also related references above from Augustine's *On Baptism*, n. 34.

Perhaps attempting to glean a "moment" of conversion from the OCIA (as, following Cieslak, we shall now refer to the RCIA) is as specious as trying to pinpoint a "moment" in which the Eucharistic bread changes into Christ's body. Perhaps the point rather is the rhythmic flow that mediates life-change in different ways for different people. The rhythm, as we have identified it, is an outward "lived experience" of each person's life, the great and small moments of society, aloneness, working, leisure, creativity, reflection, a movement we correlate with *behavior*. This outward movement is balanced in the catechumenate with an inward movement of "teaching/ reflection" of the faith, the stories and symbols, the visions and expectations of the faithful community. In this intentional gathering for teaching and learning, catechumens learn how to behave, what to believe, and who they would belong to should they take the committed step into Christian identity. This teaching/ reflection may have content which reaches from the noetic to the practical and everywhere between. Yet its effect is to impress upon the heart of the would-be Christian these contents of faith. This movement gives the norms and interpretive devices by which a person can receive, recognize, and respond to life with a Christian worldview. This creedal orientation of the teaching/reflection movement correlates it with Kreider's *belief*.

And the outward-inward tidal rhythm of life-experience and intentional teaching/reflection is punctuated by rites which give meaning, mark progress and change, and condense one's identity into an embodied (ritual) time and place. Through the rites, between and within each period of the catechumenal process, a person is-becoming his or her Christian identity. In the dramatic, "awe-inspiring" (or, as Yarnold paraphrases, "spine-chilling")[48] rites, what one has learned and become is gathered together in the context of the Christian family of faith and *mythos* or worldview, and made visible, tangible, real: in other words, symbolic, sacramental, dimensional in their apparent as well as "bigger-than-life" aspects, Real.

Without one's own life experience, as Cyril said, there is no curiosity or receptivity or longing for an interpretive worldview big enough to provide integrity. Without the intentional gathering in community to teach-learn-reflect, one does not develop the eyes to see and interpret this experience in the life-giving, creative, redemptive

---

48. Yarnold, *Awe-Inspiring*, ix.

ethos and worldview[49] of the Christian master narrative. The rhythm of these two contributes to inner and outer change.

But without the third, without the focused intensity of rites with all their communal and personal secret-public layers of meaning, without the "doing" of conversionary change, conversion would not occur in the same way. It is the liturgical doing that effects the changing identity of the person(s) as part of the ongoing conversionary rhythm. It is rite that creates *belonging*.

In a post-Christendom church that must take seriously its increased role of mediating Christian identity[50] so that those who seek to live gospel lives of discipleship can be clear who they belong to, it is essential to understand the conversionary process amidst shifts in relationship among church, state and culture. *Christian ritualizing* is key to the post-baptismal conversionary rhythm of outward experience (trying on Christian behavior) and inward learning and reflection (growing in Christian belief), which are all made real by rites that seal a sense of Christian identity (engendering belonging). The intensity of rites—liturgy—has an essential role in enabling the church—all the baptized—to claim their identity and live out their priestly ministry in the world.

And as the collusion of culture and institutional church loosens in the twenty-first century, there is an opportunity for Christians to become again the Community of the Beautiful, attracting persons by the integrity of their behavior and their belief, so that others can see how Christians love one another with courage and faithfulness. Christian ritualizing is an essential part of the ongoing conversionary process that can enable all the baptized (not just the clergy) to claim their portion in Christ's ministry, not only in preparation prior to baptism, but in continuing catechesis and conversion *after baptism*.

Those who become part of the OCIA are very aware that baptism is the *beginning* of the Christian life. At no matter what age one is baptized, however, continuing life in Christ requires growth, expansion of the Self, moving "further up and further in" as C.S. Lewis calls it. The rite of Holy Baptism begins this *baptismal process* of ongoing conversion into Christ-by-the-Spirit. Later, Part III will address the ritual-

---

49. See Geertz, "Ethos, World View, and the Analysis of Sacred Symbols," 126–41.

50. Chauvet's concern is with Christian existence and identity, in *Symbol and Sacrament*, 2–4.

making that can carry the baptized from one life-stage to another on the journey.

But what kind of growing and change need the baptized be engaged in? What theologies of "ongoing conversion" would inform the post-baptismal process of continuing animation in the Spirit of Christ? The next chapter offers two: the mystical model of *theosis*—transforming more and more into the likeness of Christ—and the eucharistic model of *response-gift*—offering one's life and one's Self as thanks-gifts to God. Our guide into *theosis* will be the second century bishop Irenaeus, and into *response-giving*, the twenty-first century sacramental theologian Louis-Marie Chauvet.

7

Theology of the Baptized as Growing and Responding

Theosis and Response-Giving

> The entire drama of history is located in the tension between this gift and this acceptance: God's passion for human beings, and the nostalgia of human beings for God.[1]

IN THE SEARCH FOR THE ROLE OF CHRISTIAN RITUALIZING IN A REALized baptismal ecclesiology, we have brought to bear Moore and Myerhoff's distinction between the doctrinal and operational efficacies of ritual as a way of revealing two essential perspectives in realizing the church as all the baptized. We have claimed, through the baptismal theologies of three church fathers and through the historic cycle of pre-Christendom, Christendom, and now post-Christendom, that both the church's sacramental mediation of God's grace in baptism and the worshipper's reception of or response to that grace are essential in a baptismal life and must be accounted for in any complete baptismal theology.

In this chapter we propose that the doctrinal and operational efficacies of baptism may find mutual coherence and accountability in the concept of the baptismal life as an operational progression. To explore the idea of baptism not only as event, but as event that launches a life-process of ongoing conversion and maturing, we shall draw upon the process of theosis, from the pre-Christendom theologian Irenaeus (in which the person made Christian at baptism is understood to grow more and more into the likeness of God throughout life) and upon the human offering of response-gift, from the post-Christendom theolo-

---

1. Corbon, *Wellspring of Worship*, 18.

gian Louis-Marie Chauvet (in which the Christian life is understood to be lived in response to God's grace given at baptism and beyond).

Both theosis and response-giving are understood here to arise out of the sacramental grace given by God in the sacrament of baptism. Their relationship to baptism is grounded in the understanding that sacrament arises out of the sacramental principle. We begin by exploring the sacramental principle as a foundation and context for then understanding the theologies of theosis and response-gift. These, along with faith development in chapter 8, will give us the theological ground for proceeding with the role of liturgizing in the ongoing process that is the baptismal life.

The Sacramental Principle

The sacramental theology of the church has focused upon the dominical sacramental moments: i.e., baptism and eucharist. The community of theologians in conversation on sacrament has been predominantly those clerical scholars and practitioners designated to create the place, time, and ethos for sacramental events for the community, and who have sought to understand what happens, how the sacraments work, what God does, and why it is important for the community to enact them at all, and in a certain way. The church has placed significant weight on these actions which have Scriptural association with Jesus' life, and since the identifying of specific sacraments with the holy number seven by scholastic Bishop of Paris Peter Lombard (c. 1100?–1160), weight has also been placed upon confirmation, reconciliation, marriage, anointing (or extreme unction), and ordination. In the Scholastic limiting of "sacrament" to these seven clerically enacted events, however, the term "sacrament" did not then connote the worshippers' participation or response, as we saw in our review of Thomas Aquinas. And further, inasmuch as the significance of these seven sacraments is considered to be clerically, institutionally, or theologically prescribed, other events that may be of equal (or, in some cases, greater) personal significance for the worshipper are defined outside the realm of "sacrament." In contrast, we shall here argue that sacrament is more broadly *the principle whereby the material can mediate the spiritual*, and that it is the fullness of baptismal life that is sacramental, ecclesial, and ministerial.

Theologians have placed the weight of their theological energy on what the (institutional) church understands sacraments to do, or officially intends them to mean—their doctrinal efficacy—rather than on what may be of personal significance for the worshipper (how it "works," operates, effectually in their lives). This is understandable for at least two reasons. First, just as early liturgical books were written to give ministers what they needed for their particular role in the liturgy (e.g., the Evangeliary [sic] for deacons,[2] the Epistolary for lectors, the Antiphonary for choirs, etc.) without including in each the whole rite and ordo, so clergy study what they need to know to conduct liturgy and make needed decisions about proper designing, planning, and implementing of baptismal and eucharistic services, and to teach others to do the same. The peculiar private meanings, or the normative meanings that carry over into the personal lives of individual worshippers,[3] are understood to be important to the church as a whole, but not of first importance among the clerical scholarly priorities. The theologians are largely clerics, and they study that which has the most import for their work on behalf of the church.

The second reason theologians have emphasized doctrinal over operational efficacy of sacraments is, ironically, because of the commonality with which clergy are constantly participating in minor sacramental events connected with the broader sacramentality of the world. This broader sacramentality has been referred to in contemporary scholarship as "the sacramental principle": the general reality that material objects and experiential circumstances signify, symbolize, or mediate the numinous. In their symbolic role, clerics and monastics are often called upon to witness, bless, and/or pray with people on the border of the holy.[4] With the relative frequency or commonality of such sacramental moments, criteria for singling out particular sacred witnessing over myriad others would be difficult to identify.

---

2. This spelling of Evangeliary is given in Cross and Livingstone, eds., *Oxford Dictionary of the Christian Church*, 485. In the eclipse of the diaconate, the Evangeliary would have been used by the priest proclaiming the Gospel.

3. Hoffman, "How Ritual Means," 78–97. To *private* and *normative*, Hoffman adds two additional ritual meanings: *official*, which are those meanings authorized by official religious bodies (corresponding to our doctrinal efficacy), and *public* meanings that are commonly held but not authorized (e.g., Passover as the occasion for a family reunion; Easter as the first day to wear spring clothes).

4. See L. William Countryman's clarifying *Living on the Border of the Holy*.

Should special attention be paid to exorcisms, house blessings, or the making of catechumens? For the particular persons involved, all these events can be of life-changing importance. Yet for the seminarian who has many subjects to master, how much time should be spent, for example, on the blessing of a prisoner, praying with the dying, blessings at childbirth? It is understandable that clerical scholarly attention has been paid to the focal sacramental events with the greatest weight in Scripture and tradition. The theological conversation around sacraments, then, has been located around the teaching and presiding roles of the clergy *vis-à-vis* the dominical sacraments (and, from the twelfth century, the five others).[5] The doctrines which are developed in theological conversation provide the institutional church with official explanations as to the meaning and effectiveness of sacraments. This we have called doctrinal efficacy.

Yet, as we have seen, the doctrinal efficacy of sacrament, necessary though it is, is insufficient to fully account for sacramental efficacy. The extrinsically recognizable and intrinsically felt impact of sacramental action in the ongoing life of the baptized person is real efficacy, whether in presence (as in our illustration of Margaret) or in its sometime absence (as for John). We have found patristic acknowledgement of operational efficacy in Augustine and in Calvin (and to a small degree in Aquinas), and we have shown the universal expectation in the early church that those opening themselves to baptism enter as changed and changing beings: changing in behavior, belonging, and belief. As we have seen from our examination of the early church, the baptismal life has been understood from the beginning to be a

---

5. Note that until Lombard, no specific number of "sacraments" was designated, but many events were understood to be sacramental, including, e.g., foot washing and coronation of a monarch. One of Lombard's Scholastic contemporaries, Hugh of St. Victor (1097–1141), named numerous sacraments in his *On the Sacraments [Mysteries] of the Christian Faith*, including water of aspersion, reception of ashes, and blessing palm branches and foliage (book II, part IX) along with monastic vows, church dedications, death, and judgment (in White, *Documents of Christian Worship*, 121). In England, Thomas Cranmer (1489–1556) wrote: "By the ancient authors there be many sacraments more than seven; for all the figures which signified Christ to come, or testify that he is come, be called sacraments, as all the figures of the old law, and the new law; *eucharistia, baptismus, pascha, dies Dominicus, lotio pedum, signum crucis, chrisma, matrimonium, ordo, sabbatum, impositio manuum, oleum, consecratio olei, lac, mel, aqua, vinum, sal, ignis, cineres, adapertio aurium, vestis candida*, and all the parables of Christ, with the prophecies of the Apocalypse, and such other, be called by the doctors *sacramenta*." Cranmer, "Questions and Answers," 524–25.

changed life, a changing life. The ongoing turning, converting, of the baptized person in the baptizing community[6] begins before baptism, and continues until death.

With Christendom, the merging of institutions of church and state muted the Christian change in behavior and belonging: Christendom organized the life of the church so that ongoing change was assumed for some (i.e., clerics, monastics) but not all. But the radicality of baptism implies now, as it did in pre-Christendom, a person changed in Christ by the Holy Spirit. As A. M. Allchin has said, "the Christian gospel cannot be simply fitted into the world as it now is. It involves its radical transformation. It means a revolution not only in our idea of God but also in our idea of humankind and of the world in which we live."[7] Thus, for a full contemporary baptismal ecclesiology, we need to look at the whole life of the baptized person as a process of change.

Based upon what we have said so far, it is possible now to contend that baptismal life—as a life of ongoing, continuing change—is normative and involves belief, behavior, and belonging. In contra-distinction to Christendom, our longing at the beginning of the third millennium in this post-Christendom church is for a realized baptismal ecclesiology, for the full engagement and empowerment, authority and ministry, of all the baptized. This implies change, not just for clerics and monastics, but for all the baptized. We need, therefore, to look at the whole of the Christian life as a process, as unfolding development and maturing into union with God-in-Christ through the active work of the Holy Spirit.[8]

Foundational to the longing of the church for the full engagement and empowerment of all the baptized as growing, changing images and ministers through Christ in the Spirit is this theological broadening of the notion of sacrament. Major liturgical theologians of the church are recognizing that the reduction of God's sacramental

---

6. See Eastman, *The Baptizing Community*. Eastman makes a step toward operational efficacy when he says, "The church is no more than God's agent in this transaction . . . [But] the church lags and wanders in its mission in direct proportion to the distance that baptism is allowed to stray from the center of ecclesial life. The Matthean formula . . . [sees the church] as the community that evangelizes, baptizes, and teaches" (4).

7. Allchin, *Participation in God*, 1.

8. This idea was generated out of a conversation with my colleague Dr. Mary McGann of the Franciscan School of Theology, Berkeley, California.

activity to seven specific events in the church obviates the sacramental nature of the church itself. The church, according to Otto Semmelroth, is the Ursakrament.[9] More fundamental than the church, however, according to Edward Schillebeeckx, is the sacramental nature of Jesus Christ, the primordial outward sign of the grace of God.[10]

Yet prior to Jesus Christ is another event of the Creator that effects what it signifies: the Creation. Theodore Runyon (United Methodist) asserts that the Ursakrament prior to Jesus Christ is Creation itself.[11] Edward Kilmartin (Roman Catholic) asserts that since God's love is woven into the very fabric of Creation, the specific sacraments are, as they were in the patristic period, "valued as particular concentrations of the sacramental nature of all creation." In order to "maintain an integrated view of the real world," we must hold "a sacramental understanding of all reality": the cosmos itself is inherently sacramental.[12] Kenan Osborne (Roman Catholic), pointing to "the sacramentality of the universe," argues for an interrelationship between God and creation, God and humanity, and locates sacramentality at the meeting of "the primordial divine disclosing" and the "human response."[13] Louis-Marie Chauvet (Roman Catholic) says that creation is inherently gift, and "responsible word": gratuitous and obligatory. "To confess creation is to attain freedom: the given of the universe is received as an offer . . . The 'reception' of the world as creation, that is, as 'gift,' implies the 'return-gift' of the offering. Thus, the confession of creation is itself charged with sacramentality."[14] And Louis Weil (Episcopal) describes what he calls, "the sacramental principle: to see God in all created things. In other words . . . God is revealed in the whole created

---

9. Kenan Osborne points out that Semmelroth deserves credit for this concept from his book *The Church as Original Sacrament* [*Die Kirche als Ursakrament*, 1953]. Just prior to this publication, Karl Rahner had referred to the church as a "radical sacrament" in a manuscript on penance. "It was Rahner's subsequent writings, together with Edward Schillebeeckx's works, that brought the idea of Jesus as the primordial sacrament and the church as a basic sacrament into international prominence." See Rahner's *Church and Sacrament* [*Kirche und Sakrament*, 1961]. In Osborne, *Christian Sacraments in a Postmodern World*, 9.

10. See Schillebeeckx, *Christ the Sacrament of the Encounter with God*.

11. Runyon, "The World as the Original Sacrament," 495–511.

12. Kilmartin, "Theology of the Sacraments," 158, 159; in Kenan Osborne, *Christian Sacraments in a Postmodern World*, 50–51.

13. Osborne, *Christian Sacraments in a Postmodern World*, 50, 121.

14. Chauvet, *Symbol and Sacrament*, 551.

world; and in that sacramental perspective, everything is understood as an access, or a transparency, to the presence and action of God . . . [O]rdinary things can be instruments of grace; . . . an object, a physical, created object can bear the holy, can be an instrument or means of grace . . . The sacramental sense is not narrowly Christian because it is grounded in a certain understanding of our humanity."[15]

Sacramentality is grounded in creation and in the human reality; its foundational theology is Incarnational. Sacraments "reveal that the physical world, far from being evil, is the domain of God's activity," and thus physical objects and actions can mediate encounter with God.[16] Sacrament is the principle by which such outward tangibles mean more than themselves and communicate invisible spiritual reality.

Upon the ground of the sacramental principle, then, we now want to look at two theological hermeneutics that assert the normativity of experiences of growth and change in response to God's grace made operative at baptism. Among several fields to which we might look,[17] in this chapter we examine theosis from mystical theology and the intersubjective rhythm of giving–receiving–thanksgiving from liturgical theology. These perspectives suggest that a baptismal theology that takes full account of the perspective of the baptized person implies an ongoing conversionary process in which pastoral liturgical rites mark points of transition in Christian maturing. If we wish to take account of the experience of the baptized, which this book argues that we must do, then these theological orientations will point us to an understanding of what transitional or transformational experiences operating in all the baptized may need to be educationally and ritually accounted for. We contend that the ongoing animation of the Christian person is essential and critical for a realized baptismal ecclesiology.

---

15. Weil, Lecture, Berkeley, CA, February 8, 2000, 8–9; see also p. 10.

16. Weil, *A Theology of Worship*, 17.

17. Other fields which would yield fruit in the area of human change include *process theology*, especially Whitehead, Lee, and Schillebeeckx; *human affectivity*, especially Aune (e.g., "Ritual Practice," "The Subject of Ritual," "To Move the Heart," "Worship in an Age of Subjectivism Revisited") and Don Saliers (e.g., *The Soul in Paraphrase, Worship as Theology, Worship Come to Its Senses*); and *gift theory*, particularly Hyde, *The Gift*; Mauss, *The Gift*; Titmuss, *The Gift Relationship*; Vaughan, *For-Giving* and "The Gift Economy"; and Weiner, *Inalienable Possessions*.

Theosis: Growing into God

> O God, who wonderfully created, and yet more wonderfully restored, the dignity of human nature: Grant that we may share the divine life of him who humbled himself to share our humanity, your Son Jesus Christ; who lives and reigns with you, in the unity of the Holy Spirit, one God, for ever and ever. Amen.
>
> —*Seventh-century Collect for the Feast of the Incarnation*[18]

The first model from the Christian Tradition we explore which explicitates the normativity of baptismal life as a life of ongoing, continuing change comes from the Greek Fathers. From the pre-Christendom church and later identified with Eastern Orthodoxy is the mystical theology of theosis: human participation in divine life. The Greek "theosis" is commonly rendered "deification" or "divinization": becoming like God, "godding," deifying, becoming divine. That theosis is a process of human becoming is exquisitely expressed by another Greek term connoting the poetics of human life, the "making" of humans into who they are created to be as children of God: theopoeisis. Theosis and theopoeisis imply that the Christian life is a process of ongoing conforming to Christ through the active work of the Holy Spirit, that Christians become more and more like God through the continual pattern of participation in holy living.[19] Theosis characterizes the Christian life. To be Christian is to be in the process of becoming godlike. Theosis is helpful to our quest for a baptismal theology

---

18. *Book of Common Prayer 1979*, collect for the second Sunday after Christmas Day and Of Incarnation, pp. 162, 200, 214, 252. Marion Hatchett writes, "[t]his collect ... dates to the Leonine sacramentary (no. 1239), the earliest of the sacramentaries, as the collect of the first Christmas Mass. The Gelasian sacramentary places it among the Christmas prayers for Matins or Vespers (no.27) and the Gregorian in 'other Prayers of the Birthday of the Lord' (no. 59). ... The petition echoes a sentence attributed to Saint Leo the Great: 'The Son of God became the Son of Man that the sons of men might become the sons of God.'" *Commentary on the American Prayer Book*, 170.

19. In his book, *Holy Living*, Jeremy Taylor (1613–67), an Anglican who leaned toward *theosis* as basic understanding of the Christian life, wrote, "Theology is rather a divine life than a divine knowledge. In heaven indeed we must first see and then love; but here on earth we must first love and love will open our eyes as well as our hearts; and we shall then see, perceive and understand." Section X, "An Act of Desire" appended to "Of Preparation to the Holy Sacrament of the Lord's Supper"; in Gordon S. Wakefield, "Anglican Spirituality," 265.

that encompasses both doctrinal and operational efficacy because it expects that what deifies is not the theology of theosis but the worshippers' experience of Christ and of the Spirit in liturgy. The result of this process is human sharing in the divine life: participation in God. While theosis has been most developed in the Eastern church, it exists in the Western church, including in Thomas Aquinas,[20] in Lutheranism,[21] and in Anglicanism.[22]

The idea of theosis is rooted in Scripture and developed in the fathers. The direct Scriptural reference is found in 2 Pet 1:4: "Thus he has given us, through these things, his precious and very great promises, so that through them you may escape from the corruption that is in the world because of lust, and may become *participants of the divine nature*." (NRSV).

The two church fathers well known to have explicitated deification are Irenaeus, Bishop of Lyons (c.130–c.200), and Athanasius, Bishop of Alexandria (c.296–373). In his work against the Valentinian heresy, Irenaeus states that God came to earth to be human in order that humans can become like God: "following the sure and true Teacher, the Word of God, Jesus Christ our Lord, who on account of his immense love was made what we are, so that we might become what he is."[23]

In her work on Irenaeus, Mary Ann Donovan writes, "This final line of the preface [to Book V] sounds a dominant theme that recurs throughout AH and traces its own path in Christian history, occurring in another form in Athanasius: 'God became a human that humans

---

20. See A. N. Williams who is convincing in her evidence for this in *The Ground of Union: Deification in Aquinas and Palamas*.

21. For example, in Lutheranism, see Mannermaa, "Theosis as a Subject of Finnish Luther Research" and Yeago, "The Bread of Life," in Williams, *The Ground of Union*, 201 n. 2. See also Braaten and Jenson, eds., *Union with Christ*, for which reference I thank Michael Aune.

22. Allchin, *Participation in God* is a cogent study of deification in Anglicanism.

23. *Adversus omnes Haereses* (*AH*) V, Preface [in *Sources Chretiennes* 153:14], transl. by Donovan, *One Right Reading?*, 142. John Keble's translation reads: "Jesus Christ our Lord: Who for His immense love's sake was made that which we are, in order that He might perfect us to be what He is" (Keble, *Five Books of Irenaeus*, 449). Only part of *AH* is preserved in the original Greek; parts also are preserved in Syriac and Armenian. The whole text is preserved in Latin. A critical edition of the Latin along with a reconstructed Greek text are extant in the French series *Sources Chrétiennes* (SC).

might become God' (De Inc[arnatione] 54)."[24] It is Athanasius who uses the term *theopoeisis*.[25] Implied in this dynamic theology is the prolepsis of the reign of God into the present life of the church, the ecclesia, the baptized. The end or *telos* of humankind, union with the divine, is already in the making, present in the process of becoming in Christ.

Illuminating of deification and integral to it are three theologies: imago Dei, Incarnation, and the Holy Spirit. It is not our task to extravagate upon the mystical theology of *theosis*, but merely to recognize it as a significant pattern in the Tradition that calls for serious (sacramental) attention to the Christian life after baptism. Our recognition will be helped by a brief look at each of the connected doctrines so that their integration in Christian life and in worship may become clear.

First, the *imago Dei*: "Then God said, 'Let us make humankind in our image, according to our likeness; . . .' So God created humankind in his image, in the image of God he created them; male and female he created them" (Gen 1:26a, 27 NRSV).

As developed in Eastern Orthodoxy, the meaning of humanity's creation in the image of God is not some external imprint, but is rather the intrinsic "participation in the divine nature."[26] According to Paul Evdokimov, "the image [of God] predestines humanity to theosis."[27] Humanity is born to be in relationship with God and with those others who also bear the imago. This is a gift that is intrinsic to the human person: by our created nature, we bear within us an orientation to the divine, a built-in longing or disposition toward the Holy One. We are

---

24. Donovan, *One Right Reading?*, 142. Athanasius: "gegone anthropos, hin hemas en eauto theopoiese," *Ad Adelphium*, 4, PG 26, col. 1077 a; cf. "Oration on the Incarnation of the Word of God," *De Incarnatione* 54, PG 25, col. 192b; cited in Meyendorff, *Christ*, 230 n. 1, and in Lossky, *Orthodox Theology*, 136 n. 36. In addition to Athanasius, Lossky also cites St. Gregory of Nazianzus, *Poem. Dogmatica*, X, 5–9, PG 37, col. 465; St. Gregory of Nyssa, "The Great Catechetical Oration," 25, PG 45, col. 65D. Lossky ends the Postscript on "Image and Likeness" by saying, "Those who are tempted by the teaching of the *felix culpa* often forget that, in destroying the domination of sin, our Savior opened to us anew the way to deification, which is the ultimate end of man. Thus the work of Christ brings with it the work of the Holy Spirit (Luke 12:49)," 137.

25. *theos gegonen anthropos hina hemas en eauto theopoiese*.

26. Meyendorff, *Christ*, 114.

27. Evdokimov, *L'Orthodoxie*; in Williams, *The Ground of Union*, 15.

born leaning into the Light, one foot firmly grounded in the Potter's holy clay.

The "likeness" of God, as distinct from the image, is not present from the beginning, but is acquired in the lived Christian life. Orthodox theologian John Breck explains that,

> Eastern patristic tradition often distinguishes between "image" and "likeness," holding the former to be the "given" of our created existence, and the latter to involve the personal struggle, in and by the Spirit, to attain God-likeness, to "be perfect" as God is perfect. The work of the Spirit . . . is ultimately to reestablish the unity between "image" and "likeness," a unity shattered by sin. This is accomplished, in biblical terms, by "taking up our cross" in the power of the Spirit. It is the Spirit who, through our personal struggle against sin . . . accomplishes within us, and entirely by grace, the inner transformation into the "likeness of Christ" which St. Paul describes as . . . the present life of believers: "We are being changed (*metamorphoymetha*) into his image" by "the Lord who is the Spirit" (or, "by the Spirit of the Lord").[28]

Breck refers to II Cor 3:17–18: "Now the Lord is the Spirit, and where the Spirit of the Lord is, there is freedom. And all of us, with unveiled faces, seeing the glory of the Lord as though reflected in a mirror, are being transformed into the same image from one degree of glory to another; for this comes from the Lord, the Spirit" (NRSV). This assimilation is deification. According to St. John of Damascus (c.675–c.749), one is "assimilated to God through virtue."

Such a distinction between the imago which is intrinsic to human being, and the likeness which is appropriated bit by bit in human becoming, may help us make sense of the lives of Margaret and John, both born human, both reborn in baptism, but with distinctive differences in the development of their likeness to God. In the funeral homily we referred to in chapter 1, the pastor had said that Margaret's baptism "took." This may now be understood as describing the ever-deepening of Margaret's likeness to God as it merged into and was fed by her participation in God as God's image. We now see that the most fitting metaphor of baptism "taking" is that of the branch grafted into the tree (Rom 11:16–24) or the vine (John 15). In the grafting, the

---

28. Breck, "Two Hands," 245–46. My thanks to Barbara Sweetland Smith for this reference.

branch receives all its nourishment from the trunk as the fluids merge. It becomes part of the tree or vine. If it grows and bears fruit, it will year by year also manifest its likeness to the whole tree, fulfilling its purpose (i.e., fruit) in relationship to the trunk and other branches. We can say that inasmuch as a person's baptism is fulfilled, the image and the likeness are merged in a person's maturing, evolving life.

The Incarnation is the second doctrine endemic to theosis. In God's becoming human, humanity itself was divinized. Holiness enfleshed implies a sanctification of the body, of the human, of creation. According to Irenaeus, it is not just the soul or the mind that has divine nature, but body as well as soul.[29] This must be the case, for in Christ, God became body, incarnate (Latin *carn-*, *caro*, flesh). God became fully human and dwelt among humans (John 1:14), infusing them with divinity. John Breck explains that "[t]rinitarian soteriology . . . is necessarily predicated on incarnational theology" and is,

> concern[ed] . . . with the transformation of human nature from a condition of sinfulness and mortality, to one of perfection and "deification." This is possible by virtue of the fact that the Son of God, through his incarnation, restores fallen human nature to its original perfection . . . The Son of God rises from the dead and ascends to glory "in the flesh" (St. Ignatius) precisely as the God-man. Thereby he raises and glorifies his own humanity. Soteriology, then, concerns not only the overcoming of sin and death; it involves as well the perfection and glorification of human nature.[30]

Intimately related to Incarnation is the third linking doctrine: that of the Holy Spirit. In the theology of deification, theosis occurs by the continuing present work of the Spirit in the life of the ecclesia personally and corporately. The equality and mutually-effecting relationship of the Son and the Spirit (which the doctrine of the Trinity intends to express) draws the human into being as alter Christus and as pneumatikos: that is, into God. John Meyendorff[31] expounds on the Spirit's role beginning with a quotation from Irenaeus: "Where the Church is, there also is the Spirit of God; and where the Spirit of God is, there is the Church, and all grace: but the Spirit is Truth."[32]

---

29. Meyendorff, *Christ*, 114.
30. Breck, "Two Hands," 242–43. The ascent-descent imagery recalls Eph 4:8–10.
31. Meyendorff, "Theosis," 470–76.
32. Irenaeus, *AH*, III.24.1: Keble's transl., *Five Books*.

Irenaeus goes on to describe the relationship between the Son and the Spirit as "the two hands of God."[33] God did not need angels nor virtues "to do the things which He had in Himself determined before to do, as though He had no Hands of His own: since to Him is ever present His Word and Wisdom, the Son and the Spirit, by whom and in whom He made all things freely and voluntarily."[34] Again, "For there assisted [God] in all things his first born and his Hands, that is, the Son and the Spirit, the Word and the Wisdom, whom all the angels serve and to whom they are subject."[35]

The church of Western Christendom is a church in which the theological role of the Holy Spirit has tended to be subsumed under the theological role of the Christ. This shift was made part of the Western *kerygma* when the "two hands of God" were reduced to one hand when the Western version of the Nicene Creed (796 or 797) added the *filioque*: the Holy Spirit was proclaimed to proceed not directly from the Father but through the mediation of the Son.[36] The operational expectation that the Holy Spirit will effect transformation through ongoing animation of the people of God requires an intentional doctrinal claim in the West that the Spirit bears a role and power equal to that of Christ's salvific role in Incarnation and Resurrection. To that end, we look further for evidence of the Spirit's equality in role with the Son.

The mutual "bimanual" empowerment of Word and Spirit are found first in the Hebrew Scriptures,[37] where God's "creative and re-

33. Irenaeus, *AH,* IV.20.1 and V.1.3, 6.1.

34. Irenaeus, *AH,* IV.20.1, Keble's transl., *Five Books.*

35. Irenaeus, *AH,* IV.7.4, Donovan's transl., *One Right Reading?*. On this, see also Donovan, *One Right Reading?* 104, 106, and chap. 10 esp. 151 n. 1. Keble's translation of this passage is: "For there ministers to Him in all that is His, His Progeny and the Image thereof, i.e., the Son and the Holy Ghost, His Word and His Wisdom: Whom all the Angels serve, and are their subjects." Other references to the Son and the Spirit as the two hands of God may be found in *AH* IV.Praef.4; V.1.3; and V.28.4. One hand is referenced in III.21.10 ("the hand of God is the Word of God": *et plasmatus est manu Dei, id est Verbo Dei . . .*).

36. The Latin *filioque* means "and the Son": "I believe in the Holy Spirit, the Lord and Giver of Life, who proceeds from the Father *and the Son . . .*" For an exposition of this issue, see Kelly, *Early Christian Creeds,* 301, 354f., 358-67, 409f.

37. For example, in Gen 1:2-3, God's Spirit and then God's Word are active: "The Spirit of God moved over the water. Then God said, 'Let there be light.'" See also Ezek 2:7: "[The Lord said,] 'Mortal man, stand up. I want to talk to you.' While the voice was speaking, God's spirit entered me and raised me to my feet, and I heard the voice continue, 'Mortal man, I am sending you to the people of Israel . . . You will tell them whatever I tell you to say.'"

demptive activity is accomplished through his *dabar* and *ruach*, his creating, revealing Word and his chastening, empowering Spirit."[38] God's word comes to the mouth of the prophets only by the inspiration of the Spirit, which gives it "both form and content."[39]

In another rendering of the intimate and mutual relationship of the Son and the Spirit, some refer to the "double sending"[40]: of the Spirit by the Son (Luke 24:49; Acts 1:5–8; John 15:26; 16:7), "but also the sending of the Son by the Spirit (Luke 1:35; 4:18; Mark 1:12; Matt 4:1)."[41] The Western church is familiar with the Son who (e.g., in John 15) promises to send the Paraclete, but often overlooks parallel initiatives of the Spirit. Breck cites these references to the Holy Spirit sending the Son: Luke 1:35: "The angel said to [Mary], 'The Holy Spirit will come upon you, and the power of the Most High will overshadow you; therefore the child to be born will be holy; he will be called Son of God'"; Luke 4:18a: "[Jesus said,] 'The Spirit of the Lord is upon me, because he has anointed me to bring good news to the poor'"; Mark 1:12: "And the Spirit immediately drove him out into the wilderness"; and Matt 4:1: "Then Jesus was led up by the Spirit into the wilderness to be tempted by the devil." Scripture thus establishes and witnesses to an equality, a mutuality, and a dual activity between the Son and the Spirit.

In addition to "two hands of God" and "double sending," yet a third way of expressing the parallelism of the Son and the Spirit was put by St. Athanasius who, in the "*Letters to Serapion*, speaks of the reciprocal in-dwelling of the Son and the Spirit within the 'immanent' Trinity as well as in the divine economy, the Trinity *ad extra*."[42]

Beyond the interrelated empowerment of the second and third Persons of the Trinity, theosis is grounded in the present and constant activity of the Holy Spirit in her own particular work. Breck points out that, "as Fr Bobrinskoy also notes, the Antiochenes, beginning with St John Chrysostom, laid particular emphasis on the role of the Spirit in

---

38. Breck, "Two Hands," 233.

39. Ibid., 234.

40. This idea is represented by Boris Bobrinskoy, *Communion du Saint-Esprit*; cited in Breck, "Two Hands," 235 n. 5.

41. Breck, "Two Hands," 235.

42. Ibid., 239, citing Bobrinskoy, *Communion du Saint-Esprit*, 37–44.

the *epiklesis*, the consecration of the Eucharist, as well as in the deification of the faithful."[43]

Seeing, then, the operation of the Spirit in the divinization of the Christian, the sanctification of the flesh through the Incarnation of the Son, and the efficacious presence of God in God's icons, humans as imago Dei who fulfill our humanity in developing our likeness to God, we are able to grasp the import of theosis on Christian existence. As we attempt to extend our imagination of a realized baptismal ecclesiology into the post-Christendom church of the West, we find that we can draw upon the theology of divinization from the undivided church of the early centuries, in which proleptic anticipation at baptism of the full stature of Christ and union of the newly-baptized with God ("initiation complete in baptism"[44]) is integrated with the continuously-present ongoing action of the Spirit in the progressively unfolding Christian life begun in baptism.

Interestingly, while it is in Eastern Christianity that theosis has been most fully theologically developed, it has clear and constant threads in the West, as well. A brilliant book by A. N. Williams demonstrates how the concept of theosis is fundamental in Thomas Aquinas' *Summa Theologiae*, not in his section on sacraments, which we have examined above, but in the First-Second part on virtues (I–II.62, I–II.65) and the First part on knowledge of God (I.12).[45] In addition to deification and participation, Thomas uses the term "deiformity" to describe the goal or *telos* of the Christian life. Deiformity is accomplished by divine assistance through the "theological virtues" (i.e., faith, hope, and especially love) by which human reason (intellect) and human will are directed toward God.[46]

While threads of theosis are woven quietly through many parts of the Western church, this theology plays a particularly significant role in Anglicanism. The English preacher Ralph Cudworth described

---

43. Ibid. Breck gives the Greek for "epiclesis" = *calling down* (or *invoking*) the Spirit.

44. See Whitaker, *Sacramental Initiation Complete in Baptism*.

45. Williams, *Ground of Union*, 34.

46. Ibid., *passim*. Williams compares *theosis* as it appears in Gregory Palamas and Thomas Aquinas as quintessential theologians of East and West, following the history of doctrinal disagreement and showing technical differences and similarities. She argues convincingly that the theology of deification can provide the ground of (re-)union between the Christian churches of East and West.

theosis in a sermon in 1647 as the point and end of God's incarnation into human form: "The Gospel is nothing else but God descending into the world in our form and conversing with us in our likeness that he might allure and draw us up to God and make us partakers of his divine form, *theos gegonen anthropos* (as Athanasius speaks) *hina hemas en eauto theopoiese*; 'God was therefore incarnated and made man that he might deify us'; that is (as St Peter expresseth it) makes us partakers of the divine nature."[47]

In a profound little book entitled *Participation in God*, A. M. Allchin has identified the thread of theosis that runs through Anglicanism. Exemplars include sixteenth-century theologians Richard Hooker (1554–1600) and Lancelot Andrewes (1556–1626); in the Methodist movement in Wales Williams Pantycelyn (1717–91) and Ann Griffiths (1776–1805), and in England Charles Wesley (1707–88)[48]; nineteenth-century Oxford Movement leader E. B. Pusey; and twentieth-century writer/theologian C. S. Lewis.

Lancelot Andrewes (1555–1626), Bishop of Winchester, is perhaps the best-known Anglican example, the better known because of Nicholas Lossky's book praising theosis in Andrewes' sermons.[49] As we have said, participation in God is possible only because in the Incarnation of God in Christ, humans are salvaged from corruption (Acts 2:27), and in the Spirit these humans, made in the image of God, are brought to the end or purpose (*telos*) for which they were created: namely, union with God, participation in God. The Incarnation, the

---

47. More and Cross, *Anglicanism*, 782–83; in Allchin, *Participation in God*, 14 (Greek transliterated by Allchin).

48. For example, Charles Wesley (and his brother John) used the term "sanctification" for this process, and wrote his theology in hymn-texts like the last two verses of this one:

> He deigns in flesh to appear/ Widest extremes to join;
> To bring our vileness near, / And make us all divine:
> And we the life of God shall know, / For God is manifest below.
>
> Made perfect first in love, / And sanctified by grace,
> We shall from earth remove, / And see his glorious face:
> Then shall his love be fully showed, / And man shall then be lost in God.

Charles Wesley, *A Rapture of Praise*, # 5, 58–59; in Allchin, *Participation in God*, 26–27.

49. Lossky, *Lancelot Andrewes*.

coming of the Holy Spirit, the imago Dei, and the sacramentality of the church, are woven together in this theology of human becoming. Lancelot Andrewes shows the marriage of the Incarnation and the Holy Spirit in this excerpt from one of his Pentecost sermons:

> [We could not say that one is greater than the other,] the ascending of our flesh, or the descending of his Spirit; *incarnatio Dei*, or *inspiratio hominis*; the mystery of [God's] incarnation or the mystery of our inspiration. For mysteries they are both, and "great mysteries of godliness" both; and in both of them "God is manifested in the flesh." In the former by the union of his Son; in the latter by the communion of his blessed Spirit . . . [W]ithout either of them we are not complete, we have not our accomplishment; but by both we have, and that fully, even by this day's royal exchange. Whereby, as before he of ours, so now we of his are made partakers. He clothed with our flesh, and we invested with his Spirit. The great promise of the Old Testament accomplished, that he should partake of our human nature; and the great and precious promise of the New, that we should be *consortes divinae naturae*, "partake his divine nature," both are this day accomplished.[50]

Allchin points out in Andrewes the "full complementarity and reciprocity" between the role of Christ and the role of the Spirit.[51]

> The once for all event of the birth of Christ finds its fulfillment in the ever-renewed process of the coming of the Spirit. Both in the life of the church and in the life of each member of the church, progress and change are as necessary as fidelity and stability . . . [W]hile the history which led up to Jesus was full of the promise of his coming, the history which follows from him is full of an even greater and more mysterious expectation, the coming of the Spirit to dwell at the very heart of humanity and of all creation . . . We are caught up in a process as yet incomplete.[52]

The point and purpose of human life is to be transformed and transfigured by the Spirit breathing, pulsing, singing at the very core of each person and of all creation. The fulfillment of this work of the Spirit is the point, the "goal" of human life—"goal" not as striving but

---

50. Lancelot Andrewes, *Complete Works*, 108–9; in Allchin, *Participation in God*, 20.

51. Allchin, *Participation in God*, 20.

52. Ibid., 21.

as becoming completely what one was created to be: "completion" = "perfection." Andrewes connects this movement toward "perfection" or completion with the journey metaphor: "The state of grace is the perfection of this life, to grow still from grace to grace, to profit in it. As to go still forward is the perfection of a traveler, to draw still nearer and nearer to his journey's end."[53]

It is perhaps not surprising that theologians who comprehend the union of God and humanity as already-but-not-yet mutual participation through the "two hands of God"—Christ and the Holy Spirit—also have strong theologies of sacrament: for it is through sacramental participation (among others) that God comes near in Christ, that the Holy Spirit breathes upon the gathered community, enacting in them who they really are in God's economy of creation and redemption. John and Charles Wesley, for example, untypically for their time, favored frequent communion. Two centuries earlier, Richard Hooker, in *Lawes of Ecclesiasticall Politie* (1553), wrote, "Sacraments are the powerful instruments of God to eternal life. For as our natural life consisteth in the union of body with soul, so our life supernatural in the union of the soul with God. And forasmuch as there is no union of God with man without that mean between both which is both, it seemeth requisite that we first consider how God is in Christ, then how Christ is in us, and how the sacraments do serve to make us partakers of Christ."[54]

Russian Orthodox theologians Nicholas and Vladimir Lossky (father and son) have written on theosis. Nicholas' significant work on Andrewes shows the connection Andrewes makes to baptism: "The final goal of spiritual life being union with God, one can say that the theology of Lancelot Andrewes is a mystical theology, as long as one elucidates the meaning of the word 'mystical.' It is not a question of an exceptional experience, reserved for a few . . . On the contrary it is a question of the interiorization of the revealed Christian mystery, to which Andrewes calls all the baptized."[55]

If the living of the Christian life, the life of all the baptized, is living in the "between times" between anamnesis and prolepsis, it is not only the reign of God that is "already but not yet": the baptized, too, are "already but not yet." We are of divine nature, in the image of God.

---

53. Lancelot Andrewes, *Complete Works*, 367; in Allchin, *Participation*, 21.
54. Hooker, *Ecclesiastical Polity*, Vol. V, 1.3; in Allchin, *Participation*, 13.
55. Lossky, *Lancelot Andrewes*, 327; in Allchin, *Participation*, 22.

Yet sin continues. What happens when we breathe the Holy Spirit in sacramental action, in acts of love in the community? We are changed, transmuted, conformed more and more to Christ. Irenaeus holds before the church the image of humanity—not just humans individually but humanity as a whole—as beginning in a child state, not fully developed. We are created children of God, and are called to be "adults of God," to progress and develop into the life for which we were made: the divine. This theology is strongly suggestive of on-going growth and development through the power of the Holy Spirit by the grace of God in the church, the Body of Christ, and in its sacramental action. To call the liturgy Divine Liturgy is to suggest that participation in liturgy is participation in the very reign of God come close, come proleptically into the present. As Alexander Schmemann explains it, "'Behold, I make all things new' (Rev 21:5). Notice that Christ does not say 'I create new things,' but 'all things new.' Such is the eschatological vision that should mark our eucharistic celebration on each Lord's Day."[56]

We ascend to the point of being able to say "Holy," to give thanks. The Lord's Day,

> is the day on which the Church assembles, locking the doors, and ascends to the point at which it becomes possible to say, "Holy, holy, holy Lord God of Sabaoth, heaven and earth are full of thy glory" . . . The world which [the newspapers] show us is certainly not full of the glory of God. If we make such an affirmation in the Liturgy, it is not just an expression of Christian optimism ("Onward, Christian soldiers"), but simply and solely because we have ascended to the point at which such a statement is indeed true, so that the only thing that remains for us to do is to give thanks to God. And in that thanksgiving we are in him and with him in his kingdom, because there is now nothing else left, because that is where our ascension has already led us.[57]

The process of deification is one that begins at baptism, in the sacramental waters of death and resurrection and anointing with the Spirit. It is a process that is very personal, which means that it is very communal.[58] It is a process of each member of the Body of Christ and

---

56. Schmemann, "Liturgy and Eschatology," 12.

57. Ibid., 12.

58. As Allchin expresses it, "Often in common usage what is personal is thought to be identical with what is individual. But the reverse is the case. For whereas when

of all the whole Body together. It is a way of purification and *kenosis*. It is the way of the cross. And it is a way of beauty and *plerosis*; it is the way of joy and intimacy and transcendence. The doctrinal efficacy of theosis creates categories of thought and understanding such that when moments of participation in holiness, in divine beauty and self-transcendent rapture occur, they may be recognized and celebrated. But the doctrinal categories, while necessary, are not themselves the experience. The operational efficacy of depths and heights, tears of anguish and tears of ecstasy, are not present in the description of theosis. The operation of the Holy Spirit occurs over time, in a life lived alone and in the community of the ecclesia, as one is changed and turned and refined; as one lives through little deaths and whose increasing greatness of heart prepares for the Great Death, one's own *transitus* or paschaltide when one is united fully with God. The joy, the beauty, the participation occurs in moments, but also in the whole of one's lived life. In the work of art that is the human creature, only in its completion can the full work be seen. Only at the funeral can we look upon the whole life lived, created, redeemed, Spirit-filled. And only in the next life is theosis complete.

Theosis implies a process of maturing in Christ. Irenaeus understands the human to be born a child of God, and the human life to be one of ongoing progress by the action of the Holy Spirit in collaboration with the willing human subject. We are God's work of art, a work-in-progress:

> How can you be a god when you have not yet become a man? How can you be perfect when you have only just been made? How can you be immortal when, in your mortal nature, you do not obey your Maker? You must hold the rank of man before you partake of the glory of God . . . If you are the handiwork of God, await the Craftsman's hand patiently; He does everything at a favorable time, favorable, that is, to you, whom He made. Offer him your heart, pliant and unresisting. Preserve the form in which the Craftsman fashioned you. Keep within you the Water which comes from Him; without it, you harden and lose the imprint of His fingers. By preserving the struc-

---

we speak of the individual we speak of each one in . . . separateness in competition with all others, when we speak of the person we speak of each one in . . . relatedness, in communion with all others. Indeed just as in God each of the three divine persons lives in and through the others, so also it is at the human level. We are members one of another. In each the whole is present." Allchin, *Participation in God*, 4.

ture, you will ascend to perfection; God's artistry will conceal the clay within you . . . Making is a property of God's generosity; being made is a property of man's nature. If, therefore, you hand over to him what is yours, faith in Him and subjection to Him, you will receive the benefit of His artistry and be God's perfect work of art. If, on the other hand, you resist Him and flee from His hands, the cause of your imperfection will lie in you . . . The light does not fail because of those who have blinded themselves; it remains the same, while the blinded are plunged in darkness by their own fault. Light never forces itself on anyone, nor does God use compulsion on anyone who refuses to accept His artistry.[59]

Baptismal liturgy creates intimate identification of persons in Christ-and-the-Spirit. Eucharist is the "recapitulation of the meaning of the whole process of incorporation into Christ's body."[60] Eucharistic liturgy reminds Christians that they are in process, already-but-not-completely the Body of Christ, and inSpires them to be who they are-and-are-becoming.

The becoming is the thing. As the doctrine has developed, theosis is a gift, a grace; and also, humans have a role. God-the-Son-and-Spirit have acted and are acting: the "image" is intrinsic and salvation is secure. But, like our illustration of John at the funeral, the "likeness" is not complete, not perfected, not fulfilled. The life work of the Christian is to turn toward holiness, to live a virtuous life, to pray (alone and liturgically) so as to participate sacramentally in the salvation already secured. Louis-Marie Chauvet will urge upon us the centrality of ethics in the Christian life: equal with sacrament and Scripture is the experience of ethical living. "Deification is ethical; it is not a state of being lost in God but of loving as he loves, being merciful as he is merciful."[61] Theosis accomplished by the two hands of God is not static. The continuing operation of the Spirit in holy living and periodic sacramental action in the community effect a dynamic becoming for the Christian who is already-but-not-yet.[62]

---

59. Irenaeus, *AH*, IV 39, 2–3. Trans. by John Saward, in *The Scandal of the Incarnation*, 72–73.

60. Louis Weil, "The Structure of Christian Community," 119.

61. Wakefield, "Anglican Spirituality," 269.

62. In holy living, the "likeness" of the virtuous Christian with the "image" imprinted in the human person at creation come closer and closer together. Worship is an essential, incarnate component of this: the Christian requires "the experience of

Further, theosis takes account of the will, the intent, and the consciousness of human persons in their personalness and subjectivity both by acknowledging their virtuous (or non-virtuous) actions and affections, and by taking seriously the persons' experience from their own point of view. "Orthodox theological reflection properly begins with the experience of Christ and the Holy Spirit within the present life of the Church," Breck explains.[63] "The content of our faith, then, is provided not only by the biblical witness. It is provided by the living experience of God, primarily in the Church's worship . . . and only then do [the Orthodox] seek to judge and confirm that experience with reference to Scripture."[64]

The doctrine of theosis, and more immediately the actual effective experience of encounter with God-in-Christ-and-the-Spirit in one's life, has major implications for post-baptismal living and for the building up of the body of Christ. Any response of the church in support of the baptized in their lives and ministry would, in response to this anthropology, expect and support this ongoing growth and transformation.[65]

Imagining a Life of Theosis for All the Baptized in the Post-Christendom Church

The church has from the beginning had a process to prepare people for the sacrament in advance of their baptism. The transformational, conversionary catechumenal process arose in the early church as an effective way to ready the soil for planting, to prepare the tree and the branch for the grafting into Christ of the newly-baptized. This rhythm of experience, reflection-and-prayer, and rite is, and has been from the

---

God in worship, particularly but not exclusively in eucharistic celebration" (Breck, "Two Hands," 232).

63. Ibid., 231.

64. Ibid., 231, 232.

65. Williams, *The Ground of Union*, notes: "we find in the patristic corpus . . . the idea of deification as progressive, a process that begins in this life, certainly, but finds its fulfillment only in the next. Irenaeus, Theophilus, Cyril of Alexandria and Damascene all portray deification in this way, and such a model would be consistent with Nyssa's notion of epectasy" (ibid., 164–65). "Aquinas tends to focus on growth in deiformity towards a culmination of theosis in the next life, while Palamas more readily alludes to divinization in this one" (ibid., 173).

early church, effective in enabling ongoing change, turning, *metanoia* toward a new way of living and loving in the body of Christ. It is a *conversionary rhythm,* a rhythm of repentance and transformation. Catechesis is about changing behavior, belonging, and belief, as discussed in chapter 6.

In terms of doctrinal theology, one might ask whether these changes occur *during* the catechumenal process, i.e., before baptism, or whether they occur *at* baptism. Both positions exist in the church. While baptism is "the nodal point of conversion,"[66] Kreider has shown two emphases: the *Apostolic Tradition*, for example, understood the changes to occur during the one-to-five years of catechesis, so that the person finally immersed in the baptismal waters was already a changed being from the person who had entered the order of catechumens years earlier. Others, like Cyprian, pointed to examples such as the Ethiopian eunuch who "was baptized by the apostle Philip, immediately, without investigation of his lifestyle, without catechism"[67] (Acts 8:37)—although whether and to what extent change occurred for the eunuch, Scripture does not tell us. Cyprian worked and struggled throughout his own catechumenate to be free of his addictions to money, power, and good food; but it was at his baptism that the victory was won and he became a free man. A struggle that seemed impossible by himself was wondrously bestowed as a gift by the God for whom nothing is impossible; and the gift began at baptism.

Yet whichever doctrine one might hold from a theological or ecclesial perspective, the important point in terms of operational efficacy is that *the persons themselves experience* becoming a new creation. Different people will have such an experience(s) at different points, both before and/or during baptism, in a moment or over time. Theologically, we can acknowledge that in this diversity, it is God-in-Christ-through-the-Spirit who acts in the life of each person. Trusting in this Holy Action, we can affirm the operational efficacy of the two hands of God in encountering each catechumen. However and whenever the person experiences the ongoing work of the Spirit, the rite of baptism celebrates both culmination and initiation of lifestyles changed and persons forming into a community of belonging, a structure of beliefs and stories, and new patterns of behavior.

---

66. Kreider, *Change*, 6.
67. Cyprian, *Ad Donatum*, 4–5; in Kreider, *Change*, 48, 60, 2.

Thus, whether or not a pre-baptismal catechesis is accomplished, and whether baptism is done as an infant, child, teen, or adult, it is not only a washing away of sin to that point and a culmination and/or celebration of a present action. Baptism is also the beginning of a journey, a walking in newness of life (Rom 6:4), an entry into a new realm. Baptism is both a summit and a source, both an end and a beginning.

If we take seriously the action of the Spirit animating the divine within us and arousing holy incarnation in the baptizing community[68] among each and all—well, then, a post-baptismal catechesis is called for, as well. For the church to take seriously its call to theosis, it must consider how it will enable each Christian's becoming-into-God. And such an enabling agent is already set before us.

The pre-baptismal catechumenal rhythm is a well-tested pattern that has been effective for two thousand years (although for several centuries in the church's history this pattern was latent and unused). Inasmuch as we understand baptism to be a culmination, a change of state, a completion, it is fitting to end the process with baptism, or with the end of mystagogical instruction. However, inasmuch as we understand baptism as the beginning of a journey into God, then it is fitting that with baptism a new rhythm begin. Or, if like Lancelot Andrewes we see baptism as that rite by which we are called to a processual (ongoing) interiorization of the revealed Christian mystery, then it is fitting that baptism begin a new process by which, with Irenaeus, we "await the Craftsman's hand," offering to God our "heart, pliant and unresisting," staying flexible, being formed and shaped by the hand—the two hands—of the Artist.

Thus, if pre-baptismal catechesis effectively leads us to the sacrament by which we are made children of God, we also need post-baptismal catechesis to effectively lead us in response to baptism through which we may be made adults of God.

Side by side with the metaphor "children of God" we place "adults of God" as a way of contrasting Irenaeus' understanding of the human person with the Augustinian view.[69] For St. Augustine, human perfection is understood as originating in God's creation of humanity, i.e.,

---

68. See Eastman's treatment on the community's role in baptism in his study, *The Baptizing Community*.

69. See Hick, *Philosophy of Religion*, 42–49. He refers to Irenaeus' *Against Heresies*, IV.37, 38.

in the past. From the state of goodness and perfection, humans "fell," and are thus in need of a savior to redeem them. The metaphor "children of God" implies and reveals not only our relationship with God as creature-to-Creator, servant-to-Lord, offspring-to-Father/Mother, but also our "genetic imprint": the imago Dei by which we inherently share in some way in the divinity of God. But through sin, the imago Dei can be hidden, encrusted, laden with distortion so that the light can fail to shine through—or even be remembered. The redemption of Christ restores the person to her or his state, still as *children* of God. As revelatory as this metaphor is, then, the metaphor "children of God" also conceals another part of the truth by failing to capture the process by which our relationship with God changes, by which we are changed "from glory into glory" as Charles Wesley's hymn expresses.[70]

In contrast, Irenaeus refers to human beings as God's work of art, beginning as a lump of clay, incomplete and in need of finishing. Human perfection for Irenaeus lies not in the past, but *in the future*, at the end of a process of growing up in Christ. Humans are born children of God: imperfect, incomplete, and needing a saving Word and Spirit to form them to become fully human. Always God's offspring in God's image, humans are called to mature in Christ (Heb 6:1), to grow up.

Irenaeus' perspective can be expressed by the additional metaphor *adult of God* which affirms the relationship with God as parent, sovereign, and creator, while also including the expectation in (for example) Paul's letter to the Corinthians that Christians will "put away childish things" (1 Cor 13:11–12) and move beyond the stage where milk suffices for food to a stage where solid food will also be required (1 Cor 3:2). We are conceived and born children of God, and we will always be God's children. At the same time, we are invited to grow more and more into the likeness of God, to take our place as co-creators, to speak and act on behalf of the coming of God's realm, growing and maturing into adults of God.

This is not a new idea. Commemorating the lives of saints as a help to following their holy examples began early and has continued through the church's two millennia. Weekly Christian worship has

---

70. See Wesley's hymn "Love Divine, all Loves excelling," which ends, "Changed from glory into glory,/ Til in heaven we take our place." *Hymnal 1982*, #657, and *United Methodist Hymnal*, #384.

been accompanied by devotional prayer at home, and at least since the printing press and Reformation, by regular Bible study. In the current era, Christian education and formation have been accomplished in myriad ways, including in Christian schools, through spiritual guidance, in Sunday School classes, on retreats, and in preparation for sacraments such as first communion, confirmation, sometimes marriage or first penance, ordination, and as we have seen in the OCIA, adult baptism.

What is new in the theology argued here is the call to order the church's life so as to allow baptism, at whatever age, to mark the beginning of an ongoing process of post-baptismal catechesis including the same transformative rhythm of experience, reflection-study-prayer, and rite, in order to tend each baptized person's growing up in God through Christ in the Spirit. The fourth-century term for post-baptismal de-briefing is *mystagogy*, continuing instruction and reflection upon the mystery in-Christ-and-the-Spirit just experienced at baptism, a term reclaimed in the twentieth century. What would it be like to shape the lives of all the baptized into an extended mystagogy? What would happen if Christians—not just the clergy, but *all the baptized*—lived, behaved, and spoke so consistently what they proclaimed that others noticed? What if the spiritual lives of the baptized were so vibrant that visitors to Sunday worship could feel it? If Andrewes' description of the body of believers being inSpired in ongoing Pentecost really matched the incarnate presence of the risen Christ?

A church willing to take seriously God's ongoing work of theosis in the lives of Christians and of the Christian community as a whole would intentionally sustain a conversionary rhythm in which personal experience is reflected upon in groups of study and prayer, and resulting ongoing growth in Christ-and-the-Spirit would be celebrated in post-baptismal ritualizations. Part Three will propose more particularly what such a rhythm might look like. Suffice it now to say that such a rhythm would have a baptismal character and would be personal and collective response to the grace given at baptism and to the ongoing deification in the community of faith by the two hands of God. If we know that, in reverse action to exorcism, the Holy Spirit is invigorating, animating, awakening, and converting, it seems that the gathering for shared storytelling, study, and prayer would be helpful for recognizing the Spirit's work in one another; and rites of movement toward transfiguration before the witness of the congregation would "make real" the Spirit's action: namely, the incrementally changed human person, freely self-offered day by day as thanks-gift to God. The intentional self-giving to God, as Christ did, is a visible sign of one's growing into God. But through the work of Louis-Marie Chauvet, the personal thanks-gift of oneself to God can be seen as a quintessential personally-experienced operationally-effective step in relational intimacy between God and those baptized into Christ by the Holy Spirit.

Response-Giving

> Mama was a beautiful quilter. She done the best work in the county. Everybody knew it. She never let nobody else touch her quilts . . .
>
> I always longed to work with her and I can tell you how plain I recall the day she said, "Sarah, you come quilt with me now if you want to."
>
> I was too short to sit in a chair and reach it, so I got my needle and thread and stood beside her. I put that needle through and pulled it back up again, then down, and my stitches were about three inches long.
>
> Papa come in about that time, he stepped back and said, "Florence, that child is flat ruinin' your quilt."
>
> Mama said, "She's doin' no kind of a thing. She's quiltin' her first quilt."
>
> He said, "Well, you're jest goin' to have to rip it all out tonight."
>
> Mama smiled at me and said, "Them stitches is going to be in that quilt when it wears out."
>
> All the time they was talkin' my stitches was getting' shorter.[71]

The mystical theology of theosis provides a theological foundation for the expectation that Christians will continue to grow up in God and into God following their baptism. Baptism initiates a life-process of *metanoia* and turning, of being made (*theopoeisis*) and formed (deiformity) ever more into the likeness of God. The baptismal life is a process in which the Two Hands of God continue to be active in the life of persons and communities who seek to live *en christos*.

---

71. Cooper and Allen, *The Quilters*, 52.

Yet the baptismal process is not only marked by God's ongoing action in the life of God's people. The people themselves have agency in this process. Louis-Marie Chauvet, French liturgical theologian, has written a significant work in which he dislodges Thomas Aquinas' schema that sacrament produces grace. Specifically countering Thomas,[72] Chauvet asserts that a relationship, including the relationship of humans to God, implies giving and receiving on both parts. Sacrament exists in a greater matrix that also includes Scripture and ethics (like the catechumenal rhythm). This greater matrix Chauvet calls "Christian existence"—not just of the ordained, but of all the baptized. The life of a baptized person, which is a person who is the recipient of God's grace, a recipient of free will and agency, implies a life which can be returned to God in response-gift. In other words, Christian existence means that Christians respond to God in thanks. The "obligatory generosity" of thanks-gifts back to God are the mark of the noble humble covenantal people of God. Against Thomas' priest-centered clerical ecclesiology, Chauvet insists that the lived life of Christians—all the baptized—includes not passive receptivity, but the active receptivity of response-giving. The worshipper, in our case the baptized person, is not an object that is merely acted upon, but is a subject who is in relationship with the God who became incarnate in Christ Jesus and seeks ongoing friendship with God's people through the Spirit's inspiration.

Within the field of lived Christian identity or existence, Chauvet places not only sacrament (which he calls "the level of thanksgiving"), but also Scripture ("the level of cognition") and ethics ("the level of action").[73] Ethics is the specific locus of a lived Christian life, a baptismal life.[74] One of the marks of this life is the intersubjective Divine-human rhythm of giving—receiving—thanks-giving. Thus, with his fellow Frenchman Jean Cauvin (Calvin) who claims that the role of

---

72. Chauvet, *Symbol and Sacrament*, chapters 1, 2, and 10, especially pp. 7–83, 377–498.

73. Chauvet, *Symbol and Sacrament*, 3.

74. I find the resonance compelling between Chauvet's Scripture and ethics = lived Christian life, celebrated in Chauvet's third component, sacrament, with Tad Guzie's "story, lived experience, festivity" which he calls "the rhythm that makes life human" (*Sacramental Basics*), as well as with the inward-outward rhythm of the catechumenate, and the post-baptismal catechumenal process proposed here. For more on this life as rhythmic, see S. M. Smith, "Spiritual Guidance."

humans is different from that of God, as we saw in chapter 1 ("it is one thing to be offered, another to be received"),[75] Chauvet can claim active receptivity for God's people as a necessary part of the divine-human relationship, the marvelous exchange (*admirabile commercium*) which is grace.[76] God acts. But, like Calvin, Chauvet considers the reception of God's action by the human to be an important and necessary part of the gift exchange. And not only does the human receive God's gifts of grace: the human person is given the dignity, the will, the longing, the capacity to offer gifts back to God. This, too, is an essential part of the divine-human relationship.

Chauvet gives significant treatment to this relationship of gift, reception, and what he calls "return-gift." I prefer the term "thanks-gift" which honors the significant use in the New Testament of the Greek *charis* = "gift," which, when God gives it, is translated *grace* (e.g., 1 Cor 16:23), and when humans give it, is translated *thanks* (e.g., 1 Cor 15:57).[77]

For Chauvet, sacraments represent the intersubjective relationship between God and humanity. In sharp contrast to Thomas, for whom God acts through the sacraments and the (lay) people are passive and acted upon, Chauvet understands a mutuality in the divine-human relationship: "In other words, the sacraments are not, in the last analysis, a play in which God assumes all the roles (or the only role); they are not a play for one actor. The 'sign' (signum), as it is presented by the celebrating Church, is the very mediation of the gift of grace."[78]

As relationships grow and change, so do God's people. Chauvet asserts that "the subject exists only in a permanent becoming, in a *never-finished* process where it has to learn, at its own expense, to be bereaved of its umbilical attachment to the Same."[79] The human being is

---

75. Calvin, *Institutes*, IV.17.33.

76. Chauvet, *Symbol and Sacrament*, 100.

77. Smith, "Receiving." I am grateful to my colleague Lester Ruth for the insight about *charis*.

78. Chauvet, *Symbol and Sacrament*, 17.

79. Ibid., 99. He continues, ". . . to renounce [the desire] to win back its lost paradise, its own origin, and the ultimate foundation which would explain its existence. To become fully human is to "consent to the presence of the absence" of God, which is to say that human finitude renders us incapable of "seiz[ing] the 'real'" on our own, apart from symbolic mediation. Its task is to consent to be in truth by accepting the

a being-in-process-of-becoming. Challenging the medieval Scholastic re-assertion of Aristotle's perfect god as *unmoved* mover (which rational humans seek to imitate), Chauvet demonstrates that *movement*, the life vector and *direction of becoming,* is as important as what is, as being. Chauvet holds Plato accountable for the philosophy that held sway in Christian theology for centuries, that being is superior to becoming, mind to body, and contemplation to action.[80] Chauvet argues at length for a renewed and more integral Christian somatology,[81] a stronger pneumatology,[82] and places *action* (*ethics*; Kreider's *behavior*) at the heart of Christian identity alongside Scripture and sacrament.

While referring to "Christian identity" and "Christian existence" instead of ecclesiology, Chauvet's thesis is that it is through the church that Christ is present in the world: the church is "the presence of the absence of God." Claiming that language makes humans "human," Chauvet compares the relationship of God to humanity to linguistic intercourse: the church is the locus of a divine-human "discourse." In repudiation of Thomas's metaphysics in which there is one subject of this discourse, God, and all others are objects acted upon, Chauvet's point is that this discourse is intersubjective: the people, too, are subjects. Without the people, there is no relationship. The covenantal conversation between God and God's people is a "discourse from which the believing subject is inseparable."[83]

One then sees the resonance of Chauvet with Calvin.[84] When there are two subjects, both give, and both receive. To deny the pos-

---

difference, the lack-in-being, *not as an inevitable evil but as the very place where its life is lived.*

80. For Chauvet's argument against past uncritical absorption of Plato into Christian theology, see esp. 22–29, 44–45. Drawing from Plato's *Philebus*, he shows how Plato compares love to shipbuilding, implying that love is a "cause." Chauvet refutes both Plato and Thomas here, pointing out that the lover "only causes the other to exist *as a beloved*" (ibid., 24), but not a loveable or as a person. Love is not a product like a ship; neither are sacraments.

81. See Chauvet, *Symbol and Sacrament,* chapter 4, "Symbol and Body," esp. 140ff.; also, 355–76, and 518–31.

82. See Chauvet, *Symbol and Sacrament,* esp. 509–31.

83. Chauvet, *Symbol and Sacrament,* 43. For a perspective on Chauvet's response-gift as an example of the "appropriation" vector in Paul Ricoeur's hermeneutic of discourse, see Smith, "Confirmation" (2000), 72–83.

84. I acknowledge my debt to Prof. Regis Duffy, sometime of the University of Notre Dame, who suggested these resonances when he offered a liturgical theology

sibility of persons' active receptivity of God's good gifts, or their response to God in thanks-gifts, is to deny that which is essential in the divine-human relationship: humanity's free will and the possibility of their thankful response to God's grace.

Chauvet attempts to get at this response-gift in terms of sacramentality by posing the term "symbolic exchange" for the covenantal giving/ receiving which is part of Christian identity. While this term can be confusing, his alternative term "obligatory generosity"[85] more aptly describes this grace-full relationship. There is a lovely irony in that the gift and the return-gift,[86] or thanks-gift,[87] are both freely offered out of generosity, and at the same time, obligatory: a duty or responsibility. Anthropologist Marcel Mauss identified this same irony, referring to "the gift, where obligation and liberty intermingle."[88] In this interactive giving/ receiving, it is not only God who acts, not only the sacraments that act as instruments of the human and the divine Christ. *Humans also act.* The sign of what was received is the response-gift, the giving back a bit (a tithe) of what was received. The action of receiving is thanks-giving, acting in gratitude (*gratias agere*).[89] This exchange does not operate in the world of market economy or *quid pro quo*, but rather in the world of symbol (thus his term "symbolic exchange"). It is "gift-reception-return-gift that structures every significant relationship, that is to say, every 'human' relationship, between partners[, between subjects]—a process which is the very process of language"[90]—or, more specifically, the discourse which is the baptismal covenant.[91]

---

seminar on Augustine, Calvin, and Chauvet (1992–93), before Chauvet's work was readily available in translation (1995).

85. Chauvet, *Symbol and Sacrament,* 101.

86. "[T]he fundamental system of 'obligatory generosity' and 'mandatory gratuitousness,' organized according to a process of gift—reception—return-gift, continues to pervade our exchanges" (Chauvet, *Symbol and Sacrament,* 103). See also 277f.; 282f.; 435.

87. Smith, "Receiving," 348, 351.

88. Mauss, *The Gift,* 65. For Chauvet's treatment of Mauss, see *Symbol and Sacrament,* 100–102.

89. Smith, "Receiving," 348–50.

90. Chauvet, *Symbol and Sacrament,* 107.

91. Here we honor the significant contribution of feminist scholars who have pointed out that such receptivity and response are endemic/ inherent in the feminine way of being. Carol Gilligan and her colleagues at the Center for the Study of Gender,

This relational giving-receiving-thanksgiving has major significance for any theology of sacrament. Who acts in sacrament? The church has always asserted that God acts. From the time of Augustine's strong response to the Donatist controversy, reviewed in the first chapter, the church has been inclined to assert that God alone acts. The priest has had an essential role, *sine qua non*: the Holy Spirit is understood to be invoked through the water and the word ("I baptize you in the name of the Father, and of the Son, and of the Holy Spirit"). Augustine himself identified that the element (in this case, water) and the formulaic word was what "made" a sacrament: the word added to the element makes a sacrament (*Accedit verbum ad elementum et fit sacramentum*).[92] Theologically, this definition has stood, and has been called upon when questions of validity and minimum requirements were needed.

However, liturgy is not a theological treatise. While it is critically important that liturgy and theology feed each other and consist with each other, liturgy is not primarily a matter of cognition, or notional assent. Liturgy is bodies interacting on behalf of and for the love of

---

Education, and Human Development at the Harvard University Graduate School of Education have noted that justice, the primary value identified by Lawrence Kohlberg in his longitudinal study (of men), is not the only primary value: *relationship* is the primary value in a majority of women studied. Kay Johnston studied eleven- to fifteen-year old boys and girls, presenting moral dilemmas from two fables: The Porcupine and the Moles, and The Dog in the Manger. While a majority of boys made a first decision based upon what was "fair," a majority of girls decided based upon what would meet most people's "needs." Belenky et al., in *Women's Ways of Knowing*, discovered what they term *connected knowing* as a primary epistemology for women. And Genevieve Vaughan has written on the "gift paradigm" which she distinguishes from any notion of "exchange." The *gift paradigm*

> is a way of constructing and interpreting reality that derives from mothering . . . [it] emphasizes the importance of giving to satisfy needs. It is need-oriented rather than profit-oriented . . . [N]urturing [and] caring . . . it is qualitatively . . . based . . . [G]iving to needs creates bonds between givers and receivers. Recognizing someone's need, and acting to satisfy it, convinces the giver of the existence of the other, while receiving something from someone else that satisfies a need proves the existence of the other to the receiver" (*For-Giving*, 30).

See also Vaughan, "The Gift Economy," 84–85.

92. "The word is added to the element, and the result is the sacrament." *Treatise on the Gospel of John* 80.3.

the Lord. The study of liturgy has come late to seminaries because it is *done* more than thought. At Nijmegen University in The Netherlands, "liturgy" is taught in the general department of "practical theology."

Terms like "practical" and "pastoral" imply activity on the part of the worshippers, that they are practicing something, or that they have pastoral needs which are being attended to or at least taken into account. It is hoped, at least at the start of the new millennium, that liturgical efficacy will not reside solely in our doctrine, but that its efficacy will operate in the lives of the worshippers. That worshippers might also act in worship, or rather interact with God, opens the messy possibility that the results of such interaction may not be able to be controlled or even known. On the other hand, divine-human interaction is effected by the Holy Spirit (whose action can certainly not be controlled, or even known). Chauvet's (and others') expectation that what happens in worship and in life is an intersubjective relationship of giving–receiving–thanksgiving between God and God's people places directly before us the reality that people have a part to play in the holy playful discourse that is liturgy.[93]

Does this mean that human beings can also take initiative in worship-acts? It seems clear that not only *can* human persons take initiative; but that if they are to respond to God in thanks, they *must* take initiative. They must sing and dance and pray and move (in life, as in worship). They must sew, like the young child in the epigraph above, changing the size of their stitches in response to the wondrous gift of being called to work on the master quilt. They must worship with the body in consecrated places and be living Christian witnesses in and to the world. As Chauvet has said, "there is no possible reception of the gift of the good news of the resurrection without the return-gift of Christian witness."[94] Worshippers must be free to witness, to give over their lives which have been given to them, in all kinds of thankful ways. They must, therefore, be free to liturgize and ritualize their response-gifts in ways no theologian has yet been able to imagine. In Part Three, a launch pad for such imagination will be laid for pro-

---

93. As Godfrey Diekmann (d. 2002) wrote in the introduction to Robert Hovda's book on presiding, *Strong, Loving and Wise*, "To borrow the witty judgment of a church historian: the Donatists may have been wrong theologically, but they were pastorally, oh, so right" (ibid., vi).

94. Chauvet, *Symbol and Sacrament,* 164–65.

spective pastoral liturgical initiatives on the part of God's people living lives of thankful action.

Next, however, we will look to a theologian who has worked in the human science of psychology to point us toward where in a person's lived experience occasions for ritualizing thanks-giving, becoming, or transition may lie.

8

Stages of Faith Development
Maturing in Christ

Do not be like children in your thinking, my brothers and sisters; be children so far as evil is concerned, but be grown up in your thinking. (1 Cor 14:20)

Foolish people! How long do you want to be foolish? How long will you enjoy making fun of knowledge? Will you never learn? (Prov 1:22, TEV)

The apostles said to Jesus, "Increase our faith." (Luke 17:5)

Human Being as Human Becoming

IN 1955, GORDON ALLPORT PUBLISHED A BOOK BASED UPON THE Terry Lectures he had given at Yale University, a book he entitled, *Becoming*. He issued a challenge to the discipline of psychology in America to be wary of the tendency of its researches to "mere accuracy if its productions are largely irrelevant to root problems."[1] One of the root problems, he suggested, is that many psychologists "fail to take an interest in the existential richness of human life."[2] What are the questions that lead to full humanity? Why would psychologists limit study to specific problems with measurable answers? Why not incline their researches to the most important question of enabling humans to become more fully human?

Allport suggested an answer to this question in often-unrecognized assumptions upon which research is based: Continental

---

1. Allport, *Becoming*, 19.
2. Ibid., 11.

psychologists (following Leibnitz) tend to understand humans as primarily active agents, he pointed out, while those of England and America (following Locke) view humans as more passive. Leibnitzian thought "maintains that the person is not a collection of acts nor simply the locus of acts; the person is the *source* of acts. And activity itself is not conceived as agitation resulting from pushes by internal or external stimulation. It is purposive. To understand what a person is, it is necessary always to refer to what [that person] may be in the future, for every state of the person is pointed in the direction of future possibilities."[3]

By contrast, English and American psychologists tend to follow the Lockean philosophy of the human mind as *tabula rasa*, waiting to be filled from outside itself. From this view, stated Allport, come the notions that what is external and visible is more fundamental than what is complex and molar; and that what is earlier is more fundamental than what comes later. Therefore, it has been possible to view the human person as motivated primarily by external forces, and to examine this assumption about humans through testing beings more simple than humans (e.g., rats).

Further, the challenge of psychology as science has been to study humans in general, as a species. The particularity of an individual is studied not for its own sake, but in order to induce what may be universally true for the human being as species. Studies of individuals, then, are not studies of the whole person, but studies of an aspect of a person so as to compare that same aspect in other persons in order to be able to generalize about the species as a whole. For example, the psychologist looks at John in order to identify one aspect of John suitable for comparison with other humans. We end up looking at traits, therefore, with no history, "no interrelations, no duration in time, no motion, no life, no variability, no uniqueness."[4] And we do not find out what is particular about John (except, perhaps, for labeling his percentiles). But after the research, we "are still in the dark concerning the nexus of John's life. A large share of our trouble lies in the fact that the elements we employ in our analyses are not true parts of the original

---

3. Ibid., 12. For a hermeneutical exploration into the notion that a person bears a reference point in the future (as well as in the past), see Paul Ricoeur on *telos* and *arche* in *Freud and Philosophy*, 342 and *passim*.

4. Ibid., 20.

whole. It is not helpful, I think, to reply that science, by its very nature, is impotent in the face of the idiomatic process of becoming."[5]

These studies lead to data that are necessarily static. No account is made of the human process of *becoming*, which process is unique to individuals, nor of motivations from within the person, such as striving or visions of the future, which are dynamic and larger than that measurable in operant experimentation. Allport reminds and challenges psychologists and all of us to examine methods and assumptions and to avoid the pitfall of misidentifying what we can see (and measure) with the totality of the vibrant process of becoming human.

> The first fact that strikes us is the uniqueness of both the process and the product. Each person is an idiom unto himself, an apparent violation of the syntax of the species . . . Now the scientific training of the psychologist leads him to look for universal processes common to the species . . . But when we are interested in guiding or predicting John's behavior, or in understanding the Johnian quality of John, we need to transcend the limitations of a psychology of species, and develop a more adequate psychology of personal growth.[6]

If Locke is a significant philosophical inhibition upon English and American psychologies of becoming and of personal growth, Plato and Aristotle continue to be significant philosophical inhibitions upon Christian theologies of becoming and of personal growth. Greek philosophy found that which was immutable to be superior to that which could change. Being was more perfect than becoming, which was constantly changing and subject to influence. That which was absolute was superior to that which was relative or dependent. While the Christian theologies of the Trinity (God as inherently relational)[7] and of the Incarnation (God as human, changing, living-dying-rising) defied these Greek influences, the Christian tradition became infused with the hierarchy of classical antiquity in which mind is understood to be superior over body (which is constantly developing, aging), reason over emotion (which fluctuates with the situation and context), and stasis or Being as higher than on-going evolution or Becoming.[8]

5. Ibid., 21.
6. Ibid., 19, 23.
7. On the Trinity, see Catherine Mowry LaCugna's book *God For Us*, and her essay "The Trinitarian Mystery of God."
8. While beyond the scope of this work, it is important to acknowledge the movement known as "process theology" which attempts to account for God's ongoing

These philosophical constructions are recognizable in Christian theology as well: God as unmoved mover, uncreated, immutable. Christian disdain for the body and for people who manifest an embodied presence (e.g., women, children) has been an unfortunate legacy of these perspectives. Is there room in Christianity, then, for a grounded theology of human becoming?

William J. Bouwsma has demonstrated the way in which the theological threads of *both* Being and Becoming have woven their way concurrently through the Christian tradition. In his article "Christian Adulthood,"[9] Bouwsma notes "that Christianity does contain a characteristic conception of healthy human maturity" which we can find if we distinguish between two strands found in historical Christianity: the idea of manhood and the idea of adulthood. Both exist in our tradition and affect our thinking (often unconsciously) about reception and response of persons, and thus our theologizing about baptismal process.

"Manhood," Bouwsma explains, comes from the Indo-European verb "to think" (Latin *mens*), and "refers to a supposedly qualitative difference between human beings and other animals," implying "entrance into a fully rational existence." This concept is "a creation of classical antiquity, and it reflects the need of classical culture to organize all experience in terms of absolute, static, and qualitative categories."[10] It tends to be gender specific, and to thereby deny full maturity to women. It is "oriented to the goal rather than the processes of human development." The "ideal man is therefore a fully rational being who pits his reason against the chaotic forces both within himself and in the world."[11]

---

creative work. Including the works of Alfred North Whitehead, Charles Hartshorne, Norman Pittenger, and Teilhard de Chardin, process theology has attended specifically to "becoming," to the process of development through time; to relatedness, relationality, and relativity; and to novelty, to the freedom of the unfolding of creation and evolution in human beings as well as in creation, suggesting the notion that God is self-creating. Ewert H. Cousins describes the three "process themes of temporality, relatedness, and novelty" with clarity in his essay "Process Models in Culture, Philosophy, and Theology," 3–20, esp. 19.

9. Bouwsma, "Christian Adulthood," 81–96. I am grateful to James Fowler for introducing me to this article, and to Louis Weil for introducing me personally to Prof. Bouwsma.

10. Ibid., 81.

11. Ibid., 82.

In contrast, *adulthood* comes from the Latin *adolescere*, "to grow up." It "implies a process rather than the possession of a particular status or specific faculty." Adulthood "is related to the anthropology of the Bible; and its suggestion of process hints at the distinctively dynamic qualities of the Hebrew language."[12]

Bouwsma finds the model of adulthood fitting for the process toward the full stature of Christ. There is a paradox "that the Christian, however ripe in years, cannot think of [one]self as a completed [hu]man. Christianity has, then, a conception of full adulthood; the goal of human development is total conformity to the [hu]manhood of Christ. But since this is a transcendent goal, the practical emphasis in Christian adulthood is on the process rather than its end."[13] The creation is "depicted as a work of time . . . Time and change, so dimly regarded in the classical world of thought, are therefore also necessarily good; the biblical God underlined their positive significance by presenting himself, after the fall, as the Lord of history."[14] The Christian is called not to avoid problems, but to grow through them. The image of pilgrim, of journeyer, expresses this sense of life as movement, change, growth. In fact, there is "a close connection between the rejection of growth and the problem of sin; the refusal to grow is, in an important sense, the source of all particular sins."[15]

If the refusal to grow can be a source of sin, then it is all the more fitting that those who have been cleansed of sin in baptism come to conscious openness to the process of maturing in Christ. Are there some guidelines for what this very human process might look like? What might be touchstones along the pathway of "adulting"? Are

---

12. Ibid., 81. Bernard Lee demonstrates the dynamic sense of process in the Hebrew language in a statement about the "name" God gave to Moses at the burning bush: "There are no tenses as such in classical Hebrew, such as our past, present, and future. It is only possible to state an action in such a way that it is presented as completed or as not completed . . . When God gave his name to Moses (Exod 3:13–15), he used verbs in the forms that indicated non-completed action: *Ehyeh asher ehyeh* . . . 'I am in the process of becoming the one who I will be'. . ." is a much closer translation. "The lack of finality in God's naming of himself has the sense of: keep an eye on *what happens*, and you will find out who I am and what I am." Lee, *The Becoming of the Church*, 209–10. Lack of finality also implicates the process of human maturing.

13. Bouwsma, "Christian Adulthood," 85. One sees parallelism here with the theopoetic earthly goal of process toward the likeness of God-in-Christ-and-the-Spirit.

14. Ibid., 86.

15. Ibid., 87.

there common identifiable moments in this process of change and incremental growth? If the openness and willingness to grow is a life-orientation of making oneself available to the work of the two hands of God and the transformational work of the Holy Spirit toward the *imago Dei*, we look now to what we may learn about this process of human development toward God, a process called *faith development.*

Theologian James W. Fowler has offered a valuable hermeneutic of meaning-development in human beings. His seminal research in identifying stages of faith development is well known among theologians, religious educators, and psychologists of religion. Built upon the theology of H. Richard Niebuhr and Paul Tillich, and using heuristically the psychological theory of Jean Piaget, Erik Erikson, and Lawrence Kohlberg, Fowler and his colleagues interviewed some 500 men and women, girls and boys, through a ten-year period[16] to induce from the interviewees' own experience, patterns of meaning-making by which they made sense of their lives within the perspective of their current worldview. As increasingly complex life situations crack open the congruence of the "world" they have come to understand, a crisis in meaning can be generated in which current patterns no longer account for the realities they experience. Such a crisis can be experienced as a kind of death, a chaotic upheaval in all they have known that provided stability and integrity. Out of this chaotic crisis, a new pattern of meaning-making arises, a new horizon of meaning, a wider worldview. In the newfound pattern, they *know* something different about life, about the Ultimate, about symbols, relationships, power, authority. This new *knowing* is, according to Fowler, new *faithing*: the new worldview or horizon of meaning is, in his term, a new *stage of faith.*

In contrast to the Lockean interpretation challenged by Allport, Fowler's research is inherently historical, suggesting a sequence or vector or movement in human evolution of meaning-making.[17] While

---

16. See Fowler, *Becoming Adult, Becoming Christian*, 51.

17. See the results of Fowler's research in his seminal work *Stages of Faith*. Fowler is overt about his following the structural developmentalists who "have resolutely approached the study of development as an *interactional* process" (*Stages*, 100). He places this position between, on the one hand, the behaviorist theories "in psychology, such as those of B. F. Skinner, [that] tend to see persons as passive and malleable, their patterns of action largely determined by influences from their environments"; and, on the other hand, the maturationist theories, a position deemphasizing environ-

concerned to uncover a common human pattern of faith development,[18] Fowler holds in strict tension with the claim of commonality the necessity of honoring the particular path of each person which varies in his or her experience of meaning-making. The "scandal of particularity," a name theologians give to the unthinkability of God's Incarnation in one human person in a specific time and place in human history, is recapitulated in the radical particularity of the life of each person God has created. Thus, the pattern of faith development stages, even if it be universal,[19] is not itself normative. Rather, it aids comprehension of persons as they "adolesce" (mature) in finding meaning in the human vocation of living in an expanding universe. And faith stage theory aids in the Christian interpretation of that vocation as one whose worthiness or meaning comes from healing redeeming, and regenerating[20] "under the pressure and power of the in-breaking kingdom of God."[21] The tension between the many and the one, between the common or universal pattern of human growing and the radical particularity of each person's journey toward God, is a creative tension that underlies Fowler's work and must underlie our understanding of the process

---

mental factors, represented by Arnold Gesell and R. J. Havighurst who "view growth or development as primarily the unfolding of innately programmed organismic capacities" (ibid., 100). Rather, Fowler locates himself between these poles and within the "structural-developmental interactional approach" which views "development as resulting from the interchange between an active, innovative subject and a dynamic, changing environment" (ibid., 100).

18. Fowler begins with a foundational assumption about human nature as having a need for *meaning* (a position shared, for example, by Ernest Becker who calls humanity *homo poeta*, the meaning-maker (ibid., 4). Thus, faith or the quest for meaning is a human universal ("I believe faith is a human universal" ibid., xiii), while the way we understand them (i.e., stages in faith development) is a construct which is not itself endemic to the human condition.

19. While "universality" is a goal and a claim typically made by stage theory in whatever area of development is studied, Fowler has generally not asserted this claim for faith development. In the *magnum opus* of 1981, *Stages of Faith,* Fowler wrote, "I do not feel warranted in making claims of 'universality' for our stages, beyond the contention that the formal descriptions of them are generalizable and can be tested cross-culturally" (ibid., 100). This agnostic stance was reiterated a decade later: "We believe that the stages are sequential and invariant. We do not have sufficient data to indicate the extent of their universality or cross-cultural validity," in *Weaving the New Creation*, 17.

20. This is Fowler's summary of H. Richard Niebuhr's thesis. See *Faith Development and Pastoral Care*, 21.

21. Fowler, *Faith Development and Pastoral Care*, 21.

of personal growth and evolution. We will look again at the question of the one and the many in the last chapter. Here, however, we must communicate Fowler's continuous emphatic assertion on behalf of the uniqueness of each person that the description of faith stages is not in any way intended to evaluate a person's faith before God: "[i]n no way will we be suggesting that a person characterized by one of the less developed stages is any less a person than one described by a more developed stage"[22] or should be so judged by themselves or others. At the same time, and because Fowler examines the common process of human maturation, he does claim a kind of evolution (or revolution)[23] that there are

> patterns characterizing persons' construals of self-other, self-self, self-world, and self-Ultimate environment relations . . . Stages of selfhood and faith . . . refer to typical patterns of construal that we have come to understand as deriving from systematically integrated operations of [in this case] knowing, valuing, and meaning construction . . . [To identify these as stages is to claim that these patterns] exhibit a certain formal uniformity in a range of persons. It is to claim that there is a developmental sequence of such systems of integrated operations. Further, it is to claim that the developmental sequence exhibits a series of qualitatively distinguishable patterns and that each pattern adds successively something qualitatively new and more complexly developed to the patterns that come before it.[24]

In sum, Fowler states that in "continuity with the constructive developmental tradition, faith stages are held to be *invariant, sequential* and *hierarchical*. I do not claim for these stages *universality.*"[25]

With Fowler, then, and taking seriously Allport's *caveat*, we identify these stages not for the sake of generalizing about humans as species, but rather to give a human sciences perspective on human beings as processual, as necessarily changing and becoming; and also to engender, for those concerned for the ongoing animation of the

22. Fowler, *Faith Development and Pastoral Care*, 57.

23. By "evolution" I do not imply linearity. Fowler's metaphor for the journey is a *spiral* (see Fowler, *Stages*, 274–75 *passim*). In *Becoming Adult, Becoming Christian*, Fowler refers to "predictable stages or *revolutions* in the life of meaning-making" (52; emphasis mine).

24. Fowler, *Faith Development and Pastoral Care*, 57.

25. Fowler, *Faithful Change*, 57.

baptized, a theological faith perspective on some constitutive elements of the baptismal process. Therefore, while Fowler has not limited his research nor his conclusions to Christian interpretations of faith, our use of Fowler will be in the specifically Christian context of the lived life of baptized persons. Further, it will not be necessary for us here to plumb the depths of stage theory, its variants, its critics,[26] nor its breadth. For stage theory has burgeoned in such studies as stages of cognitive development,[27] moral development,[28] ego development;[29] stages of loving,[30] of social perspective-taking,[31] of a man's life,[32] of women's lives,[33] of black men's lives.[34] There are stages of personality development[35] and of fetal/infantile development.[36] Nor is it our task here to present a comprehensive outline of the many ways in which the human journey may be interpreted. Rather, we bring to bear Fowler's theological interpretation of psychological theories for patterns bearing upon theology's fundamental root questions of ultimacy and meaning and the evolutionary ways in which these questions are integrated into changing human beings in the creative processual work of art that is a lived human life.

In order, then, to grasp the vector of maturing in "faithing" or meaning-making which James Fowler has discovered, and to identify its implications for a realized baptismal ecclesiology accounting for the experience of the baptized, we shall proceed as follows. First we will define the term "faith." Second, we shall look briefly at the seven

---

26. For gender critiques, for example, see Carol Gilligan's study of women's moral development *In a Different Voice*; for a critique of ritual assumptions, see liturgical theologian Catherine Vincie's "Gender Analysis and Christian Initiation," 505–30.

27. For a succinct summary of the stages, see Jean Piaget, "Piaget's Theory."

28. Kohlberg, *The Philosophy of Moral Development*; Gilligan and Brown, *Meeting at the Crossroads*.

29. Loevinger, *Ego Development*.

30. Keen, *The Passionate Life*.

31. Selman, "The Developmental Conceptions of Interpersonal Relations," and Selman, "Social Cognitive Understanding."

32. Levinson, et al, *The Seasons of a Man's Life*.

33. Gilligan, *In a Different Voice*.

34. Gooden, "The Adult Development of Black Men." Gooden's teacher was Daniel Levinson.

35. Erikson, *Childhood and Society*, esp. chapter 7.

36. Stern, *The Interpersonal World of the Infant*.

stages of faith as Fowler has described them, paying particular attention to three aspects: relationship with symbols, locus of authority, and perspective-taking, while noting the ever-widening bounds of social awareness. And third, we shall examine transitions between the stages for an understanding of what enables or inhibits the passage from one horizon of meaning to another, and how this understanding can contribute to growth and maturing in the baptismal process.

Faith—That Which Develops and Matures

The common problems of the human condition include the issues of finitude, vulnerability, "cosmic aloneness,"[37] and "ontological anxiety."[38] The creation of integrity in the face of human angst, Fowler calls *faith*: "faith is a way of construing, interpreting, and responding to the factors of contingency, finitude, and ultimacy in our lives."[39]

Drawing first upon theologians Paul Tillich and H. Richard Niebuhr, Fowler raises the fundamental question of "ultimate concern,"[40] the human need for "an overarching, integrating, and grounding trust in a center of value and power sufficiently worthy to give our lives unity and meaning."[41] Fowler seeks a word *not tied to particular noetic contents* which describes "a person's or group's way of moving into the force field of life. It is our way of finding coherence in and giving meaning to the multiple forces and relations that make up our lives. Faith is a person's way of seeing him- or herself in relation to others against a background of shared meaning and purpose."[42]

Faith (Latin: *fides*; also *credo, credere*; Greek: *pistis*) is the deepest kind of knowing, the source of confidence which can fill the human soul. Fowler quotes Wilfred Cantwell Smith's word study on *credo*

---

37. Fowler, *Becoming Adult, Becoming Christian*, 51.
38. Tillich's term. In ibid., 53.
39. Ibid., 52.
40. Tillich, *Dynamics of Faith*, 1–8.
41. This description represents Fowler's accounting of H. Richard Niebuhr, in Fowler, *Stages*, 5. In ibid., 34 n. 4, Fowler explains that his idea is found in Niebuhr's "Faith on Earth" (unpub. ms. of seven chapters), intended originally for publication with what became Niebuhr's *Radical Monotheism and Western Culture* but was rejected by the publishers (see Fowler, *Stages*, 5). For a summary of "Faith on Earth" see Fowler's treatment of H. R. Niebuhr, *To See the Kingdom*, chap. 5.
42. Fowler, *Stages*, 4.

which in the West came to refer to notional assent without requiring a commitment of the heart = of the total person. Originally, however, *credo*

> is a compound from *cor, cordia*, "heart" (as in English "cordial," "accord," "concord," and the like; compare also, from the closely parallel Greek cognate *kardia*, the English derivatives "cardiac," "electrocardiogram," etc.), plus *do*, "put, place, set," also "give." The first meaning of the compound in classical Latin had been and its primary meaning continued to be "to entrust, to commit, to trust something to someone," and of money, to lend. A secondary meaning in secular usage was "to trust in," "to rely upon," "to place confidence in."[43]

Therefore, Fowler gives this summary of the questions of faith as he means it: "On what or whom do you set your heart? To what vision of right-relatedness between humans, nature, and the transcendent are you loyal? What hope and what ground of hope animate you and give shape to the force field of your life and to how you move into it?"[44]

In a later work, Fowler elaborates that faith includes unconscious as well as conscious awareness, and emotional dispositions as well as cognitive content and processes.[45] Faith is

> 1. . . . the most fundamental category in the human question for relation to transcendence. Faith, it appears, is generic, a universal feature of human living, recognizably similar everywhere despite the remarkable variety of forms and contents of religious practice and belief.
>
> 2. Each of the major religious traditions studied speaks about faith . . . [which] involves an alignment of the will, a resting of the heart, in accordance with a vision of transcendent value and power, one's ultimate concern.
>
> 3. Faith . . . is not a separate dimension of life . . . [but] an orientation of the total person, giving purpose and goal to one's hopes and striving, thoughts and actions.[46]

With Fowler, then, I shall use the term *faith* to mean the moral, affective, aesthetic dispositional orientation to knowing, valuing, and

---

43. Wilfred Cantwell Smith, *Faith and Belief*, 76. In Fowler, *Stages*, 12.
44. Fowler, *Stages*, 14.
45. Fowler, *Faithful Change*, 55.
46. Fowler, *Stages*, 14.

committing,[47] and the set of conditions necessary for a conceptional horizon of meaning by which the cosmic and ultimate are conceived of and claimed to be true. A person's capacity to conceptualize; a person's ability to relate to symbols; the breadth of a person's perspective and social awareness; along with the ability to locate one's own relationship with ultimate power, authority, and goodness, all affect a person's meaning-quest. As suggested in the title of his 1996 work, the life of faith is a life of "faithful change." Let us now explore the results of Professor Fowler's research on the movement of that change in a human life.

Stages of Faith Development[48]

The questions Fowler and his colleagues put to the interviewees in their study were intended to ask persons, how do they "awaken to and begin to form (and be formed) in the life stances of trust and loyalty, of belief and commitment that carry them into the force fields of their lives? Are there predictable stages or revolutions in the life of meaning-making? Must we, in order to become fully adult and to be fully human, have a deep-going and abiding trust in and loyalty to some cause or causes, greater in value and importance than ourselves?"[49] Is there a series of human operations "of knowing and valuing,"[50] irrespective of what or who would be known or valued? What constitutes human meaning-making given the common human circumstances of "contingency, finitude, and ultimacy"?[51] If persons are not *tabula rasa* but purposive agents, active creators "composing a life"[52] within the framework of an *arche* and a *telos*,[53] what must come to be put in place—developed—for

---

47. Fowler, *Faith Development and Pastoral Care*, 67.

48. These stages of "becoming a self" are called in Fowler's *Faith Development and Pastoral Care* "Stages in Selfhood and Faith" (p. 53).

49. Fowler, *Becoming Adult, Becoming Christian*, 51–52.

50. Ibid., 52.

51. Ibid.

52. See Mary Catherine Bateson, *Composing a Life*. An unauthorized sub-title of Bateson's book: *Life as a Work in Progress—The Improvisations of Five Extraordinary Women*.

53. Arche = beginning; telos = end or aim. See Ricoeur, *Freud and Philosophy*, 342, 459ff; as dialectic of progression and regression, 493, and chapter III.4 (494–551).

the human person to live fruitfully, *meaningfully*? "Are there predictable stages or revolutions in the life of meaning-making?"[54]

Fowler and his colleagues sought "a successive progression of increasingly complex, differentiated, and comprehensive modes of knowing and valuing."[55] Let us now identify these progressive stages with the purpose of coming to understand the vortices of valuing and knowing that operate beneath our conscious awareness in the process of human becoming.

1. Primal Faith

Developed more fully after the publication of the initiating volume *Stages of Faith*, the stage of *Primal faith* begins with birth and usually extends to the first two years of life.[56] Robert Kegan refers to the self developed in this stage as "the incorporative self" in which all experiences are incorporated into the infant's subjectivity. The bounds of social awareness, then, are limited to the child's own skin. The infant is not able to distinguish self from other, and is "constituted by its reflexes, its sensing, its moving."[57] There is no "perspective" in this stage.

Daniel Stern has identified four distinct sub-stages during this period which Fowler has incorporated into his stage theory:[58] the *emergent self* (birth to c. two months) in which formation of the imagination begins; the *core self* (two to six months) which Fowler sees as the *body self* and links to the birth of ritualization; the *intersubjective self* (seven to fifteen months) when awareness of feeling in self and others develops which grounds the possibility of emotional intimacy,

---

54. Fowler, *Becoming Adult, Becoming Christian*, 52.

55. Ibid., 57. See also Fowler, *Faithful Change*, 56–57: "The varying stages of faith can be differentiated in relation to the degrees of complexity, of comprehensiveness, of internal differentiation, and of flexibility that their operations of knowing and valuing manifest."

56. In this section, I am following Fowler, *Faith Development and Pastoral Care* [*Faith Development*], 57–59, and Fowler, *Faithful Change*, 20–46.

57. Fowler, *Faith Development*, 58. Fowler follows Robert Kegan's *The Evolving Self*.

58. See Fowler, *Faithful Change*, 25–43. Fowler draws upon Daniel Stern's *The Interpersonal World of the Infant*.

a stage Fowler links to the birth of the soul;[59] and the *verbal self* (fifteen to twenty-four months), linked to the birth of symbolization.

This fourth sub-stage opens a new world, and brings the person to the brink of a next stage in development. When a child begins to be able to name objects external to herself, her relationship with the world around her changes dramatically. The "rise and use of verbal symbols is exhilarating and liberating, and yet it is full of potential for alienation, as well as for communication."[60] In agonizing childhood situations of disrespect, shame, or abuse, a "false self" begins to develop at this time.[61] On the other hand, with "the emergence of the verbal self, meaning is communicated by language and symbol. Meaning is created *between* others and the child in new levels of mutuality."[62] This, Fowler points out, is Martin Buber's I-Thou quality of relationship. At the same time, language-symbols become part of ritualizations, and ritualizations can overcome the alienation arising from "primitive agonies"[63] or from misuse of language.[64] Fowler cites an example from Katherine Nelson and Jerome Brunner:

> [U]pon the birth of a younger brother, the two-year-old sister devises all sorts of ways to keep the father present with her at bedtime. At his eventual departure, she adopts his tone and mannerisms in an ongoing monologue. Besides practicing his language patterns, she is demonstrating her internalization of her father's total presence. If successful, the child gains agency—she keeps Dad present. She gains autonomy, being able to relinquish his physical presence. She gains communion, because she now participates in his symbol system and mannerisms, all by way of this simple bedtime ritual . . . This, then, is the opposite of alienation; it keeps her from having to con-

---

59. Fowler, *Faithful Change*, 33.

60. Ibid., 39. See also Rappaport, "Liturgies and Lies," on verbal symbolization as the beginning possibility of the specific kind of alienation which is speaking untruths.

61. Fowler, *Faithful Change*, 42–43.

62. Ibid., 43.

63. Stern, in ibid., 41.

64. See Barbara Brown Taylor, *When God is Silent*, for the interesting point that misuse of language leads to deception and to the inability of persons to trust what others say, or even speech itself. She uses examples from advertising, such as, "Be all you can be: drink soda pop." "Place your security in the right place—our bank." In primal faith, if the words "I love you" were accompanied by shaming activity, confusion and disintegrity would result in the child. This can distort the child's formation and exacerbate the formation of a dissociative or false self.

struct a false self. The emanating power of becoming, coming up from below [from its inner source, *arche*,] meets with the transcendent or the numinous power of the future [*telos*] in language and ritual, and a relatively true self is consolidated in an early interpersonal relationship.[65]

This spontaneous ritualization provided an embodied stability for the child, a guard against alienation. As she grows, both in the regular unfolding of processes and in her setting and matrix of relationships, she will soon demonstrate another orientation toward value and power which Fowler has named "intuitive-projective faith."

2. Intuitive-Projective Faith

The impulsive self develops along with "a style of meaning-making" Fowler calls Intuitive-Projective faith, beginning about the time language is formed for a youngster. Robert Kegan's[66] shorthand for this stage is "I am my impulses." Here is Fowler's succinct description of this phase:

> This stage represents an emotional and perceptual ordering of experience. Imagination, not yet disciplined by consistent logical operations, responds to story, symbol, dream, and experience. It attempts to form images that can hold and order the mixture of feelings and impressions evoked by the child's encounters with the newness of both everyday reality and the penumbra of mystery that surrounds and pervades it. Death emerges as a source of danger and mystery. Experiences of power and powerlessness orient children to a frequently deep existential concern about questions of security, safety, and the power of those upon whom they rely for protection. Owing to a naive egocentrism, children do not consistently differentiate their perspectives from those of others. Because of this lack of perspective taking, and in virtue of an as yet unreliable understanding of cause-and-effect relations, children construct and reconstruct events in episodic fashion. While appreciative of stories and capable of becoming deeply engrossed in them, they are seldom able to reconstruct very adequately the narrative pattern and detail of a story. The reconstruc-

---

65. Fowler, *Faithful Change*, 43–44. This story is cited Stern, *The Interpersonal World of the Infant*, 172–74.

66. See Kegan, *The Evolving Self*.

tions they make take on an episodic quality, and in them fantasy and make-believe are not distinguished from factuality. Constructions of faith at this stage are drawn to symbols and images of visible power and size. There is an appreciation for stories that represent the powers of good and evil in unambiguous fashion.[67]

The child, as far as emotions and self-control are concerned, does not *have* (in the sense of possess or control) impulses; rather, the child *is* its impulses. The child is constituted by—is embedded in—its logical fallacies, its egocentrism, its imagination, its perceptions, its internal contradictions of desire and fear of punishment. Tantrums, for example, are not something a four-year-old has. More appropriately we might say the tantrum has the four-year-old; he or she is internal to it. Tantrums are in a sense a logical expression of the impulsive child who is thwarted or frustrated by a world that he or she cannot fully interpret or make sense of.[68]

While it is not given that every child will out-grow this stage, Fowler's recounted interviews do not provide examples of adults remaining in intuitive-projective faith, which is most typical of children aged three to seven.[69] While intuitive-projective faith is the "stage of first self-awareness," there is still not the possibility of taking a perspective beyond one's own.[70] For example, in an interview with Freddy, a four-year-old from a Roman Catholic family, Freddy was asked, "Can you tell me what God looks like?"

> *Freddy:* "He has a light shirt on, he has brown hair, he had brown eyelashes . . ." At this point Freddy brought in two small statues of Christ which he showed to the interviewer. After remarking about the statues she asked him, "Does everybody think that God looks like that?" Freddy's answer, suggesting a typical inability to construct other perspectives, is arresting: "Mmm—not when he gets a haircut."[71]

Children first encounter the mystery of death at this stage. As food for the imagination, which is a primary source of meaning, chil-

---

67. Fowler, *Faith Development*, 59.
68. Ibid., 60.
69. Fowler, *Stages*, 133.
70. Ibid.
71. Ibid., 127.

dren are helped by "access to the symbols, stories, and shared liturgical life of a religious tradition" by which she or he is awakened "to an expanded horizon of meanings . . . [and provided with] sources of guidance and reassurance."[72]

The transition from one stage to the next may occur from physiological change, from the flow of circumstances, or from some precipitating crisis of meaning. In the latter, change may be propelled by a cracking of the skin which held life's meanings together, beginning the molting of change gladly or unbidden. The transition from intuitive-projective faith to mythic-literal faith usually occurs over a two-year period beginning commonly at the age of five to seven. Here is an example of one child's molting that began as a crisis of meaning.[73]

> A five-year-old boy, big for his age but naive in other ways, sat with three seven-year-old boys. The seven-year-olds had been teaching the younger boy to "cuss" (to use mild profanity and "dirty" terms). Glad at feeling included and "big" with his new-found vocabulary, the younger boy made a crucial mistake. He asked the older boys what Santa Claus was going to bring them for Christmas. Scoffing, the seven-year-olds said, "You don't believe in Santa Claus do you Tommy?" "Naw," answered Tommy, absorbing crushing news. While Tommy struggled internally to accommodate a newly flattened and secularized world, Billy, on whose front steps they were sitting, went into his house and returned with a small green parakeet his aunt had given him. The parakeet was sick. As Billy held it in his fat, freckled hand, its head kept falling to one side. After the boys contemplated the sad looking bird for a few moments, Dickie, the slyest and most hard-hearted of the older boys, said, "Let's kill it. It's going to die anyway. We might as well put it out of its misery." Buddy, a handsome, soft-eyed lad, looked at the bird and then at its owner. He asked, "Do you want to kill it?" After a pause, Billy, who only recently had become the bird's owner, said, "Yeah! Let's kill it." Tommy wasn't consulted about the matter, and after his earlier experience of embarrassment was not about to speak. He watched as Billy tightened his grip on the frail body of the bird and then forcefully slapped its listing head against the cement step. "Thwack . . . Thwack . . . Thwack, Thwack, Thwack, Thwack, Thwack." And there was death, broken-necked, pop-eyed, and limp.

72. Fowler, *Becoming Adult, Becoming Christian*, 55.
73. *Faithful Change*, 68. The example that follows is found pp. 68–69.

> In young Tommy's life and faith, this sequence of events, occurring with older boys he admired, initiated a period of transition out of the Intuitive-Projective stage and into the construction of a Mythic-Literal stage . . . Tommy's dramatic experiences and learnings on that December afternoon began a process, deeply fraught with emotion, of looking in new ways at many things his family and church had taught him. He began to think in new ways about God, death, and the evil good people can do.[74]

The direction of changes in Tommy's life is not pre-determined. The people and teachings that will guide him to reinterpret his life, which paint the color of his newly-molted "skin," are not given. But a new skin it will be, a narrative skin, fed by mythic stories.

3. *Mythic-Literal*

The Mythic-Literal style of meaning-making is associated with the "ability to narratize one's experience . . . [and] the ability to bind our experiences into meaning through the medium of stories."[75] At this stage Fowler notes in a mythic-literal child "the almost exclusive reliance on narrative as the means of organizing . . . meanings, the central importance of reciprocity as the principle governing divine-human relations . . . the overall anthropological character of . . . meaningful symbols and the literalism involved in her reliance upon those symbols."[76]

Robert Kegan calls a person in the mythic-literal stage "the imperial self" because the dominant self-orientation is "I am my needs and desires."[77] At the same time, in this stage one is able to step outside one's own perspective to take the perspective of another. Fowler calls this *simple perspective taking*.[78] It is the ability to imagine a perspective other than one's own that makes *story* so delightful and significant. Persons can only tell a story if they can imagine points of view other than their own; and in taking another perspective, one's "world" or horizon of meaning is broadened. Indeed, the term "mythic" for this

---

74. Ibid., 68–69.
75. Fowler, *Stages*, 136.
76. Ibid., 148–49.
77. Fowler, *Faithful Change*, 62–63.
78. Fowler, *Stages*, 244.

stage comes from the love of myth and narrative, and its central role as point of reference and interpretation for life experiences. This relates to the term "literal" in that meaning is bound up in the physicality of the symbol. Distance or conceptual reflection upon symbols and stories is not possible for those in this stage. Thus, "meaning is both carried and 'trapped' in the narrative."[79]

While the person's social awareness is now able to embrace a group wider than oneself and one's parents or immediate family, the breadth is limited to "those like us" in terms of religion, race, class, tribe, or family.

The world composed in this stage is related to its accompanying stage of moral development that, at least for boys, is grounded in fairness based upon equality and reciprocity.[80] Locus of authority continues to be external in this stage, located outside oneself, especially in persons with authoritative roles.

Most school children manifest this stage of faith development. Some do not pass through this stage as their lives unfold. One adult interviewed, Mrs. W., seemed to be aware that her faith was childlike, and she communicated the painful sense that her faith might not be adequate to carry her though ambiguous and dangerous situations, either in the world or in her own psychic-emotional life.[81] In a later work, Fowler posits evidence that "suggests that the majority of adults in our society arrest or equilibrate in either the Mythic-Literal or the [next] Synthetic-Conventional stage."[82]

A sign that a person is transitioning to the next phase is the widening of perspective-taking. Some gain the ability to recognize that the other person sees from a point of view different from one's own. Beyond the simplicity of taking another perspective oneself, a person moving toward synthetic-conventional faith becomes able to take the next leap to "see" that the others have distinct perceptions

---

79. Ibid., 149.

80. Ibid., 149. Fowler's work here is based upon the work of Lawrence Kohlberg. Carol Gilligan and others have identified a second way of moral orientation, one more typical in girls than in boys: valuing *relationship* over *justice*. While not delineating stages *per se*, for articles showing how girls valued harmony over a reciprocal sense of fairness in moral decision-making, see Gilligan, et al., eds., *Mapping the Moral Domain*.

81. Fowler, *Stages*, 146–49, esp. 149.

82. Fowler, *Weaving*, 21.

of their own. Stunningly, one comes to *see oneself from another's perspective*. This self-consciousness does not occur before the ages of ten to thirteen (if at all). Fowler uses a couplet to describe this *mutual* perspective-taking:

> I see you seeing me:
> I see the me I think you see.[83]

The transition to the next phase is then characterized by Fowler as follows:

> A factor initiating transition to [Synthetic-Conventional Faith] is the implicit clash or contradictions in stories that leads to reflection on meanings. The transition to formal operational thought makes such reflection possible and necessary. Previous literalism breaks down; new "cognitive conceit" (Elkind) leads to disillusionment with previous teachers and teachings. Conflicts between authoritative stories (Genesis on creation versus evolutionary theory) must be faced. The emergence of mutual interpersonal perspective taking ("I see you seeing me; I see me as you see me; I see you seeing me seeing you.") creates the need for a more personal relationship with the unifying power of the ultimate environment.[84]

In the coming to terms with these crises, conflict in authoritative stories, and new insights or questions posed which stimulate reflection and reexamination of one's position, a molting transformative movement begins to occur. Fowler characterizes the style of meaning-making which follows as one in which the person identifies with the community of the person's primary identity.

4. Synthetic-Conventional Faith

Synthetic-Conventional faith is the stage of the interpersonal self: "I am my relationships and roles." This stage is commonly associated with puberty and adolescence, although there are many adults for whom "it becomes a permanent place of equilibrium. It structures the ultimate environment in interpersonal terms . . . It is a 'conformatist' stage . . . tuned to the expectations and judgments of significant others."[85]

---

83. Fowler, *Stages*, 153.
84. Ibid., 150.
85. Ibid., 172.

With the ability to see oneself from the perspective of the other comes the birth of self-consciousness. Now, how one is seen by others *matters*. One begins to rely on others as "mirrors," and to come to love oneself as loved by others. But not only can persons perceive themselves as they imagines the other seeing them, but

> You see you according to me:
> You see the you you think I see.[86]

With this level of intersubjectivity comes a sensitivity toward others. The "tremendous power our perceptions of others' perceptions [and] evaluations of us have upon our forming sense of self"[87] has been called the "tyranny of the 'they.'"[88] What psychologists call "projection" arises out of this "mutual interpersonal perspective taking."[89]

Related to this ability for simultaneous consciousness of "seeing others see us" and "seeing ourselves as we think others see us" is the capability for formal operational thinking as Piaget identified it. At this stage, "meta-thinking" is possible. Reflection and analysis, along with interpersonal perspective taking, means that the person can not only enter the world of a story told, but can also step outside that world and analyze the story itself. This new meta-story enables imagination about one's own possible futures along with a beginning reflection upon who "we" are who share a particular mythic story.

The bounds of social awareness are wider as well, given that those who mirror the person are not limited to family or those like oneself. Peers and adults from outside one's primary identity group also mirror the adolescent. And when these mirrored expectations and reflections of self don't match with each other or with one's own view of self, an "identity crisis" (Erik Erikson's term) ensues.[90] A risk in this stage is "the danger of becoming permanently dependent upon and subject to what Sharon Parks calls the 'tyranny of the they.'" Authority continues to be located outside the self, in this tyrannical "they," for example,

---

86. Ibid., 153.
87. Electronic conversation with James Fowler, April 18, 2002.
88. Sharon Parks, "Faith Development and Imagination," in Fowler, *Stages*, 154.
89. Fowler, *Stages*, 153.
90. Ibid., 154.

or in institutions (e.g., of society or government). Social relations are constructed "as extensions of interpersonal relationships."[91]

Symbols function as if they *are* the thing symbolized (and cannot reflectively be separated).[92] This is related to the level of "tacit knowing": of operating beliefs and assumptions, even strongly held values, which have never been subject to reflection. Demythologization is experienced as a significant threat to meaning and "an assault on the sacred itself."[93] Further, there is in this stage an over-identification of symbol with the thing symbolized. For example, the flag would be understood to *be* the nation, and untoward treatment of this symbol would to a person in this stage be considered treasonous. The bread on the altar *is* in a literal way the Body of Christ. While the reverential treatment of symbols would be an important aspect of living out this style of meaning-making and faith, Fowler also notes that the other side of this reality also functions: when symbols cease to hold sacred meaning, the sacrality itself is experienced as absent. In the course of social trivialization of sacred symbols (through advertising, bald humor, etc.), those in Synthetic-Conventional faith who rely upon the revered symbols as *the* bearer of the sacred, can suffer anomie. When the sacred is emptied, "the vacuum of meaning and of meaningful symbolic representations results in rampant anxiety and neuroses and in a resurgence of interest in all kinds of occult and spiritualistic phenomena."[94]

For an example of the non-analytical style of finding meaning in the collective synthesis, we note the reply when Mr. D. was asked about his beliefs and values: "There is really very little that I could tell you. I am really not much of a thinker; my views are quite the same as those of any teamster, or any working man."[95]

It is this quality of non-analysis from which the term "conventional" comes: his individual faith "is seen as being everybody's faith system,"[96] a commonly held convention. His views are not the result of a reflective process by which he has labored to integrate his experi-

91. Ibid., 162.
92. Ibid., 163.
93. Ibid., 163.
94. Ibid., 164.
95. Ibid., 165.
96. Ibid., 167.

ence with a life-orientation or a worldview. Rather, he has accepted the synthetic view of the group with whom he identifies. Any discussion of his values is held not "to distinguish himself, or to examine the values, or to be sure that his views are correct. Rather, in such discussion he seeks to establish a sense of commonality or relatedness with the other person present."[97] This is conventional faith. "The norm lies in the conventional pattern of life of those who constitute 'everybody.'"[98] Authority, thus, is external to oneself: e.g., in institutions, Scripture, one's parents, one's group.

At this stage, the world is experienced as wider and more complex than in the previous stage. "Faith must provide a coherent orientation in the midst of that more complex and diverse range of involvements. Faith must synthesize values and information; it must provide a basis for identity and outlook."[99]

> The dangers or deficiencies in this stage are twofold. The expectations and evaluations of others can be so compellingly internalized (and sacralized) that later autonomy of judgment and action can be jeopardized; or interpersonal betrayals can give rise either to nihilistic despair about a personal principle of ultimate being or to a compensatory intimacy with God unrelated to mundane relations.
>
> Factors contributing to the breakdown of [this stage] and to readiness for transition may include: serious clashes or contradictions between valued authority sources; marked changes, by officially sanctioned leaders, or policies or practices previously deemed sacred and unbreachable (for example, in the Catholic church changing the mass from Latin to the vernacular, or no longer requiring abstinence from meat on Friday); the encounter with experiences or perspectives that lead to critical reflection on how one's beliefs and values have formed and changed, and on how "relative" they are to one's particular group or background. Frequently the experience of "leaving home"—emotionally or physically, or both—precipitates the kind of examination of self, background, and life-guiding values that gives rise to stage transition at this point.[100]

---

97. Ibid.
98. Ibid., 171.
99. Ibid., 172.
100. Ibid., 173.

5. Individuative-Reflective

According to Kegan, this stage represents "the institutional self."

The transition from synthetic-conventional to individuative-reflective faith may often happen when one is faced with a situation that is outside the realm of the familiar. Such "leaving home" causes one to see (and contextualize) for the first time how one's life and growing up have been. When one's own certain knowledge of the Real comes face to face with situations which cannot be accounted for by that reality, there is conflict: cognitive and valuational dissonance. In this dissonance, a shift can occur. One's view may widen, reflection begin, and assumptions be challenged. The example of Jack is given: "In going to the army Jack left home, both emotionally and geographically. As he encountered the ideologically potent and threatening teachings of the Panthers, it drove him, for the first time, to look with critical awareness at the assumptive system of values he and his family had shared with most of their neighbors as he grew up."[101]

Often going to college represents this leaving home. But what makes the transition is the alternative groups one encounters. If the army or college has groups that reinforce the conventionality of thinking, then "dependence on external authority and derivative group identity" of synthetic-conventional faith will remain.[102]

Rather,

> for a genuine move to [Individuative-Reflective faith] to occur there must be an interruption of reliance on external sources of authority. The "tyranny of the 'they'"—or the potential for it—must be undermined. In addition to the kind of critical reflection on one's previous assumptive or tacit system of values ... there must be, for [Individuative-Reflection faith], a relocation of authority within the self. While others and their judgments will remain important to the Individuative-Reflective person, their expectations, advice, and counsel will be submitted to an internal panel of experts who reserve the right to choose and who are prepared to take responsibility for their choices. I sometimes call this the emergence of an *executive ego*. The two essential features of the emergence of [this] Stage

---

101. Ibid., 177.
102. Ibid., 178.

> . . . are the critical distancing from one's previous assumptive value system and the emergence of an executive ego.[103]

Fowler goes on to note that many will make one move but not the other: through overseas travel perhaps, their perspective will broaden, providing critical distancing and reflection upon one's assumptions, but without an interruption of "their reliance on external sources of authority."[104]

Full groundedness in Individuative-Reflective faith finds persons with a clear differentiation of their perspective from others' perspectives. "Third-person perspective" enables them to recognize not only their perspective and the other's distinct perspective, but a third "observer" point of view, which helps Individuative-Reflective persons recognize the value and limits of their contribution in the wider whole. Through this seeing, they are able to claim their own authority. Further, Individuative-Reflective persons begin to take reflective and moral responsibility for their actions and choices, and for their perspectives. They begin to recognize their own responsibility for their self-perceptions, and thus to be able to hold their perspective "with full recognition of how others are likely to respond to or evaluate them."[105]

It is in this way that the locus of authority begins to reside within individuative-reflective persons instead of external to themselves.[106] Therefore, they no longer project their perspectives or personal relations upon all others. Their bounds of social awareness have extended to recognize and honor the complex institutional and social systems of society, and to allow the rules and laws of those systems to affect and take claim over their own actions and priorities. This is the stage of "law and order," of doing what the rules say, of going "by the book."[107]

Their grasp of symbols is also affected by the ability to differentiate between their own personal views of reality and the views of others. They are, on the one hand, freed from over-identification of symbols with things symbolized. On the other hand, the stage legalisms and literalisms lean instead toward a radical separation of symbol from thing symbolized. Able to ask critical questions such as, "why

103. Ibid., 179.
104. Ibid.
105. Electronic conversation with James Fowler, April 18, 2002.
106. Fowler, *Faith Development*, 68–69.
107. Fowler, *Stages*, 180.

does this symbol mean that?" "How does it mediate reality?" one has the freedom and the challenge of demythologization. This represents a kind of fall from innocence, a departure from first naiveté of encounter with symbolic power. The risk is that the Individuative-Reflective person may so split the symbol from the thing symbolized that over-identification may be replaced with seeing no relationship between them. Here, bread is bread, and *not* the Body of Christ; the flag is fabric with no reason for treating it differently from any other fabric. Tillich refers to the symbol's inability to mediate the transcendent for such a person as a "broken symbol."[108]

While there is a loss, there is also the gain of "[m]eanings previously tacitly held becom[ing] explicit" with the possibility of regaining a more creative tensive relationship in the next phase.[109]

This stage of faith may occur in early- to mid-twenties. However, many adults come to this stage, if at all, sometime at mid-life. The transition "can be precipitated by changes in primary relationships, such as a divorce, the death of a parent or parents or children growing up and leaving home. Or it can result from challenges of moving, changing jobs, or the experience of the breakdown or inadequacy of one's synthetic-conventional faith."[110] The transition is thus a vulnerable time for any human, including those living the baptismal process. The question as to the role of liturgy or liturgizing seems especially pregnant at this turning point:

> This transition represents an upheaval in one's life at any point and can be protracted in its process for five to seven years or longer. It typically is less severe for young adults, however, coming in that era as a natural accompaniment of leaving home and of the construction of a first, provisional adult life structure. When the transition occurs in the late thirties or early forties it often brings greater struggles. This is because of its impact upon the more established and elaborated system of relationships and roles that constitute an adult life structure.
>
> *The movement from [Synthetic-Conventional to] Individuative-Reflective faith is particularly critical for it is in this transition that the late adolescent or adult must begin to take seriously the burden of responsibility for his or her own commit-*

---

108. Tillich, *Dynamics of Faith*, chapter 2; in Fowler, *Stages*, 180.
109. Fowler, *Stages*, 181.
110. Ibid.

ments, lifestyle, beliefs and attitudes . . . [T]he person must face certain unavoidable tensions: individuality versus being defined by a group or group membership; subjectivity and the power of one's strongly felt but unexamined feelings versus objectivity and the requirement of critical reflection; self-fulfillment or self-actualization as a primary concern versus service to and being for others; the question of being committed to the relative versus struggle with the possibility of an absolute.[111]

A danger in this transition can come from "an excessive confidence in the conscious mind and in critical thought" which can express itself in a narcissism that presumes one's own perception of reality to be "the" Reality. The inability to recognize the truth in the perspectives of others represents an arrest in this stage.[112] The passage both to and from this stage, therefore, is important, critical, and yet vulnerable and fraught with fearsome dangers for the person. As we saw earlier, many adults in this culture are unable to make the transition to the next stage.

What are the kinds of things that precipitate or enable or cause shifts in one's perspective taking, one's locus of authority, one's boundaries as to who "we" are, or one's relationship with symbols, which would enable passage to the next stage? Fowler gives this synopsis of the influences that nudge a person toward a deepening reconfigurement of their construal of ultimate meaning, of the locus of valuing and power toward the next stage:

Restless with the self-images and outlook maintained by [this stage], the person ready for transition finds him- or herself attending to what may feel like anarchic and disturbing inner voices. Elements from a childish past, images and energies from a deeper self, a gnawing sense of the sterility and flatness of the meanings one serves—any or all of these may signal readiness for something new. Stories, symbols, myths, and paradoxes from one's own or other traditions may insist on breaking in upon the neatness of the previous faith. Disillusionment with one's compromises and recognition that life is more complex than [this stage's] logic of clear distinctions and abstract concepts can comprehend, press one toward a more dialectical and multileveled approach to life truth.[113]

111. Ibid., 181–82. Emphasis in original.
112. Ibid., 182–83.
113. Ibid., 183. Emphasis in original.

When one's "God is too small"; when the prejudices taught by one's family cannot with integrity be maintained in one's own relationships; one becomes ready for some kind of inner-outer reconfiguring. When it occurs, the person becomes able to hold together tensive experience in a greater reality and mythos. This ability to integrate gives to the next stage its name: *Conjunctive faith*.

6. Conjunctive Faith

Kegan's shorthand for this stage is "the inter-individual self," and Fowler's, the "tensional self."[114] In this stage, the disparity between the symbol and the thing symbolized of the previous stage are re-integrated, not in a mythic or synthetic merger, but a new tensive relationship, in which the person is able to live in the tension without struggling to resolve it. Symbols are able, for persons with conjunctive faith, to simultaneously conceal and reveal the holy.[115] If the demythologization of reflective faith represents the fall from innocence, conjunctive faith is the stage of what Paul Ricoeur calls the *second naiveté:* a new innocence and wisdom, like Dorothy and her friends when the Wizard of Oz is seen both for what he literally really is ("only a man") and for what he symbolically really is (the wizard) in the compelling power to draw creatures in hope toward a new life. In conjunctive faith is found the "postcritical desire to resubmit to the initiative of the symbolic."[116] Symbols may hold a more profound meaning for persons in this stage, since the tensive metaphoric paradox of symbol is also found in cognitive and perspective-taking capabilities. Such a relationship with reality is beyond "either/or" and requires holding two unlike or contradictory realities side-by-side at the same time. Fowler calls this both/and thinking "dialogical knowing": "In dialogical knowing the multiplex structure of the world is invited to disclose itself . . . The knower seeks to accommodate her or his knowing to the structure of that which is being known before imposing her or his own categories upon it . . . [with a] willingness to let reality speak its word, regard-

---

114. Fowler, *Faith Development*, 75.
115. See Lakoff and Johnson, *Metaphors We Live By*.
116. Fowler, *Stages*, 187–88. See also Fowler, *Faith Development*, 73.

less of the impact of that word on the security or self-esteem of the knower."[117]

Here, one is free to take other perspectives than one's own and to recognize their truth claims on their own terms. Here, too, the bounds of social awareness stretch to include the different, the "other," including those outside one's own group. The bounds stretch toward including all humanity as "us." With this wider horizon of perspective, community, and truth, one's authority-base cannot be invested in any one limited, finite person or institution, each of which has limited perspective. As the person leans toward critical-spiritual authority with a wider view, the locus of authority is now located within the person's own conscience and heart. The person her- or himself is widened and stretched, and becomes greater as wider truths are apprehended.

In this widening, as self-centeredness begins to wane, I am reminded of Paul Ricoeur's hermeneutical description of one's changing interaction with text. At first, one participates, coming to a text with one's own idea of what one will find there (pre-understanding), attaching or projecting our own experience onto what we read in the text. The next "moment" Ricoeur describes is that of distancing oneself from the text—creating a detachment, a "space between oneself and the text—in order to comprehend on its own terms the meaning that arises from the "world" out of which the text itself was written. If this move is made, then there is a third possibility: that of appropriating the truth of the text into one's own life. This is a movement toward freedom for the reader of receiving a new self. As Ricoeur puts it, "I exchange the *me, master* of itself, for the *self, disciple* of the text."[118] One begins to grasp the relativized position of oneself in the world: at once small, insignificant and relative, and also influential and of ultimate importance. In this space there can be "a new reclaiming and reworking of one's past."[119] This also involves an "opening to the voices of

---

117. Fowler, *Stages*, 185.

118. Ricoeur, "Phenomenology and Hermeneutics," 113 (emphasis Ricoeur's). It is interesting to note that Ricoeur understands meaning to be generated through the interaction, the interlocution, of a person with a text and the "world" to which it refers. I am intrigued by the resonance of Ricoeur's movement from participation to distanciation to appropriation, with Fowler's stages of synthetic-convention personalizing, through individuative-reflective analyzing, to conjunctive integrating.

119. Fowler, *Stages*, 197.

one's 'deeper self'"[120] and an apprehension of paradox. One recognizes that the truth that can be known and/or articulated is only partial. All of these parts are conjoined in the person who reaches this level of maturity.

> Unusual before mid-life, Stage 5 knows the sacrament of defeat and the reality of irrevocable commitments and acts. What the previous stage struggled to clarify, in terms of the boundaries of self and outlook, this stage now makes porous and permeable. Alive to paradox and the truth in apparent contradictions, this stage strives to unify opposites in mind and experience. It generates and maintains vulnerability to the strange truths of those who are "other." Ready for closeness to that which is different and threatening to self and outlook (including new depths of experience in spirituality and religious revelation), this stage's commitment to justice is freed from the confines of tribe, class, religious community or nation. And with the seriousness that can arise when life is more than half over, this stage is ready to spend and be spent for the cause of conserving and cultivating the possibility of others' generating identity and meaning.[121]

7. *Universalizing Faith*

Fowler calls the person in this stage the "God-grounded self." "The self is no longer the prime reference point from which the knowing and valuing of faith are carried out. Figure and ground are reversed."[122] Life is loved, but held lightly.[123] The "bases of identity, knowing (epistemology), and valuing (axiology) are transformed" as a universalizing person lives a life of willing self-emptying or kenosis.[124]

Fowler has developed his understanding of this stage in the years since *Stages of Faith* was published. His research has shown that persons come to this stage, if at all, no earlier than mid-life. These are the wisdom years:

---

120. Ibid., 198.
121. Ibid.
122. Fowler, *Faith Development*, 75.
123. Fowler, *Stages*, 201.
124. Fowler, *Faith Development*, 75.

Beyond paradox and polarities, persons in this stage are grounded in a oneness with the power of being. Their visions and commitments free them for a passionate yet detached spending of the self in love, devoted to overcoming division, oppression, and violence, and an effective anticipatory response to an inbreaking commonwealth of love and justice.[125]

As I understand it, the Universalizing stage of faith is a kind of completion of a process of decentering from self that begins in childhood with the Mythic-Literal stage with its advent of simple perspective taking, where the child begins to see things from others' points of view. Gradually across the stages, that taking of the perspective of others widens to the point where persons best described by the Universalizing stage have completed that process of decentering from self. You could say they have identified with or they have come to participate in the perspective of God. They begin to see and value *through* God rather than from the self. This does not mean that the self is not valued: the self is included in God's loving and valuing of all creation. But the self is no longer the center from which one's valuing is done; it's done from an identification with God.[126]

Faith Development and the Baptismal Process

What have we learned from this exploration into stages of the human quest for meaning, of the movement of faithing? First, from stage theory in general and James Fowler's research into stages of faith in particular, it is clear from this human sciences perspective that life is indeed processual: that is, while it is not possible to predict the process of any particular human, it is possible to point in general to tidal movements in the human life of faith, to patterns of what may happen. Further, changes are stimulated differently: some changes occur from simple physiological growth, and some from typical cultural or life circumstances; others occur out of crises.

Second, it is clear from this research that change in a human life is both given and not given. Some changes occur from the simple fact of physiological growth. Some occur from typical cultural or life circumstances, like the "leaving home" that often occurs around the age

---

125. Fowler, *Weaving*, 18.
126. Fowler, *Weaving*, 113–14.

of eighteen (but may not), and often occurs again when one leaves one's marriage home in later years and moves to a retirement community, and for some may occur at other points as well. Two examples will illustrate a stage-change that did not occur and one that happened much later than the typical. (By "later than typical," however, we are describing, not prescribing. We reiterate Fowler's and Allport's concern to avoid a sense that there is a "schedule" or a "right progression" that all people "should" follow.) These examples underline that there is nothing "lock-step" about these—that the sequence of stages does not mean that everyone passes through all of them, but that changes may happen, or may not, and in different timings.

We recall the account of Mrs. W. who lived her life in the mythic-literal way of organizing her meanings, a style she may have come to with others as a school-aged child. Mrs. W.'s centers of value and power were articulated in personal stories of things that happened to her, with her family as her "world." She characterized herself as a child, revealing in the interview that she "is pretty painfully aware that her form of faith does not serve her very well as an orientation in a complex and dangerous world."[127] For many reasons, her maturation arrested at an early stage; stage passage beyond that in general did not occur. Changes may not happen.

Fowler recounts the story of another woman who was very busy in her career without much time for reflection. In retirement, at sixty-seven, she had taken up some other activities, including joining a church. Mrs. M. was approached through her church by a graduate student assigned to do a two-hour interview. At the end of the time, it was "clear that there was much more that they needed to talk about. The visiting student approached his professor on Monday and explained that Ms. M. seemed to need to talk more about the matters discussed in the interview. Some of these matters, he sensed, would involve dealing with pain, grief, and the struggle of making meaning." The professor agreed, and the student went back repeatedly for six weeks of conversation. "As they talked, she dismantled the strong conventional faith she had formed as an adolescent and young adult in her Lutheran church many years ago. In the light of her long years of service in other societies and countries, her encounters with other religious traditions, her confrontation of evil and tragedy in human af-

---

127. Fowler, *Stages*, 149.

fairs, and her long, career-absorbed avoidance of facing her own deep loneliness, she needed to revisit and fundamentally rework her faith."[128]

The student provided a "safe space," a "holding environment" "where she could take her deepest beliefs and convictional grounding and bring them into critical interchange with the rich range of her life experiences and some deep sources of pain and grief they held.[129] In this case, the transition from synthetic-conventional to individuative-reflective faith, claiming the locus of authority within herself, happened not in young adulthood, but much later, in retirement, at a moment of profound readiness through the encounter with a sensitive, receptive, caring listener.

From faith stages, we learn, then, that life is a process, and that different kinds and quantities of changes may occur for different people on varying timelines. We draw a third inference from the fact that some transitions, however, are sparked by crisis, and that the content of the change is not prescribed. Here we recall the example of Tommy who was thrust from intuitive-projective into mythic-literal faith following an encounter with older boys who disabused him of Santa's existence and killed a pet parakeet before his eyes. What happened to Tommy after that? The third inference we take from faith development theory is that the direction of change is not pre-ordered. Change can be life giving or not; it can expand our skin or tighten it. Death, whether of persons, dreams, or meaning-constructs, can crack our developmental skin and thrust us to new meaning-configurations. Considering the contents of these new structures is not the work of faith development theory. It is, however, the concern of the baptized who live a life of becoming. Will their incremental moltings and movements turn their disillusionments to hope or to hard-heartedness?

Fowler's work on the stages, the meaning-factors which comprise them (e.g., locus of authority, relationship to symbol, perspective-taking, bounds of social awareness), and the transitional occurrences which engender them, stimulates our imagination as to what might support baptized persons in faithful becoming. What kinds of relationship, activity, intervention, interpretation might enable baptized persons in their life-long quest for meaning and integration? Some have already considered answers to this question. For example, those

---

128. Fowler, *Faithful Change*, 71.
129. Ibid., 70–71.

concerned with Christian formation conduct classes, support prayer groups, lead work-trips and mission trips, teach Scripture. These form the basis of interpretation and integration of life experiences such as the examples we have recounted. They enable the tidal rhythm of experience in the world and experience in the church. And weekly worship in the church is a basic, fundamental, crucial, and essential part of this rhythm.

What, however, is the role of other liturgy, or ritual, if any, in this process? What is the implication of faith development and its stimuli for other non-weekly liturgies such as occurred in the catechumenate? What is the role if any of Christian liturgizing in light of the skin-cracking occurrences that can (or could not) lead to growth? Our final exploration in seeking insight into this question is an exploration into ritual theory. This is the topic of Part Three.

PART THREE

Making Rituals for Baptismal Fulfillment and the Enlivening of the Church

~ Turning to Part Three

BAPTISM IS EFFECTIVE. THOSE WHO BELIEVE THAT GOD ACTS IN BAPtism have sure and certain trust in the sacrament's efficacy, because it is *God* who acts: and God is all-powerful, all-merciful, sovereign, and trustworthy; and on top of all that, God loves us. With God in charge, then, the effects of Holy Baptism occur whether or not the ones baptized are conscious of the results. And the foundational effects of baptism are wondrous: union with Christ in his death and resurrection, the gift of the Holy Spirit, conversion, pardoning, cleansing, incorporation into the body of Christ (the church), and serving thereby as a sign of the proleptic in-breaking of the reign of God.[1]

But what about that consciousness? What about the experience of those baptized—will their lives be effectively different as a result? Will their churches care about whether they have operational efficacy as well? Will they live a Christian existence that is identifiable to themselves or to others? Would others witnessing their lives acknowledge that their baptism "took"?

Those denominations that conduct exclusively believers' baptism assume that the one baptized will be conscious, indeed has already been conscious, of God's action. Awareness of God's active presence is a pre-requisite for baptism, which is one's response to God, signified through a baptismal confession of faith (and a changed life). A certain operational efficacy is built in. Denominations that also conduct infant baptism, however, trust the same effects, but the experience of the baptized is claimed proleptically, with hopes for its unfolding experience over the course of the persons' lives. But like the stories of Margaret and John told in the first chapter, sometimes the effects of baptism are obviously experienced and witnessed in persons' lives. And sometimes, they are not.

---

1. These are the ecumenically-agreed-upon meanings identified in the *Baptism, Eucharist, Ministry* document, Faith and Order Paper #111 (Geneva: World Council of Churches, 1982), *Baptism* II.

Does it matter? Should the contemporary post-Christendom churches be concerned as to whether or not the baptized have actual experiences of Christian living, of a Christian existence? And if so, what model might guide the churches? And what is the role of worship, or liturgy, or Christian ritualization in such a post-baptismal process of ongoing conversionary experience into Christ-by-the-Spirit?

In Part One, the question was raised as to whether actual working, operating experience in the lives of the baptized was expected in the Christian Tradition. Theologies of three patriarchs who practiced family and/or infant baptism were examined. All of them, Augustine, Aquinas, and Calvin, were found (to varying extents) to claim not only doctrinal but *also* operational efficacy in the lived experience of those baptized into Christ by the grace of the Holy Spirit. The expectation of conscious, lived experience of the baptized life has roots in the Tradition.

In Part Two, models and theologies were offered for the baptismal process of deepening experience in Christian existence, whether one is baptized as an infant or later as a conscious believer. The conversionary process in the (pre-Christendom) early church in which rituals marked growth in Christ was given as a model for the contemporary (post-Christendom) churches. The RCIA and other pre-baptismal catechumenal processes have been reclaimed in some churches today to provide conversionary experiences by which to apprehend the story, ethics, and liturgical-sacramental celebration as marks of Christian existence. The catechumenate, which is a model of Christian formation through ongoing study and life-reflection in a rhythm punctuated by ritual action, was proposed for use in today's post-Christendom for *the baptismal process of post-baptismal ongoing conversion.*

Ongoing conversion was then shown to be not merely a nice idea, but endemic to the life of those covenanted to Christ by the Spirit in baptism; for they are called to *theosis*, to growing more and more into the likeness of God-in-Christ. Not only that, but this rich and intimate transformation into Christ need not leave a growing Christian passive in the face of such grace, but gives the possibility of offering one's life back to God, day by day as *thanks-gift*. Such response-giving is, in addition to *theosis*, a theology of intersubjective relationship with God-in-Christ-and-the-Spirit that would be well fed by ritualizing moments of vulnerability and change, and when one needs, desires, or longs for a very conscious experience of God. A summary of Fowler's faith development theory concluded Part Two, offering specific marks of maturing in faith, and pointing out the vulnerable transitions which seem to call out for ritual action to mediate safe passage to the next stage: a larger life, a bigger heart, and a greater worldview.

These models and theologies were proposed as focal points for the energy and mission of the contemporary, post-Christendom church *so that the church can be realized in the fullness of ministry of all the baptized who make up the church*. Part Three, then, suggests a ritual role in the work toward realized baptismal ecclesiology: *making ritual to carry the baptized* across vulnerable moments when one's faith is likely either to shrink or to expand. If all the baptized are nurtured ritually to continue growing into God-in-Christ-by-the-Spirit, they will fulfill their ministries in Christ, and the church will be fully animated and realized.

Such a (post-)baptismal process is proposed using ritualization (chapter 9), even though this is mostly not done in the churches and some may thereby think it *should not* be done (chapter 10). For those convinced and ready to support the full ministry of the laity through ritualizing passages, healing, and vocational change, however, five principles are offered in chapter 11 as guidelines for their creation. Finally, as a counter to a concern about providing specific rituals for the particular circumstances of individual Christians, especially in an age of narcissistic "ME-ism," chapter 12 shows how the one and the many are related in a way that caring for the one can also be an instance of caring for the many.

9

Ritual Theory and Christian Ritualization

The Design[1] of Ritual Strategies

> [R]itual communication is not just an alternative way of expressing something but the expression of things that cannot be expressed in any other way.[2]

WORSHIP AND LITURGY IS PART OF THE LARGER HUMAN CATEGORY called *ritual*. But many Christian leaders did not like the idea of "reducing" holy Christian worship to "ritual." The study of ritual was mostly the work of anthropologists who researched other cultures by recording their "primitive" rituals. It took a twentieth-century postcolonial perspective to recognize that ritual was not just something indigenous peoples or first nations conducted. Ritual, rather, is endemic to all human cultures. Studying how ritual works can be enlightening for any culture and for any religion. In this chapter, six researchers in the late-twentieth-century new field of "ritual studies" will be explored for the insights they offer to Christian liturgy, and specifically, to Christian ritualization. The first theorist is Catherine Bell, mother of ritual studies; then Ronald Grimes, its father; then Theodore Jennings on ritual knowledge, Mary Collins on changing theology by ritual practice, Roland Delattre on ritual competence, and Michael Aune on ritual practice as developer of personhood.

---

1. I acknowledge my debt to Michael B. Aune for the term "design." See his "Ritual Practice," 170.

2. Bell, *Ritual Theory, Ritual Practice* (*RTRP*), 111, referring to Stanley Tambiah.

Catherine Bell

Ritual is so basic to being human that people are often unconscious of their own ritual patterns. But attempts to define ritual have failed. Anthropologists and ritual theorists did not accept anyone else's definition, so each wrote a new one—which did not function any better than the ones before. It was *Catherine Bell* who quit trying to define it.

Against theorizing that ritual is an isolatable thing, "some object to be analyzed," and against theorizing that ritual is a generalizable aspect of every activity, "some subjectivity to be fathomed," Catherine Bell has proposed that ritual, as practice, should appropriately be studied in its *doing*. In her *Ritual Theory, Ritual Practice*, she argues for a new way of practicing the theory of ritual:[3] by "[c]onfronting the ritual act itself," and looking there for "how ritual activities, in their doing, generate distinctions between what is or is not acceptable ritual."[4] It is from Bell that I introduce the term *ritualization* to refer to non-traditional ecclesial enactments conducted for and on behalf of those in the post-baptismal process of faith development, response-giving, and theosis.

Rather than seek a theoretical definition of ritual, a scholarly practice among ritual theorists and anthropologists which, however, has not yielded a satisfactory or universally accepted result, Bell took a different approach, recognizing how ritualization is not *au fond* a separate activity, but can be a part of any activity as it is practiced.[5] Because ritual is a *practice,* she turned toward *describing how it operates as practice,* identifying four aspects of practice (and thereby ritualization): it is *strategic, situated* (context-dependent), *misrecognized* (its operation is unconscious to the participants), and *redemptively hegemonic* (shifting power relationships).[6] The term "ritualization" is helpful because it frees her (and us) from presuming whether or not there is a full liturgy occurring, whether or not there is a large number of people *vs.* one or two, and whether or not there is a designated

---

3. Bell, *RTRP*, 13, and 13–66.

4. Ibid., 80.

5. See Bell's critique of the process by which definitions of ritual have been theoretically constructed but which conceal how it operates as a practice: *RTRP*, Part I, 13–66.

6. Ibid., 81–88.

person in charge. It frees students of ritual to think broadly about the huge variety of circumstances in which power may be shifted from person to person or God to person, and to apprehend the wide range and circumstances of ritualizing activity. Each of these four attributes will be fleshed out in turn.

First, ritual is *strategic:* specifically, it creates strategic contrasts that privilege the ritual action over the common non-ritual one. Bell describes ritualization as "*a way of acting that specifically establishes a privileged contrast.*"[7] Ritual is not "an action" or "a type of action," but *a way of acting* in a particular context that strategically privileges or frames certain behaviors over others, resulting in empowerment even though participants may not recognize that this is occurring. We offer three examples of privileged contrasts, two examples from Bell (one liturgical and one familial) and a third from Lawrence Hoffman. It will be valuable in reading each of these to notice how the strategic distinctions drawn are quite particular to the contexts, and how power or meaning or significance is leveraged through "interplay and contrast with other" more ordinary ways of acting.[8]

The first example is the contrast between the Christian eucharistic meal and an ordinary meal. Both are meals; but the Christian eucharist is distinguished from a common family meal, for example, in the usually much larger number of people who come to dine; in the configuration of the table and chairs; in its frequency (weekly instead of daily or several times a day); and in its amount of food (inadequate amount for actual bodily nourishment). In these ways (and others), the eucharist is "set apart" from an average meal, such that it bears meaning and power that ordinary meals do not. She notes that such ritualization privileges *this* meal over others, and gives it power, symbolic dominance, privilege, significance, meaning.

> Theoretically, ritualization of the meal could employ a different set of strategies to differentiate it from conventional eating, such as holding the meal only once in a person's lifetime or with too much food for normal nourishment. The choice of strategies would depend in part on which ones could most effectively render the meal symbolically dominant to its conventional counterparts. The choice would also depend on the particular "work" the ritualized acts aimed to accomplish in a

7. Ibid., 90 (emphasis added).
8. Ibid., 90.

situation. Given this analysis, ritualization could involve the exact repetition of a centuries-old tradition or deliberately radical innovation and improvisation, as in certain forms of liturgical experimentation or performance art.[9]

In terms of the "basic principle of privileged differentiation,"[10] what sets this meal apart and thus makes it holy is the way it is done that is special, distinct, extraordinary, and thereby "other." This creates a strategic distinction from, and relationship with, the particular time and place and situation to which it serves as contrast.

Typical characteristics of the Christian eucharist, such as its formality or the invariance of its text, could themselves serve as strategies which differentiate it from the ordinary in particular contexts. In other cultures (and denominations), for example, its informality, and even improvisation of its text, could draw contrasting distinctions to make the meal significant, dominant, or privileged. "For example, the formal activities of gathering for a Catholic mass distinguish this "meal" from daily eating activities, but the informality of a mass celebrated in a private home with a folk guitar and kitchen utensils is meant to set up another contrast ([e.g.,] the spontaneous authentic celebration versus the formal and inauthentic mass) which the informal service expects to dominate. It is only necessary that the cultural context include some consensus concerning the opposition and relative values of personal sincerity and intimate participation vis-à-vis routinized and impersonal participation."[11]

Her second example contrasts the ordinary supplying of gym socks to a child from the special, ritualized giving of, say, argyle socks for a birthday gift, even to that same child:

> These activities are differentiated in the very doing and derive their significance from the contrast implicitly set up between them. Routine giving plays off ritualized giving and vice versa; they define each other. *The Christian mass and the gift are not models for a normal meal or family shopping;*[12] *they are strategic*

---

9. Ibid., 90–91.
10. Ibid., 91.
11. Ibid., 92.
12. A reference to Clifford Geertz's point that cultural patterns are both "models of" relationships that exist and "models for" other relationships that could exist: reflections of what is and guidance for what might well be. "[C]ulture patterns have an intrinsic double aspect: they give meaning, that is, objective conceptual form,

versions of them. Yet this is not to say that ritualization is simply acting differently. Otherwise, buying mismatched socks at a bargain table—an act that may communicate simply insofar as it differs from a routine set of expectations—would qualify as ritual.[13]

The significance, power, and importance occurs *in the doing*, rather than intrinsically in the interpretation. A third example of contrast will illustrate. An empowerment or solemnity or intimacy, for example, may be given to meals preceded by the ritualization of prayer. Yet such prayer before eating has been interpreted, on the one hand, as "asking God's blessing on the food," and/or on the persons eating, such that they become "more sacred" than without the prayer. In contrast, Lawrence Hoffman has described the historic interpretation of table blessing as separating out the food about to be eaten from the realm of the sacred creation into the realm of profane (i.e., ordinary) so that it may fittingly and unblasphemously be eaten. Yet whichever interpretation is used, the ritualized blessing prayer distinguishes that meal from those with no prayer, and engenders importance, power, and/or meaning. "Much of Jewish life . . . revolves about acknowledging the distinction between the two realms: knowing where a blessing is in order, and where not; whether someone or something possesses sanctity, or its opposite. The very function of blessings over food, for example, is the releasing of holy produce from the earth (which belongs to God) so that it is no longer holy, but profane, and can thus be consumed by equally profane creatures (ourselves) living in a profane state."[14]

To summarize, "the significance of ritual behavior lies not in being an entirely separate way of acting but in how such activities constitute themselves as different and in contrast to other activities." "Acting ritually is first and foremost a matter of nuanced contrasts and the evocation of strategic, value-laden distinctions. Viewed as practice,

---

to social psychological reality both by shaping themselves to it and by shaping it to themselves." "Religion as a Cultural System," 93. See Bell's critique of Geertz, *RTRP*, 25–37 and *passim*.

13. Bell, *RTRP*, 91. Emphasis added.

14. Hoffman elaborates upon ritualization as drawing distinctions in *Beyond the Text*, 174. He goes on: "The world is made of holy space, holy time, holy people, holy acts, and holy things—and their opposites: that much has been at the core of classical Jewish identity . . . So the study of liturgy ought first to ask how liturgical rituals encode the world for those who ritualize." See especially chapters 8 ("Conclusion: A Holistic View of Liturgy," 172–82) and 2 ("*Havdalah*: A Case of Categories," 20–45).

ritualization involves the very drawing, in and through the activity itself, of a privileged distinction between ways of acting, specifically between those acts being performed and those being contrasted, mimed, or implicated somehow. That is, intrinsic to ritualization are strategies for differentiating itself."[15]

In addition to ritualization as practice being strategic, Bell identifies three other attributes. The second is that it is *situational*: "much of what is important to it cannot be grasped outside of the specific context in which it occurs."[16] Ritualization is contextual; it is inculturated; its meaning and power come out of the circumstances that give rise to it. An action, such as throwing a chalice to the ground, in one context may mean betrayal or excommunication; in another, it may be the celebrative seal of marriage vows just taken. Remembering that ritualizing is contextual inhibits the tendency to attach an absolute ahistorical meaning to any action or symbol, and thus to reify meanings. It further challenges the suggestion that "objective" outside observers might be able to apprehend the full meaning of a ritualization.

Third, drawing upon Pierre Bourdieu, Bell identifies as intrinsic to practice, and thereby to ritual practice, the *misrecognition* of the participants as to how the ritual action is making meaning for them. We have referred to Paul Tillich's notation that to be conscious of a symbol's power is to find that power lost, or broken.[17] Ritualization "works" inasmuch as participants do not see that it works or how it works: there is "misrecognition of its limits and constraints, and of the relationship between its ends and its means."[18]

And fourth, Bell generates the phrase *redemptive hegemony* to describe that power moves in the course of ritual acting.[19] In the privileging of some actions over others, power and importance are mediated in the contrast. "[R]itualization is first and foremost a strategy for the construction of certain types of power relationships effective within

15. Bell, *RTRP*, 90.
16. Ibid., 81.
17. Tillich, *Dynamics of Faith,* chapter 3, "Symbols of Faith," esp. 42–45. For more on this notion, see Neville, *The Truth of Broken Symbols*, x n. 3, 4.
18. Bell, *RTRP*, 82.
19. Bell generated this term as "a synthesis of Kenelm Burridge's notion of the 'redemptive process' and Antonio Gramsci's notion of 'hegemony.'" Ibid., 83. She cites Gramsci, *The Modern Prince*, 174–76 and 186–87; and Burridge, *New Heaven, New Earth*, 4–8.

particular social organizations."[20] This fourth attribute of practice involves "the motivational dynamics of agency, the will to act."[21] Bell understands hegemony to imply "a lived system of meanings, a more or less unified moral order, which is confirmed and nuanced in experience to construct a person's sense of reality and identity. [This involves a] practical awareness of the world [a]s a lived ordering of power, a construal of power that is also, inevitably, a misconstrual since it is power as envisioned and encountered in very particular situations. . . . [H]egemony [is] not only . . . a lived consciousness and moral order, but also . . . a prestige order."[22] Bell combines this notion of hegemony with Burridge's definition of the redemptive process in which persons "attempt to discharge their obligations in relation to the moral imperatives of the community."[23]

In ritualization, then, a person or community can literally be empowered. In the distinguishing of some things, actions, people, and words from the ordinary, significance and importance—and power—accrue to them. Power is reordered. Redemptive hegemony "denotes the way in which reality is experienced as a natural weave of constraint and possibility, the fabric of day-to-day dispositions and decisions experienced as a field for strategic action. Rather than an embracing ideological vision of the whole, it conveys a biased, nuanced rendering of the ordering of power so as to facilitate the envisioning of personal empowerment through activity in the perceived system."[24] "As such, of course, the redemptive hegemony of practice does not reflect reality more or less effectively; it creates it more or less effectively."[25]

We have, then, from Bell, a term that refers to a way of acting, which empowers people in particular circumstances in an interplay with the ordinary by drawing strategic contrasts. Ritualization "*does things*"[26] that need doing and that cannot be done in other ways. This brief discussion of Bell's insights into studying ritual as practice reveals

20. Bell, *RTRP*, 197.
21. Ibid., 83.
22. Ibid. Bell cites David Laitin, *Hegemony and Culture*, 19.
23. Burridge, *New Heaven, New Earth*, 6; quoted in Bell, *RTRP*, 84.
24. Bell, *RTRP*, 84.
25. Ibid., 85.
26. Ibid., 111. Roland Delattre calls this "going through motions," which is "spiritually formative" for persons. "Ritual Resourcefulness," 282.

some things about how *ritualization* works. This term and concept can enable us to conceive of how post-baptismal enactments on behalf of baptized persons can be effective in empowering them on the journey of maturing in Christ.

Ronald Grimes

If Bell is a theoretician of practice, studying with the dispassion of a social scientist how practice works, *Ronald L. Grimes* lives more over the line of theorizing into the practice of ritualizing.[27] As anthropologist and field student, Grimes has observed rites and ritualizations, critiqued them, and conducted them. As Grimes describes it, "[r]itual criticism is the interpretation of a rite or ritual system with a view to implicating its practice"[28]—a feedback system wherein what we learn from reflecting upon one rite we may use as we design the next one. Among the principles Grimes has been in process of formulating since he founded the Ritual Studies group at the AAR in 1977[29] is that of *ritualizing*, which he calls "the process whereby ritual creativity is exercised."[30]

The notion of *ritual creativity* or *generative ritualizing* is of interest to Christian liturgists, both in its embrace and in its resistance. Free church pastors, who generate their own Sunday orders of worship, tend to be ready to be creative, and are likely to embrace Grimes' notion of nascent ritual (even though the term "ritual" may be resisted as implying ritual*ism* or empty, meaningless action).[31] In contrast, liturgical pastors, who carry out denominational liturgical orders for the sake of continuity with the received tradition, tend toward a positive view of liturgy and ritual. At the same time, following Tillich's point

---

27. For a helpful synopsis and comparison of the thinking of Catherine Bell, Ronald Grimes, and others, see Mitchell, *Liturgy Digest* (1993), 2–151.

28. Grimes, *Deeply Into the Bone*, 293. See also Grimes, *Ritual Criticism*, 16.

29. See Smith, *Christian Ritualizing*, Part I, chapter 1, n.4 for a brief history of the field of ritual studies and its intersection with liturgical studies.

30. Grimes, "Defining Nascent Ritual," 55.

31. But note the general resistance of evangelicals to positive ideas of liturgy or ritual. Yet for an evangelical treatment of ritual theory and ritual in Scripture, see Klingbeil, *Bridging the Gap* (2007), a work which sets the stage for openness. He concludes with the suggestion that ritual elements "may enable us to communicate profound theology in ways that are easily remembered and memorized," 236.

that symbols cannot be invented,[32] they may not be eager to "invent" rituals.

Nonetheless, even the briefest excursion into history reveals that certain innovation, or at least strategic contrast, has been a constant part of Christian liturgy. In Milan, for example, the baptismal liturgy included foot washing; we have no records of this practice in other locations, nor is it typically done today. Grimes has variously referred to the result of ritualizing as "nascent ritual"[33] and "emerging ritual."[34] Some neophyte ritualizing is "intentionally chosen," he points out, "but others arise spontaneously or preconsciously"[35] (Bell: *misrecognition*). People invent ritualizations for all kinds of occasions. Here is one of Grimes' examples: "Emerging ritual is what transpires when an intertribal group of native Canadians and Native Americans has to invent a rite to rebury ancestral bones repatriated from the 18,000 native skeletons held by the Smithsonian institution."[36]

Ritualizing is also what occurs when a President is inaugurated; when roadside places are marked where loved ones were killed; with dancing in the streets when a city's baseball team wins the World Series or country's rugby team wins the World Cup; keeping silence at the Tomb of the Unknown Soldier; breaking into Spirit-filled song.[37]

We make a move, now, from the practice of studying about ritualization to proposing the practice of ritualization: from the *descriptive* perspective of social science, to the *prescriptive* perspective of what Grimes calls ritual criticism.[38] Grimes' category of nascent or emerg-

---

32. "Symbols cannot be produced intentionally—this is the fifth characteristic. They grow out of the individual or collective unconscious and cannot function without being accepted by the unconscious dimension of our being." Tillich, *Dynamics of Faith*, 43.

33. Grimes, "Defining Nascent Ritual."

34. Grimes, "Emerging Ritual," 23–37.

35. Grimes, "Defining Nascent Ritual," 56.

36. Grimes, "Emerging Ritual," 23.

37. In another example, it is what occurred on March 11, 2002, when, on the six-month anniversary of the destruction of the twin towers of the World Trade Center in New York City, two spotlight beams were placed where the towers had been, so that two columns of light replaced the towers for a solemn ceremony.

38. As John Witvliet has clarified, liturgists have much to learn from social scientists, but their purpose is distinct. "For liturgists, far more so than anthropologists, approach their work with a vested interest in promoting certain ideals... *In contrast, liturgists who aspire to a pastoral function in an ecclesial community intend not only*

ing ritual offers us a category within which to consider the very real ongoing and significant practices of people who generate ritualizations, both secular and religious.

Theodore Jennings

Grimes is not the only one to identify this generative character of ritualization. *Theodore Jennings*, a systematic theologian, writes that ritual is a source of knowledge. In an essay entitled "On Ritual Knowledge," Jennings writes that as ritual functions noetically, ritual repetition transmits knowledge; but *ritual variation generates new knowledge*. He states that "ritual action is a way of gaining knowledge"[39] which is generated through shifts and changes in ritual action. For those who might be inclined to assert that ritual (or liturgy) is unchangeable, Jennings argues that even so-called repetitive ritual actions do vary: "A diachronic perspective on ritual, together with a cross-cultural comparison of putatively identical rituals, brings to light considerable variation which cannot be accounted for by the view of ritual action as sheer repetition."[40]

Thus, as ritual actions change and modify, new knowledge is created for the participants. This is true, he avers, because ritual is "an autonomous . . . mode of the religious imagination"[41]—not merely derivative, not senseless, but rather may serve as a noetic "mode of inquiry and discovery."[42] As Mark Searle expressed it, ritual participants come away with new knowledge that "dawns upon" the participants[43] in the course of its enactment, which is "a bodily action which alters the

---

to describe existing ritual practice but also to envision a liturgical ideal, to diagnose ritual pathology, to discern exemplary ritual improvisations, and to prescribe appropriate ritual adaptation . . . [L]iturgists are ultimately about the business of *prescription*, of carrying out *an essentially normative discipline.*" "For Our Own Purposes," 24 (emphasis in original). Liturgy is, in a sense, applied theology. As Witvliet, and others (ibid., 19) have pointed out, liturgists must be good self-observers and good participant observers so as to recognize the values they bring to liturgical assessment. But liturgists use ritual studies and other social sciences for support in what is primarily a practical theological discipline, not a scientific one.

39. Jennings, "On Ritual Knowledge," 112.
40. Ibid., 113.
41. Ibid., 114.
42. Ibid., 112.
43. Searle, "Ritual," 57.

world or the place of the ritual participant in the world."[44] According to Jennings, the way knowledge is gained in ritual "is primarily corporeal rather than cerebral, primarily active rather than contemplative, primarily transformative rather than speculative."[45] Knowledge is generated in embodied doing and acting, through engagement (not detachment),[46] and through altering the world—for not only children but also adults come to know the world by shaping it, engaging with it, encountering and modifying it.[47] In ritual change there is generated new knowledge, new meaning, additional or "a surplus" of meaning as Paul Ricoeur would say.[48] Therefore, ritual forms as they repeat and as they vary, are "basic to theological reflection"[49]; and more than reflection, ritual "teaches one . . . how to conduct oneself outside the ritual space . . . a ritual is 'falsified' to the extent to which it cannot serve as a paradigm for significant action outside the ritual itself."[50] Jennings calls this "praxological" knowledge.[51] Implied for those concerned with the ongoing life of the baptized is that ritualization generates certain kinds of knowledge that may be fruitful for ongoing conversion and formation more and more into the likeness of God.

Roland Delattre

In addition to Grimes and Jennings, *Roland Delattre* asserts that what is needed in the current era is not merely ritual but "ritual competence":[52] the ability to ritualize. In his article "Ritual Resourcefulness and

44. Jennings, "On Ritual Knowledge," 115.

45. Ibid.

46. Ibid., 116.

47. "[T]he world is known by being changed or transformed . . . [R]itual does not depict the world so much as it founds or creates the world." Jennings, "On Ritual Knowledge," 116.

48. The published version of a series of lectures Ricoeur gave at Texas Christian University in 1973 was entitled, *Interpretation Theory: Discourse and the Surplus of Meaning*.

49. Jennings, "On Ritual Knowledge," 111.

50. Ibid., 118–19. Lawrence A. Hoffman calls this transfer of "the way we act in ritual" to "the way we act in the world outside of ritual" ritual's *normative meaning*. The ethical implications are clear. Hoffman, "How Ritual Means," 78–97.

51. Jennings, "On Ritual Knowledge," 123.

52. Delattre, "Ritual Resourcefulness," 285, 294.

Cultural Pluralism," Delattre makes this claim: "In a pluralistic culture such as our own, what is required is not simply the mastery of a particular series of ritual performances, but the development of a virtual repertoire of ritual capacities together with both individual and collective resourcefulness in mobilizing them."[53]

Delattre calls for rites generated in public life, both on behalf of sub-cultural groups, and also ritualizations which will enable civility among a common though culturally diverse humanity. This requires a knowledge of how to ritualize, a skill which for many families is not on the list of things to teach the children or things to learn growing up.

Mary Collins

Mary Collins belongs to a religious group which cultivates ritual competence. A Benedictine sister and liturgical scholar, she recounts how a group of (ritually competent) religious women evolved a contemporary theology of religious profession through the process of developing and enacting their rites.[54] Because the rite of monastic profession for women had been historically merged with a rite for consecration of virgins,[55] some actions, words, gestures, and symbols came not to fit with post-Vatican II liturgical theology and the focus and intent of contemporary professing women. Beginning to doff the male-generated, male-led, male-theologized construction of "women's spiritual identity in terms of physical virginity or its absence," women have begun to take charge of their own vow-taking and to set the terms of their vocational commitment to God within their own communities. And through 214 documentations of monastic profession rites over a twenty-five-year period,[56] Collins has found that this process of reclaiming and theologizing has occurred *through ritualizing*. "Unlike their male counterparts who reformed their rites by producing new texts, the women have reformed their liturgical rites [of monastic profession] through [embodied] ritualizing . . . [T]he particular mon-

---

53. Delattre, "Ritual Resourcefulness," 281–82.
54. Collins, "An Adventuresome Hypothesis," 37–49.
55. Ibid., 43.
56. Ibid., 42.

asteries have been directly involved in this work of conserving and producing an authentic tradition of women's monastic profession."[57]

We find, then, from Ronald Grimes and others a *theory of nascent or generative ritualizing* that legitimates and accounts for the phenomenon of ritual change and development. The concept of generative ritual and its verb *to ritualize* suggest a category of thinking for liturgically-inclined persons wishing to pastor persons struggling to mature through stages of baptismal life and to respond in thanksgiving to God. Bell's elucidation of four ways ritualization operates to reorder power implies that rites originating outside the seven sacraments named by Lombard could be employed by the church on behalf of the baptized. And Grimes teaches *ritual criticism* as a practice of interpreting ritualizations in order to develop them and make them operationally effective.

Michael Aune

Finally, from *Michael Aune*, a liturgical theologian who comes to ritual studies from the standpoint of ritual critic,[58] comes the point that religious ritual "can be an interpretation of 'what it means to be a particular kind of person.'"[59] According to Aune, ritualization "involves a changed technology of power as well as a different moral economy of the self."[60] Related to individual becoming is the becoming of a particular kind of community,[61] which both derives from and leads to the former. The empowerment that occurs in ritualizing includes "divine power, now available in word and sacrament," to ritual participants, effecting change in the person(s), creating faith, empowering for ethical response. Jennings' praxological knowledge that carries over into life

---

57. Ibid., 45.

58. Aune, "The Subject of Ritual," 149: "How I became a ritual critic," and *passim*.

59. "The Subject of Ritual." Aune takes the quotation from Howard Eilberg-Schwartz, paper delivered to the Religious Studies group of the American Academy of Religion, San Francisco, 1992. Becoming a particular kind of person is also the concern of Don Saliers, who writes about cultivating religious affection, inner orientations and dispositions, in *The Soul in Paraphrase* and *Worship Come to its Senses*. Aune explores this notion in depth in his book *'To Move the Heart'*: for example, 63, 106ff.

60. Aune, "Ritual Practice," 160.

61. Ibid., 161.

after liturgy is, according to Aune, "an experiential knowledge that orients a person to others, to the world, and to God[62]—which is the essence of operational efficacy.[63] This is a key concept since this is the point of adulting in Christ, or theosis: it is to *become* fully human, to grow and change more and more into the likeness of God-in-Christ-and-the-Spirit. It is to become a particular kind of person, one who is oriented as Christ is oriented, toward truth, hope, awe, delight,[64] gratitude, holy fear and repentance, joy, love of God and neighbor.[65] Aune opens up for us Luther's associate in the Reformation, Philip Melanchthon, who wrote with lucidity two perspectives, which correlate to the terms doctrinal efficacy and operational efficacy. Melanchthon refers to dialectic and rhetoric: *docere*, the teaching of what we need to learn, and *movere*, the exciting of the passion to act, the awakening of a disposition of heart or orientation of a life: "[D]ialectics must be used to show what virtue is, and what are its causes, its degrees, and its effects. But when [Melanchthon] exhorts people to be virtuous, the principles of rhetoric must be followed. When we discourse about penance, the principles of dialectics must be used to teach [women and] men what penance is and what are its degrees. But the principles of rhetoric must be used to exhort [people] to do penance."[66]

---

62. Ibid., 166.

63. I am indebted to Michael Aune who first brought to my attention Moore's and Myerhoff's distinction between operational and doctrinal efficacy. See, for example, Aune, "Ritual Practice," 157–58 *passim*. At the same time, the Lutheran understanding of the Word as embodied extends the impact of doctrinal efficacy into the operational. As Aune says, "[I]f God's own self has been given to the world, it follows that what we have traditionally called doctrine constitutes an invitation to entrust ourselves to this world's ongoing history with God and our experience of it. Doctrine is much more than a list of items to be believed. It is an activity . . . of interpretation and transmission of the ongoing experience of God's redeeming presence in Christ." Aune, "Ritual Practice," 172–73.

64. These are the four Christian dispositions suggested by Don Saliers in *Worship Come to Its Senses*.

65. These are the religious affections Don Saliers includes in *The Soul in Paraphrase*.

66. LaFontaine, "Melanchthon's 'Elementorum Rhetorices,'" 85–86. In Aune, *"To Move the Heart,"* 27.

Conclusion

Returning, then, to our claim that non-traditional ecclesial enactments in the post-baptismal Christian life can and should occur because of the very dynamism of adulting-in-Christ, we are strengthened in our proposal by ritual theories of ritual generation and that knowledge can arise out of such ritualizing. As the baptized find themselves at a moment of seeking or conversion into the next step in Christ, or in situations of weakness, or at a life crisis or turning-point, we can begin to imagine how some pastoral persons, with the competence to engender ritualizing strategies, and who know the baptized in their particular context, might be able to assist them in generating ritualizations which could strengthen them, empower them to let go or to reach toward something new, or to mark a new spiritual place or conviction or commitment at the brink of which they find themselves. Let us, then, turn to the baptized life. What is the role of liturgy, or rather, as we shall now call it, *Christian ecclesial ritualization*, in the ongoing conversion and maturing of the baptized in Christ-and-the-Holy Spirit?

10

Praxological Becoming and Ritual Competence
A Call for Baptismal Ingemination

A Proposal: Christian Ritualizing as Post-Baptismal Practice for Becoming like God

TO BE BAPTIZED IS TO BE UNITED WITH CHRIST IN HIS DEATH AND resurrection and to be incorporated into Christ's body, the church, the *ecclesia,* the ones "called out." It is to be washed, cleansed, and freed of sin, made a new creation. Once baptized, always baptized: one cannot be "un-baptized." One's state is forever changed. Like being married or birthing a child, there is no undoing the fact that one's state has been changed.

But in order for this change in status of one baptized to be overtly made real, to be *realized,* to be witnessed, and yes, to "take," more is required. Not from God: for God has acted, and the change has been made. But more is required *from the baptized in order for this change to be made manifest.* To *realize* the church as the baptized, to make baptismal ecclesiology *real,* requires its operational effectiveness, its working out in the world.[1]

---

1. Even in denominations where the most common practice is infant baptism, adult baptism continues to be theologically normative, since discipleship in Christ always arises out of *freedom* and signifies *conversion or turning* (*metanoia,* repentance) from one's former way to Christ, the Way. Infants cannot freely choose Christ; they cannot intend to turn; newborns have no personal sin to turn from. The expectation is always that the child will grow in the Christian faith, and in the fullness of time *will* freely choose, and make a profession of faith. As the BEM document points out, to baptize infants outside the community of faith, or where there is no reasonable promise of their being raised so as to follow the Way of Christ, is to practice *indiscriminate baptism.* Such baptism outside the proleptic probability of free choice and faith profession later truncates doctrinal effectiveness and loosens the possibility of

What is this "more" that is baptism being "made real"? We have seen that it is an ongoing process of *maturing in faith* (Fowler), *growing into God* (theosis) in continuing *conversion*. And throughout this process of becoming, baptism continues to be made real in intentional *offering back to God* one's life in *thanks-giving, as response-gift*. Baptism, in other words, not only culminates a conversionary process (when there is one), but it also intends to *begin a post-baptismal process of deification and self-offering in response to God's baptismal grace*.

Inasmuch as the churches claim this process as part of ministry, the realization of baptismal ecclesiology will grow. Inasmuch as the churches intentionally enable the baptized to *practice their becoming in Christ by the Spirit*, the baptized will come to realize more and more their part in Christ's ministry and will be able to lean into the growing into which the Spirit invites them.

How shall the baptized practice their becoming? How might the churches enable the *praxological becoming* of the baptized? The early catechumenate marked stages in pre-baptismal conversion with rites, reclaimed in the contemporary catechumenate as rites of admission and enrollment, leading up to the rite of Holy Baptism. And recent ritual studies show how ritual can effect a change that cannot be done in any other way. Praxological becoming, then, will happen *ritually*. Rituals of passage, healing, and vocational change can enable the baptismal maturing process of ongoing sanctification and self-offering.

In the last chapter, we introduced Ronald Grimes' definition of ritual criticism as interpretation of a ritual system with a view to implicating its practice.[2] It is in such a prescriptive mode of ritual criticism that we propose adapting the pre-baptismal catechumenal practice of liturgical ritualization as an intentional post-baptismal practice for the baptized to enable them to embody more and more fully the reign of God. We propose the intentional re-casting of the catechumenal

---

experiential effectiveness. Baptism signifies an intimate relationship with Jesus Christ in the Holy Spirit, and it is the church's responsibility not to condone baptism where this meaning is not either extant or proleptically likely. That is, like other covenants in which God initiates but does not force a response, baptism is a covenant initiated by God and offered as gift—and calls for a relational *response-gift*. See my article, "Confirmation" (2000), parsing the liturgical hermeneutics of needful human response to God's graceful gift in baptism.

2. "*Ritual criticism is the interpretation of a rite or ritual system with a view to implicating its practice*. Because ritual criticism is itself a practice, it implies a politics and an ethic, as well as an aesthetic or poetics" (Grimes, *Ritual Criticism*, 16).

model toward an ongoing process for the baptized that they may grow into the likeness of God and that their part in Christ's ministry in the world may deepen, from baptism at whatever age to their second baptism at death. The rhythm of life-experience and prayer-study is a central part of this process, although naming touchstones of that part of the rhythm is not our task here.[3] It is, however, our liturgical task to consider the role and practice of punctiliar ritualization in this post-baptismal theopoetic rhythm. Based upon our findings in the Tradition, and in Irenaeus, Chauvet, and Fowler, we are ready to assert for the churches' worshipful sacramental life:

> It is fitting in the post-Christendom church to engage in creating and conducting appropriate ritualizations for the baptized in support of their adulting process of theosis, for the sake of realizing the church as constituted of all the baptized. *These ritualizations would enable response to baptismal grace at significant moments in a Christian life. They would employ strategic contrasts, use of symbols, and contextual propriety, so as to hold doctrinal and operational efficacies as equally significant.*

This proposal is timely now, in the twenty-first-century, as North America moves away from Christendom. For in Christendom in general, it was not deemed necessary to work with individual baptized persons to awaken them and intentionally support them in their discipleship. It seemed to happen as a matter of course. The ones who wanted to give themselves over to a purposeful openness to the Spirit tended to enter "religious life" as clergy or monastics (living in community as priority) or apostolic religious (ministerial work as priority), while mainstream baptized were ironically considered "secular" Christians. People showed up at church or didn't, followed the church's calendar or didn't. But when the dominant culture expressed Christian values and symbols, it did not seem necessary to approach individual Christians' joys or agonies with pastoral or liturgical guidance or mediation. Christian interpretations of life's pains and gifts were generally available, and people seemed to know well enough how to support one another.

---

3. In addition to myriad Christian education curricula that are effective for Sunday School and church camp, there are several programs with a wider compass which draw participants into the connection between faith and life. Examples include *Education for Ministry* with its method of theological reflection (University of the South, TN; Episcopal); the *Crossways Series* and *The Divine Drama* (Augsburg-Fortress, Lutheran); and the *Kerygma* series (Presbyterian).

Now, however, the situation has changed. In the marketplace of religious ideas, people may assume Jesus died and was reincarnated, or his body died but his Spirit didn't—leaving the Jewish-Christian understanding of resurrection generally unavailable, even to the baptized who are covenanted into this very died-and-resurrected Christ.

Yet the flow of "Christian existence" (Chauvet), which is the sacramental "rhythm that makes life human" (Guzie), includes story (of which Scripture is primary touchstone) and ethics (including reflection on the lived experience of ethical decisions)—which are pulled together, condensed, and realized by *liturgical celebration* (Guzie: "festivity"; Chauvet: "sacrament").

In the next chapter, I will offer five principles for grounding intentionally-created ritualizations of passage, healing, and vocational change as three typically significant moments in Christian ecclesial life. However, it is first important to attend to two critiques that may leave some unsure whether this post-Christendom proposal of intentional ritual-making is justified: one critique from each end of the liturgical spectrum.

Attending to Two Critiques

From *the liturgical end* may come reservations at the idea of "making up" rituals. After all, we have already noted Tillich's point that symbols cannot be engendered by a person because they arise out of the collective (or individual) unconscious; and since symbol is the smallest unit of ritual (as Victor Turner asserted),[4] liturgical critics will also challenge the idea of creating rituals. The sacraments of the church are *received*, not "made up," the argument goes.

From the *evangelical or free church end* may come reservations at the idea of rituals or liturgies as helpful at all. After all, the sixteenth-century Reformation extricated Protestants from *ritualism*, from medieval priest-craft where "hocus pocus" was said in a language the people did not understand, and some magic change was said to occur. There can be resistance to any kind of worshipful "formula" where the same thing "must" be repeated week by week, and there is belief (and sometimes, experience) that "traditional worship is boring." The critique, then, is that engaging some form of "ritual" to help carry persons across dangerous passages or painful woundedness, or even into

---

4. Turner, *The Forest of Symbols*, 19.

God-given work, is suspect. Until the end of the twentieth century, Protestant chaplains used word—conversation, pastoral counseling—to help people, eschewing ritual actions like anointing, chanting, or blessing. Besides, has not over-attachment to ritual patterns blinded church leaders to the central role of the Holy Spirit in caring for persons? It is the Holy Spirit who enables care for people, not ritual, the argument goes.

Both these critiques are valuable and point to errors lurking on each extreme. There is indeed a risk, as the evangelical critique would note, of being too rigid or reified about ritual action, even jumping to a ritual "solution" without adequately listening and comprehending what is at stake for the vulnerable focal person. And the Holy Spirit is indeed a central Player in any sacramental or ritual effectiveness. To trust in ritual action itself, without turning to the Referent and Source of ritual efficacy, can indeed lead to empty or meaningless action. Some evangelical and/or free church critics will argue against intentionally generating rites because ritual is bad, empty, dead, and meaningless. They will argue that the sixteenth-century Reformation was fought to eliminate the problem of dead ritual. Reformers rightly challenged priestly authority from one historic period when many priests did abuse their ritual power, and they claimed biblical authority instead.

Yet Jesus was one who honored the religious rituals, while altering them for the sake of healing and giving life. For example, he prayed for the ten lepers, and then sent them to the priest for the proper ritual action (Luke 17:12–19). He honored and fulfilled the Sabbath, although for the sake of enabling fullness of life, he healed the bent-over woman on that day, reminding onlookers that animals were still allowed to drink on the Sabbath (Luke 13:10–17). He kept in mind the *purpose* of the structure, rituals, and laws, using them to fulfill their true purpose.

Thus, while ritual action (and any pattern used legalistically apart from the spirit of its purpose) can indeed be empty or meaningless, nonetheless, as servant for life-giving compassion, ritual can also be a powerful mediator of the Spirit of God. And honoring this critique from the evangelical extreme should not adumbrate the very real Spirit-filled giftedness possible in corporate worshipful ritual action. To refuse to acknowledge the powerful ways the Holy Spirit moves through the collective action of Christians gathered together in ritual structure is to deny the necessity of weekly worship. The churches' primary corporate action is to gather in the Lord's name on the day of Resurrection (or the Sabbath day), week by week, in order to praise God and to be renewed before God by the Word and Holy Spirit. Whatever the style of worship, whether authorized or free, traditional or contemporary, the people of God *do worship together weekly*. Christians have a *worshipful, liturgical way of life*, even though the variety may be great. It is fitting that this festival, sacramental way of life be extrapolated toward periodic ritualizations for the sake of enabling the ones baptized into Christ to turn toward and live ever more deeply into Christ, by the Holy Spirit.

The first (liturgical) critique, calling for reserve in "making up" rituals, also points to an honest risk. Being too cavalier about ritual action, too quick to jump to ritual solutions, can lead to a functional mentality of presuming that saying the right prayer or engaging the right symbol will have the desired effect, even without faith or prayerful or loving intention. Bell has shown that ritual shifts and mediates power, but for good or ill. Ritual action is powerful. There is danger in ritualizing out of ego, or without ritual knowledge, or apart from prayer.

Other liturgical critics will argue against intentionally generating rites because they understand that Christian symbol and ritual is "handed down" (the meaning of "tradition"), and has authority because its source finally is God. Yet not all symbols are received.

It is true that fundamental or *archetypal* symbols, what Victor Turner called "dominant" symbols,[5] do arise out of a collective and are not under the control of an individual. These, like water, fire, mother, circles, earth, are common to the human family. Paul Tillich simply called these "symbols" because they participate in what they point to.[6] Water, for example, is an archetypal symbol for cleansing because washing with water actually makes things clean. Fire is a symbol of purity because the heat of fire literally refines and purifies.

---

5. My definitions are similar to but not the same as those Turner named in his study of Ndembu ritual. The symbols he called *dominant* have a meaning that they retain from rite to rite. *Instrumental* symbols are used to attain a goal in a particular ritual context. See "Symbols in Ndembu Ritual," 30–32, 45; on dominant symbols, see also ibid., 22. On the process of *symbolization*, see Langer, *Philosophy in a New Key*.

6. Tillich's definition of symbol, something that participates in that to which it points, is similar to Thomas Aquinas's definition of *sacrament*: sacraments effect what they signify, or (as we have seen in Thomas) effect by signifying.

However, there are also particular or *localized* symbols that are not necessarily handed down. Such context-specific symbols, what Turner called "instrumental" symbols, arise out of meaning-associations people make for one another day by day. A striking example of such a localized symbol was a high quality cigar given to my colleague on her last visit to an elderly man in the parish, just before he died. They had shared a long-standing practice of smoking together whenever they would visit. But she saved this last cigar, and smoked it during his funeral sermon. It was a very moving symbol of this man, of caring, of giving one's best, of friendship continuing after death, even of communion. It was perfect in that situation. But a cigar smoked during a funeral sermon in most situations would be demeaning, insulting, even violating of the deceased.

The practice of making metaphors and engaging them to operate in people's lives is a symbolic function needed for meaning-making. Regis Duffy has given the term *symbolic competence* to one of the skills needed among effective pastors.[7] Liturgical structures are also indeed handed down, but recent scholarship has been disabusive of the idea that the work of today's liturgists is to exactly reproduce the *ur-liturgy* of the past, presumably prescribed by Christ himself. To the contrary, Paul Bradshaw has demonstrated that there is no evidence of an *ur-liturgy*.[8] At a lecture once when speaker and respondents were discussing how to be sure "*The* Liturgy" was being followed, Bradshaw challenged the group with the reply, "There *is no 'the liturgy!*'"[9]

Catherine Bell also studied the way in which ritual legitimates "tradition" even while changing it. It is the very nature of ritual, she noted, to adapt to its context, as well as to change its context by its performance. As she put it, "The role of myth and ritual in oral societies

---

7. Regis Duffy, *An American Emmaus*, uses the term "symbolic competence." Kenan Osborne writes, "Regis Duffy, in an essay on the sacraments, has a section on the future of sacrament. In this forward glance to the third millennium, he indicates that there are three major unresolved issues for the mission of the church:

1. The cultural context of evangelization and sacrament.
2. the role of the Holy Spirit and its ecumenical corollaries;
3. symbolic competence in a post-industrial age and its corollary, the responsible reception of sacraments" (Regis Duffy, "Sacraments," 2:205ff., in Osborne, *Christian Sacraments*, 39).

8. Bradshaw, *Search for the Origins of Christian Liturgy*.
9. Bradshaw at the University of Notre Dame, South Bend, Indiana, 1992–93.

is to enhance, enforce, and codify cultural attitudes, something they can do best if they are continually brought into some sort of fit with the current circumstances of the community . . . In this social context, the authority of the ritual expert and the authority of the ritual itself are rooted in tradition—yet tradition is something that exists nowhere but in its flexible embodiment in memory and in current cultural life."[10]

Thus, respect for the received tradition is good, and both reserve and care are part of the symbolic and ritual competences needed for the making of life-giving, prayerful, holy Christian ritual. Yet the worry about violating meaning and authority in creating rituals can best be served not by resistance to engendering rites, but rather by exercising and cultivating prayerful, Spirit-filled openness, as well as thoughtful, studied competence in the process of making rites in order to lead the baptized toward their maturation, healing, and Christ-like living. Aware of risks, pastors can avoid dangers and turn toward deeper sacramental living. The worshipful, liturgical way of life Christians may be unaware they are living has, nonetheless, cultivated a ritual sensibility among many. To dare to engage in ritualizing moments of dangerous opportunity indeed requires a humble spirit as well as *ritual competence*—but humility and ritual competence can be developed. The principles in the next chapter intend to serve the goal of ritual competence as a step in mitigating these risks.

We can honor the two critiques, then, by avoiding both extremes. And we can honor the church's ritual knowledge resulting from its worshipful/ liturgical way of life, and the prospective ritual competence of its ritual leaders, through the making of rituals of passage, healing, and vocation. Such competent rite-making can open the way for churches to enable the baptized to grow into God, to arouse them in their own self-giving, to strengthen them in offering their God-given gifts, and to enliven the whole church through the ministry of all the baptized, the full Body of Christ.

The call to ritualizing changes and dangers and sanctifying moments in the baptized life is a call to a middle way between these two errors. Ironically, the extreme risks lead to a middle ground that can be a common ground for those on both the liturgical and evangelical/ free ends. The rigidity feared on one end, and the over-functionality risked on the other end, are both put to rest with a look at the tradi-

10. Bell, "Authority of Ritual Experts," 106.

tion, which did not start with rigidity, either in its practice or in its theology. Neither the idea that liturgy is received and should not be "messed with," nor the idea that ritual is a bad word because it is used against those trying to worship in Spirit and in Truth, is finally supported by the tradition.

A final look at the unexpected historical variety and diversity of ritualization related to baptism, and the evolution of its interpretation, may free both liturgically- and evangelically-oriented Christians to recognize not only the value but the critical importance of engaging in ritualization for the sake of opening and sustaining the baptized to grow more and more into the shape of Christ and into the fulfillment of his ministry.

Rigidity and Flexibility in the Received Baptismal Tradition

The history of theology and practice of baptism is part of the history of sacramental theology as it has intersected with the evolution of philosophy in order to understand and articulate what sacrament is, and how and when it works. This history of understanding and interpretation is a history of analysis through division of concepts into reified and definable components. In the early fifth century, for example, Augustine pointed to three factors which conjoin to make a sacrament: word, element, and faith. Examining baptism in his commentary on John 15:3, he says,

> Take away the word and what is water but water? The word is joined to the element and the result is a sacrament, itself becoming, in a sense, a visible word as well. For in that very word, whereas the actual sound is transitory, the power remains . . . Whence this power of water so exalted as to bathe the body and cleanse the soul, if it is not through the action of the word; not because it is spoken, but because it is believed? . . . This word of faith is of such efficacy in the Church of God that it washes clean not only the one who believes in the word, the one who presents [the child for baptism], the one who sprinkles [the child], but the child itself, be it ever so tiny, even though it is as yet incapable of believing.[11]

11. *Treatise on the Gospel of John*, 80:3, on John 15:3 (c. 416): PL 35:1840, emphasis added: "*Accedit verbum ad elementum.*" Translated in *St. Augustine: Homilies on the Gospel of John*.

Augustine recognized a relationship between the word, the action, and the faith, to create a powerful and effective "visible word" which not only changed the one baptized, but spilled over onto other participants in the rite. Augustine pointed to *what* contributed to the meaningful power of God's sacramental action: word, action, faith. He was not concerned about *how* the meaning was specifically effected, however.

But by the ninth century, philosophical theologians began to try to pin down exactly how sacrament worked and to concretize or reify how Christ was present. These struggles for sacramental understanding are most obvious in the arguments related to Holy Communion or eucharist. The attempt to locate Christ's presence in a specific "thing" contributed to the discussion, for example, as to not merely *that* the bread was Christ present, but *how* the bread was turned into the body of Christ. One of the earliest treatises extant is that of Paschasius Radbertus—monk (and later abbot) of the Abbey at Corbie (France)— who wrote "On the Body and Blood of the Lord" in which he took up these questions. His answer to the question of *how* Christ was present was that the historical Jesus was *physically* present *in the bread and wine*, which, following consecration, only looked like bread and wine but were "really" flesh and blood. To say otherwise was to suggest that Christ was present in figure or image (*figura*) but not in truth (*veritas*). For Radbertus, Christ's physical presence was required in order for Christ to be really present in truth.[12]

But Radbertus' interpretation was not the only theological perspective. In contrast, his fellow monk, Ratramnus, understood the essential "thing" (*res*) to be the "invisible divine thing signified" (not the physical earthly presence); and mediating the "invisible divine" were the bread and wine, which were the *sacramentum*: the "visible earthly sign."[13] For Ratramnus, it was not necessary to believe that chewing the wafer would crunch Jesus' bones in order to believe that Christ was really present, since to be present in figure *was* to be present in truth.[14]

The conversation over the understanding as to how Christ was really present became more polemical as it continued into the eleventh

---

12. For a lucid exposition of this controversy, see Mitchell, *Cult and Controversy*, 73–86; 137–51.

13. Ibid., 143.

14. From the faith development perspective, we might distinguish these points of view as individuative-reflective and conjunctive, respectively.

century. It also expanded into the question of *when* the bread and wine became the body of Christ: Did the words of consecration have to be said over both the bread and the wine for either to be consecrated (the position of Peter Cantor), or was the bread consecrated after the word spoken over the bread, and the wine subsequently consecrated after the wine word (the position of Stephen Langton)?[15] As a result of such arguments and analysis, theological investment in one position or another increased. The struggle to understand the mystery began itself to reify, and the theological constructs and hypotheses came to be identified as tenets of faith. Consensus tended to be hammered out, and by "the mid-twelfth century, most western theologians could agree that bread and wine are really changed into Christ's body and blood, and that the change happens in virtue of the words of Christ [cf. Matt 26:26–29, Mark 14:22–25, Luke 22:14–20, 1 Cor 11:23–25] spoken by the priest in the eucharistic prayer."[16] Since this was a time of full Christendom, there was no longer the heterodox parallel existence of several interpretations. Rather, those who were able to perceive other answers or who came to different conclusions were often labeled heretics, persecuted, and forced to recant. This discouraged creative thinking, and a kind of theological legalism set in.

Beyond questions of Christ's real presence in the eucharist were theological speculations as to *how many* ritual actions counted as sacraments (e.g., over fifty; thirty; seven; two),[17] and as to what precisely invokes or causes or enables—or, at any rate, is the condition by which we can be assured of—the action of the Holy Spirit (e.g., when the priest, properly ordained, with at least one other person present, says the proper words with the element and gesture). And the line of their thinking structured the churches' relationship with the thing thought about (in this case, baptism), and affected baptismal practice—which further influenced baptismal belief. Theology and practice of baptism were mutually affected by this evolution in thinking.

For example, many students of worship and liturgy are unaware of the variety of baptismal practices in the early church and assume that

15. Mitchell, *Cult and Controversy*, 151–56.
16. Ibid., 151.
17. Cranmer names twenty-one, then adds all the parables of Christ and the prophecies of the Hebrew Scriptures; Hugh of St. Victor includes some thirty; Peter Lombard named seven; the Reformers named two dominical sacraments, Holy Baptism and Holy Communion.

what is practiced today are "standard" practices of baptism handed down—but which were not actually standard at all. As we have noted, at Milan and in Gaul *foot washing* was a common part of baptism.[18] The fourth-century *mystagogical catecheses*—sermons by four theologians that reveal fourth-century theologies of baptism—were not, in fact, all written for post-baptismal mystagogy. In Antioch, the mystagogical sermons by John Chrysostom and Theodore of Mopsuestia were given *before* baptism as procatechesis, instead of after baptism like those of Ambrose of Milan and Cyril of Jerusalem.[19] At Rome, there were three *anointings* during baptism: two before immersion and one after,[20] while in Gaul there was only one anointing, after baptism.[21] In the catechumenate, there were *varying practices* including exorcisms, memorization of the creed, public scrutinies, fasting, confession, and preparatory bathing. And these are the ritualizations that are known to us. It seems probable that there were a variety of additional catechumenal ritualizations particular to the location of preparation. There was not a single set of practices in the early church, but a *variety*.

If the Holy Spirit moves where she will, which our theology proclaims that she does, we will not be surprised by these widely varying practices, all of which are part of a *process* of catechizing-toward-baptism. We see that in different places, with different bishops, subcultures, and urban or rural life-styles, the strategies used to set apart one activity or one group of people from the ordinary also varied. For example, in Jerusalem, the very place of Jesus' passion, Christians worshipped at the various sites of the passion events. These "stational" liturgies were possible and fitting in Jerusalem.[22] Such strategic and

---

18. J. D. C. Fisher suggests that *pedilavium* was the practice also in the British Isles from the sixth to the twelfth century. Also in the British Isles, as in Gaul, there was no laying on of hands as there was at Rome. Fisher, *Baptism in the Medieval West*, 84.

19. Yarnold, *The Awe-Inspiring Rites of Initiation*, 150, 167.

20. *Apostolic Tradition*, para. 21.

21. Fisher, *Christian Initiation*, 78. See also Winkler, "Confirmation or Chrismation?" 2–17.

22. Wilkinson, *Egeria* 30–37. As an example, Egeria (a fourth-century pilgrim to Jerusalem who was perhaps a nun) reports that on Palm Sunday, "they do everything as usual at the Anastasis [site of the resurrection] and the Cross from cock-crow to daybreak, and then as usual assemble in the Great Church known as the Martyrium because it is on Golgotha behind the Cross, where the Lord was put to death. When the service in the Great Church has taken place in the usual way, before the dismissal, the archdeacon makes this announcement: 'during this week, starting tomorrow, let

contextualized ritualizations enabled vibrant if varying processes of preparing and enabling persons to live the life to which they were called in Christ. Post-baptismal theosis, this book argues, would benefit from the same contextually-varied ritualizing process.

Recognizing that baptism culminates a catechumenal process yet inaugurates a process of deification in baptismal life, let us hold in mind strategic and contextualized possibilities for supporting theosis by looking again at some accounts of catechumenal ritualizations leading up to baptism.[23] We recall that the rhythmic *flow* of catechumenal formation included regular meetings with the bishop and/or catechist to study the Hebrew Bible and New Testament; the primary Christian metaphors and symbols; Jesus' teachings; and the practical teachings of the Christian life.[24] The rhythmic *ebb* was everyday living in the world, requiring new patterns of relating to people; new disciplines of purity of thought, eating, dress, and behavior; sometimes new friends and/or new jobs. Punctuating this rhythm, and intensifying it through its redemptive hegemonic strengthening, were *ritualizations* such as:

- recitation of the creed
- confession of sins
- exorcism
- removing job, relationships, life-patterns which are inconsistent with life in the Christian community
- setting apart in the order of catechumens with a new title—"catechumen"
- new fathers and mothers (Egeria's name for godparents: 45.2)
- keeping the rites secret (e.g., appropriated in Milan [Ambrose] and Jerusalem [Cyril], but not in Antioch).
- putting in one's name (enrollment)
- desisting from gluttony

---

us meet at three in the afternoon at the Martyrium' . . . And he makes another announcement: 'At one o'clock today let us be ready on the Eleona.' After the dismissal in the Great Church, the Martyrium, the bishop is taken with singing to the Anastasis. They do in the Anastasis the things which usually follow the Sunday dismissal in the martyrium, and then everyone goes home and eats a quick meal, so as to be ready by one o'clock at the Eleona church on the mount of Olives, the place of the cave where the Lord used to teach" (30.1–3).

23. Here I draw especially from J. D. C. Fisher, *Christian Initiation*; Wilkinson, *Egeria*; Yarnold, *Awesome Rites*; and Kreider, *Change*.

24. Kreider, *Change*, 26–28; Egeria 46.1–6 (in Wilkinson, *Egeria*, 144–45).

- being called by one's name
- removing clothes, ornaments, and descending naked into living water
- having one's body anointed in exorcism
- having one's body anointed in thanksgiving
- having one's body clothed in a new garment
- having one's ears opened
- having one's feet washed
- receiving salt on the tongue
- processing out of the baptistery to a common room where people awaited
- being received for the first time at the Table
- receiving milk and honey as well as bread and wine at Holy Communion
- participating in other ritualizations never before available to the candidate (i.e., prayers of the faithful)
- returning daily for the next fifty days to continue instruction

If the catechumenal process is the beginning of a process of becoming a particular kind of person, culminating in baptism as a complex of rites, then the ritualizing process *initiated* at baptism is one of continuing to become a person more and more in the likeness of God through Christ in the Spirit. This process of being a baptized person is a process to become a *new* person beyond what one was, a praxological becoming of a sanctified person-in-Christ-and-the-Holy Spirit,[25] growing into God up to the baptism of death.

This process needs a name. I call it the *(post-) baptismal process*. Ritualizing in the post-baptismal process parallels that in the catechumenal process in this way: multiple ritualizations strategically distinguish and privilege some activities, values, persons, behaviors over others, such that turning, changing, and empowering occurs toward a particular way of being and becoming. Some of these ritualizations, effective over time with a variety of people, may develop a structure that is generally replicated, becoming more formalized "rites."

Yet even if ritualizations in one place should become standard, as Jennings pointed out above, the particulars of these rites may change nonetheless, as baptism itself has done over the centuries. Consider

25. Aune, "The Subject of Ritual," 150.

the stunning extent of changes and variations in these central aspects of baptism over 2,000 years:

- amounts of water (from submersion to sprinkling)
- who is present (private, public)
- who conducts the rites (bishop, priest, lay people, midwives)
- type of font (river to "bird bath")[26]
- location of event (outdoors, baptistery, door of church, sanctuary, birthing room)
- time of the year and day of the week conducted (Easter/Pentecost to any Sunday to any day)
- what is worn (no clothes, white clothes, dressy or special clothes, any clothes)

The strategies for setting apart the baptizands, for enabling their growing, for contextualizing their learning, for embracing them in the community, and for placing them in the way of God, in other words, have varied. In this day, liturgists continue to work to identify and use strategies that operate effectively in their given situations. It is striking that the rite called "baptism," from the Greek "to wash," has claimed a historic and theological continuity in spite of all the changes and variations in every aspect of the sacrament. Persons wanting to bear the name "Christian" are baptized. They participate in a sacrament for which, in spite of the huge diversity of practices, continuity is claimed:

- persons come for baptism (either on their own or are brought by their parents and godparents) to a designated person;
- designated baptizer speaks some words (most commonly a Trinitarian formula, but not always),[27] in the active or pas-

---

26. See Stauffer, *Re-Imagining Baptismal Fonts*, a videotape showing the history and theology of baptismal symbology through a study of fonts from the earliest times to the present.

27. See Duck, *Gender and the Name of God*, 123–37, on the history of the baptismal formulae including in the name of the Trinity (Matt 28:19–20) and in the name of Jesus (Acts 2:38).

sive ("I baptize you" or "You are baptized"),[28] declarative or interrogative;[29]

- baptizer speaks words in conjunction with the application of water (although the spilling of a martyr's blood is also called baptism).[30]

If we vary one aspect, i.e., foot washing, or signation with the cross, or amount of water, have we compromised the rite of baptism as a whole? The history of continuity in the midst of wide diversity suggests not. Even the term "rite" came, in the sixth century, to refer not to enactment but to the (often invariant or authorized) *text* of a liturgy, or in an even more specific usage, to the text of a *part* of a liturgy, a single word-element-gesture.[31] Thus, "the baptismal rite," for example, a term often used synonymously with "the water rite," is distinguished from the anointing rite that preceded or followed it and from the meal rite which consummated it. But in much early church practice, *all these constituted Holy Baptism*. "Baptism" referred to *a whole set of preparations and rites which took place over time.* The ones baptized were initiated *and were able to experience their initiation,* since they lived in a *process of change over time.*

The difference between the early process and the "one event" expectation that has come down to us leads to a confusion of categories: baptism is at once "full initiation" (including the anointing or handlaying, later called "Confirmation," and first Eucharist) and "one-third

---

28. The active voice is used today in the Western churches; the passive voice, used in Orthodox churches, was noted in the fourth century by St. John Chrysostom, *Baptismal Instructions*, Ancient Christian Writers, 31 (1963), para. 13–14: "therefore, John the Baptist told us, for our instruction, that man does not baptize us, but God . . . For this reason, when the priest is baptizing, he does not say, 'I baptize so-and-so,' but, 'So-and-so is baptized in the name of the Father and of the Son and of the Holy Spirit.'" In Whitaker, *Documents of the Baptismal Liturgy*, 36.

29. Duck 136–37; Kelly, *Early Christian Creeds*, 30–49.

30. As Jesus said to the disciples, "You will drink my cup and will be baptized with the baptism with which I am baptized" (*cf.* Mark 10:38–39).

31. See, for example, this definition in a liturgical glossary: "Rite. The authorized order and text of a public liturgical service." Guilbert, *Words*, 57. Rite is contrasted with "ceremony" or "ceremonial," "the actions, postures, and practices of public worship, as distinguished from ritual, which denotes the prescribed form of words used in such worship." Ibid., 14. Such distinction occurred following the shift from oral to literate society with the invention of movable type (Johannes Gutenberg: c. 1390–1468).

of initiation";[32] the Spirit both is and is not present at the water rite; and the preparatory activities for baptism (e.g., fasting, silence[33]) are categorized separately, not as part of the rite, but as preceding it. Thus, in our cognitive categories, in our thinking about action, we are able to imagine and speak of—and thus to *practice*—"baptism" as an isolated immersion attached to a verbal phrase *apart from* the conversion leading up to it, the community mediating it,[34] the signation sealing it, the meal consummating it, and the life resulting from it.

In the early catechumenate, on the other hand, we find myriad ritualizations, without the definitional restriction of attempting to categorize them into sacrament or not, whether they contain elements distinguishing them from other human activity or not so that we would know whether they are sacred or not. While the oral culture of the early church contributed to this flexibility, in contrast to contem-

---

32. Given this theological problem, including the practical question as to whether the initial sequence should hold and those baptized as infants should refrain from eucharist until after Confirmation (the position of the Episcopal Church through the 1928 *Book of Common Prayer*) or until the age of reason (the position of the Roman Catholic Church), twentieth-century worship books resolved the problem, though in different ways. The Episcopal Church determined that "Christian Initiation [is] complete in baptism," so that Holy Communion is available immediately, and Confirmation was reconstrued as the first [unrepeatable] renewal of baptismal vows at a public profession of faith (though other renewals of baptism are available and repeatable). The words at baptismal signation are, "You are sealed *by the Holy Spirit* in baptism," acknowledging the Spirit's presence, which makes initiation complete. The Roman Church went the other way, signating infants on the crown of the head, and awaiting signation on the forehead until Confirmation, when the prayer for the Holy Spirit is said; and the role of Confirmation *in initiation* is specified in the new Roman rite (1971); see Susan Marie Smith, "Confirmation: A Suggestion from Liturgical Hermeneutics" (1998). See also Fuller, "Confirmation," 17; Stevick on distinguishing "Confirmation A" (anointing with the Holy Spirit, which is clearly initiatory) from Confirmation B (confirming as an adult the baptismal promises made on one's behalf as an infant, which in 1979 was declared *not* initiatory), in "Supplement" and *Baptismal Moments*; and Whitaker, "Christian Initiation Complete in Baptism."

33. See Justin Martyr, c. 160 in his *First Apology* 61: Those preparing for baptism "are taught to pray and ask God, while fasting, for the forgiveness of their sins: and we pray and fast with them." Also Tertullian, c. 198 in *De Baptismo*, 20.9: "Those who are at the point of entering upon baptism ought to pray, with frequent prayers, fastings, bendings of the knee, and all-night vigils, along with the confession of all their sins, so as to make a copy of the baptism of John." In Whitaker, ed., *Documents of the Baptismal Liturgy*, 2, 9.

34. See A. Theodore Eastman's good treatment of the relationship between the baptizand and the community by which and into which the person is baptized: *The Baptizing Community*, esp. 4–5, 31–54.

porary written text which can (and sometimes should) be followed to the letter,[35] ritual itself is a flexible structure which contributes to change in meaning. Again, from her ritual research, Catherine Bell pointed out that tradition "is something that exists nowhere but in the its flexible embodiment in memory and in current cultural life."[36]

Rituals of Ingemination in Response to Baptism, the Keystone Sacrament

If the catechumenal rites (i.e., admission, enrollment) marked movement toward conversion in preparation for Holy Baptism, ritualizing in the post-baptismal process will mark movement through changes and chances toward *theosis*, ongoing conversion and maturing in the baptized life *in response to baptismal grace*. While there may be many such rites, I suggest the churches be intentional about noticing need and offering rites for the baptized in times of transition, healing, and vocational change. These may be called ritualizations of *theosis* or *theopoeisis*; they have been called by Theodore Eastman ritualizations of *ingemination*.

> *Ingemination* is a stage that may occur once or twice or many times during the life of a Christian. The word means redoubling, repeating, or reiterating. Ingemination is what [I] referred to earlier as renewal. There are, as I have contended, many turning points in one's spiritual development. The pastoral and educational life of the church is meant to help a person prepare for those turning points so that he [or she] may be able to traverse them creatively and reiterate his or her baptismal commitment with new understanding and deeper faith.[37]

---

35. See Bell, "Authority of Ritual Experts," esp. 104–9.

36. Bell, "Authority of Ritual Experts," 106. See also Mary Collins, "An Adventuresome Hypothesis," on how ritual practice in the late twentieth century changed the meaning of women's religious vows, which had been focused on virginity and on becoming the "bride of Christ" (symbols included wearing of veils, shaving off of hair), to a focus on vocation in Christ without such overt sexual connotations.

37. Eastman, *Baptizing Community*, 94. Bishop Eastman's book was written following the revision of the Episcopal *Book of Common Prayer* in 1979 to flesh out the parochial implications of its baptismal theology. His concern is that "few clergy have made significant changes in the way they prepare candidates and sponsors for baptism, even though the operative formularies declare it to represent 'full initiation.'" Ibid., 4.

Eastman, a bishop in the Episcopal Church (USA), wrote his book *The Baptizing Community* following the 1979 revision of the *Book of Common Prayer*, in order to encourage "parish life [to be] reordered to reflect the educational and missionary demands that the reformation of Christian initiation requires." The purpose of the book is "to explore what it would mean for a congregation to develop a comprehensive attitude toward Holy Baptism as the keystone sacrament."[38]

It is significant that Eastman recognizes that ingemination requires liturgical expression. Eastman, drawing upon the 1979 *BCP*, specifies its liturgical expression by naming the three rites given in the *Book:* Confirmation, reception into the Episcopal Church, and reaffirmation of baptismal vows. While these three are indeed necessary liturgical expressions, it is my contention here that their texts and rubrics in the *BCP* are an inadequate expression of the fullness of what must happen liturgically if each of the baptized *ecclesia* will take her or his place as a fully-engaged member of the Body of Christ so functioning in the world. I am calling for ritual resourcefulness and competence beyond what is prescribed in the 1979 *Book of Common Prayer*. At the same time, however, in claiming with Chauvet the inherent thanks-responsiveness of Christians to divine grace, the fifth principle for generating such ritualizations (in the next chapter) is that *rites in the post-baptismal process should acknowledge in word and sign their response to baptismal grace*. In this way, then, *every ritualization in the post-baptismal process is a kind of renewal of baptismal vows* as a response to God's grace bestowed at baptism.

There is no way that enough books of prayer or worship or blessings or occasional services or rituals could finally cover the full breadth of ritualization needed for operational efficacy in the lives of all the baptized. Yet the continuing Incarnation of the Word of God in the Body of Christ is by the Holy Spirit ever present in ways and places that are not apprehendable by the human imagination. One of those

---

38. Ibid., 4, 5, 94. Because the 1979 Episcopal *Book of Common Prayer* is his point of reference, Bishop Eastman ends the preceding paragraph by saying, "The liturgical expressions of ingemination are confirmation, reception [into the Episcopal Church], and reaffirmation [of baptismal vows]." I here propose a wider range of rites of ingemination (transition, healing, vocational change). However, the fifth principle of ritualization proposed in the next chapter is that each ritualization be made referent to (and in response to) the grace of God received in baptism. In this way, all ritualizations in the post-baptismal process are rites of renewal of baptismal vows.

ways by which the Spirit of God breathes incarnationally into the life of human beings is ritually. I therefore assert that the churches have not just liturgies, not just orders of worship, not just sacraments to offer, but *a liturgical way of life*—that is, liturgy for living.[39] The church is the continuing incarnation of Christ on earth. What this church is given to offer is the competence, the experience, the tradition of a ritualizing way of life by which what ritual does is made available for the mediation of the Christian mythos. This is why the churches need to *claim their ritual knowledge derived from the churches' existing worshipful/liturgical way of life*. Pastors and lay leaders know more than they think they know about ritual making. It is time to claim it and offer it.

At the same time, the need is so vast and the practice so thin and the danger so great that *it is essential that pastors and lay leaders intentionally develop ritual competence* (including ritual resourcefulness and symbolic competence). In his article "Ritual Resourcefulness and Cultural Pluralism," Roland Delattre says, "In a pluralistic culture such as our own, what is required is not simply the mastery of a particular series of ritual performances, but the development of a virtual repertoire of ritual capacities together with both individual and collective resourcefulness in mobilizing them."[40] Theoretical and practical education for ritual and symbolic competencies is thereby called for in the church. As Yves Congar wrote in his rethinking of the theology of laity and ministries: "the Church's liturgy, however sacred, rich, and nourishing, does not seem to take up sufficiently the concrete life of men [and women] as it unfolds within the structures of a 'secular city' nor the activities of a secularized civilization. The need for the 'holy' which [women and] men always experience . . . seek[s] other forms of expression."[41]

If it is ritual which can set apart activities so that humans can be imbued with power from the Holy, or claim power they could not have in the political sphere, then what is fitting for the ongoing life of the baptized as the church supports them in deification, in becoming more and more like Christ? It is time for the churches to claim the role of liturgy in what I have called realized baptismal ecclesiology.

---

39. The Episcopal Church's Teaching Series volume on liturgy bears this provocative and fitting title. See Weil and Price, *Liturgy for Living*.

40. Delattre, "Ritual Resourcefulness," 281–82.

41. Congar, "My Pathfindings in the Theology of Laity and Ministries," 185.

Christian ritualizing in the baptismal process is what will enable baptism, by which one is united to Christ in death and resurrection and sealed by the Holy Spirit, to "take."

Based upon theological insights from faith development, theosis, and response-giving, I propose three types of ritualizations which the church might employ for the specific intention of attending to the post-baptismal formation of Christians into Christ: ritualizations for molting-moments, when a stage-transition is immanent, which I call ritualizations of *life-passage*; for freedom from sticking-places which keep one from the likeness of God: *healing*; and committing of one's work as thanks-gift to God: *vocation*. Amidst myriad possibilities, these three seem essential if the church—that is, the baptized—be freed to claim their place in the Body of Christ and carry out their ministries in the world. While I do not preclude the possibility of such ritualizations becoming full textualized rites published in euchologies, my focus here is not to develop three rites but rather to identify three foci for contextualized ritualization. There is great benefit in pursuing quite specific ritualizations in these areas for the privileging of growth and maturing in Christ of particular baptized persons. In the course of commenting upon these three types of ritualizations as appropriate for intentional ritualizing for ongoing conversion, I shall offer five principles for pastors and lay leaders to claim as they move toward their own ritual competence in generating Christian ritualizations for the baptismal process.

11

Five Principles for Christian Ritualizing in the Baptismal Process

Making Rites for Life Passage, Healing, and Vocational Change

HAVING DEMONSTRATED THE IMPORTANCE IN POST-CHRISTENDOM of supporting the continuing conversion and maturation into Christ by the Spirit through the practice of Christian ritualization, we now explore three touchstone moments in a Christian life that would typically be assisted by competent rite-making. Unfolding in the discussion of these three vulnerable turning points will be five principles for guiding the making of such life-giving, growth-supporting ritualizations. Here are these five principles summarized:

Summary of Principles for Conducting Competent Christian Ritualizations

1. The starting point for ritualizations in the baptismal process is the focal person(s) for whom the ritual will be designed.
2. In planning a ritualization for the baptismal process, one must bear responsibility for making manifest the presence of the church.
3. The Paschal Mystery in the person's life is identified as it is already present by the grace of the Holy Spirit.
4. The full mystery of death and life is incarnated in the ritualization through the juxtaposition of contraries.
5. Because baptism is the keystone sacrament and point of departure for post-baptismal theopoetic ritualization, the relationship of the action to baptism should be clear in the

ritual symbolization and enactment (e.g., that it is a renewal of baptismal vows, or a step within those vows, or a thanks-gift in response to baptismal grace).

Ritualizations for Life Passage

From the faith development work of James Fowler, we are able to recognize patterns, stages that are generally common in human beings. It is not the preciseness or universality of this claim that concerns us here, but the research that reveals that humans grow, become, adolesce, adult—and that general sequencing of this process can be identified. What we noticed most significantly in our study of Fowler's work for our purposes was the crisis, the molting, which breaks open one stage into the next. That is, while anthropologists have classically named four biogenetic stages which are commonly ritualized in many cultures, i.e., birth, puberty, reproduction (e.g., marriage), and death, what we have inferred from Fowler is that any number of crises may crack a worldview, whether the crisis be biogenetic, psychosocial (cf. Erik Erikson), cognitional (cf. Jean Piaget), moral (cf. Lawrence Kohlberg and Carol Gilligan), or any number of others. In the vulnerable moment of a life crisis, there may—or may not—occur growth, integration, meaning, perspective, or communal attachment.

Put another way, just as there may not be a fixed set of attributes by which we can recognize, "Ah, this is a ritual!," so there may not be a fixed pattern by which we can definitively say, "Ah, Sharon will be entering a new stage of development next week." Rather, a crisis that challenges or creates a conflict with authority, or the bounds of one's social group, or the power of a symbol, leads one to a precipice. Whether the person remains stuck at the edge or is able to pass to an adjacent terrain is not pre-determined. It is in this situation that a competent ritualization could be the bridge or means of passage to solid ground. Some crises do seem to come with the age and circumstances of life, such as in the example of Tommy and the seven-year-olds; and a life-passage ritualization could open a prospective dead end into a new, deeper, life-giving path.

Reporting and reflecting upon some of these precipice rites and the theologies they embody is a volume edited by Paul Bradshaw and Lawrence Hoffman entitled *Life Cycles in Jewish and Christian*

Worship. At the end of Hoffman's opening essay, he considers "life cycle as personal identity," quoting Erik Erikson's epilogue to *Young Man Luther*: "Society . . . must support the primary function of every individual ego, which is to transform instinctual energy into patterns of action, into character, into style—in short, into an identity with a core of integrity . . . At a given age, a human being . . . becomes ready and eager to face a new life task, that is, a set of choices and tests which are in some traditional way prescribed and prepared . . . by society's structure."[1] Hoffman continues, "In Martin Luther's case, adolescence had been determinative; for others it would be other challenges."[2]

It is this that suggests a liturgical role for the baptismal process. Life thresholds occur, moments that are determinative for one's character, one's life direction, one's sense of self, and one's relationship with others, with God, and with the world. To make manifest the reality that *all the baptized* make up the church (not just the pastors), it would be important to offer support so that these determinative moments would not be ignored, nor would the Tommies be left utterly alone to risk such moments leading to anomie or alienation. Rather, such moments or crises would be ritualized toward Christ in the Spirit.

Perhaps the question "what is the role of liturgy?" in light of the strategic nature of ritualization, may give way to "what is the role of the liturgist?" What is the role of a liturgist, a ritualizer, a spiritual leader with ritual competence? Here, it would be to recognize "moments" or situations as potentially determinative, and to enable them to be ritualized in a way that is life-giving. For example, as for Martin Luther, teen years are crucially determinative for many. The question for the liturgist is, we propose, not "Which of the given sacraments of the church should be (or may legitimately be) applied to this person?" but rather, "How might we generate a ritualization for *this* person in *this* situation to enable her or him to *come* more fully into the likeness of Christ by the Spirit?" Existing rites might be assessed, then, not only for their theology, as important as that is (doctrinal efficacy), but also for their effectiveness in helping the teenager in crisis negotiate a passage into deeper experiences of freedom, life, justice, mercy, and love (operational efficacy). It would no longer be necessary, for example, to ask the question, "How old should (or young could) a person be in

---

1. Hoffman, "Life Cycle as Religious Metaphor," 8.
2. Ibid., 8.

order to be confirmed?" but rather, "Given this person's need at this moment, and given the meaning of confirmation, is it confirmation or some other rite or ritualization that would be most appropriate, most helpful, most effective?" Elsewhere, I have identified three rites used for teens, all of which were effective in their respective contexts (Rite 13, confirmation, a post-baptismal enrollment).[3] Others might be developed.

But teen moments are not determinative for everyone, nor are they the only ones that are determinative. Any number of turning points could be critical within a person's life. For example, for many people, divorce is painfully determinative. People frequently leave the church at the moment of divorce. The deep brokenness of a covenantal relationship, the breaking apart of a family, the broken promise, the societal stigma, estrangement from intimacy, the breadth and weight of life-changes resulting (e.g., moving, financial ups and downs, child-care, child custody, holiday patterns), along with a future unknown and unimagined—these will almost invariably break open one's relationship with God: ending it, starting it, or in any case, changing it. An imperative for the liturgist attending to the baptismal process would be to ritualize this moment in a way that relates it to the gospel and enables a life-giving encounter with the Holy One.

There are some who might argue against the need for a particularized ritualization of passage for an individual on the basis of an assumption that "the Church already has all the passage rites needed: baptism, marriage, renewal of baptism—and eucharist." This argument asserts that crisis moments, and other moments, are brought to Christ at the eucharist; for isn't this the regular moment when one's identity is assured and reassured, when we become again the Body of Christ, being cleansed and forgiven of all that is impure and not-of-God?

I venture to say that there is no Christian liturgist who does not live daily the conviction that the primary gathering of the people of God on the Lord's Day, the *dies domine*, the *dominicum*, is the primary and essential moment of turning again to God, of experiencing one's identity as part of the *ecclesia* of God, the Body of Christ, the Pentecost people filled with the Spirit.[4] A major part of the work of a liturgist is

---

3. For these examples and an exploration of the meaning of confirmation as authorized in the Episcopal *1979 Book of Common Prayer*, see Susan Marie Smith, "Confirmation as Perlocutionary Response," 72–83.

4. See, for example, Gordon Lathrop, *Holy Things*, esp. 36–43.

to enable the weekly service of Word and Table to effect operationally what it signifies doctrinally. The Easter people celebrate Christ's resurrection weekly, and bring with them to this moment of "Sabbath time" all the burdens and anxieties, all the hopes and joys, of daily life to be offered to God. They come, too, in their priestly ministry, bringing the cares and concerns of the world, which they also offer to God. Much has been written about the eucharist which unites Christians across time and culture, frees them from sin, empowers them for ministry, and animates them to care for neighbor. Weekly worship in the community of faith is foundational and essential.[5]

And weekly eucharist, we claim, is a fundamental part of the baptismal process because of the intimate and essential relationship between baptism and eucharist. Theology of baptism proclaims that one's sins are put away, and one emerges from the water as pure as the day one was born. It is a new birth. In eucharist, one is again freed from sin through the recitation of the Lord's Prayer ("forgive us our sins"), in corporate confession, and in the receiving again of Christ at the Holy Table and in the assembled community. Baptism marks conversion, and eucharist is the meal which sustains the converted. As Monika Hellwig expresses it, "[t]he great sacrament of repentance ... is the Church itself. The transformed and transforming community"[6] itself enables the baptized to remember who they are in living *anamnesis*. Thus baptism, eucharist, and the church are all means and therefore signs of repentance and reconciliation, and thereby of Christ's ministry in the world. Holy Communion continues the forgiveness, the union with Christ, and the corporate identity initiated in baptism. Regular participation at the holy feast of the Lord's Supper may indeed mediate experiences of sanctification, sustain growth, and enable passage.

But operationally speaking, sometimes more specific rites are needed. Even Jesus was willing to offer a second touch to a man whose healing required additional attention (Mark 8:22–26). There is no discredit to the sacrament of Holy Communion to suggest that it may not be sufficient to every person for every passage. Baptism forgives sins; but it did not take long in the early church for leaders to realize that

5. "[W]eek by week and month by month, on a hundred thousand successive Sundays, faithfully, unfailingly, across all the parishes of christendom, the pastors have done this just to *make* the *plebs sancta Dei*—the holy common people of God." Dix, *The Shape of the Liturgy*, 744.

6. Hellwig, *Sign of Reconciliation and Conversion*, 28.

baptism did *not* mean that persons would never sin again. A second touch was needed for forgiveness following baptism, and the church provided it, without any sense of discredit to the effectiveness of God's forgiveness of sin at baptism.

At first, the church provided one additional opportunity to repent.[7] By the fifth century, it was common to offer a weekly opportunity to name one's sin and be absolved.[8] It was the experiential need of the people which led to the patterns of reconciliation, sometimes public, sometimes private. The weakness and need of God's people did not reflect poorly upon God, as though God's action had been ineffective; nor upon the rite of baptism, as though it had failed; nor upon the eucharist, as though it were weak; nor upon the church, as though it were inadequate where it should not have been. It is true that the church along with all humans and their institutions are finally inadequate, for such is the nature of sin and the finitude of humanity. The church and its sacraments have come into being (among other reasons) *because* of human weakness and human need, to help sinners. God accommodates to human weakness, including human need for penitence and forgiveness, even after baptism.

---

7. Ibid., 36ff. It is interesting that the first approach to facing post-baptismal sin was to originate a *progression* from sin to reconciliation, a process parallel to the catechumenal process with stages or grades. In the catechumenate, we recall, there were four stages: one was first a *seeker or inquirer,* then in the second stage a *catechumen,* then a *candidate,* and after baptism, a *neophyte* during the period of mystagogy. The period of time in each stage varied from place to place but also person to person. Discernment was involved on the part of the candidate, the bishop, and the sponsors.

Similarly, in the order of penitents there were five gradations, named for their relationship to the community at the Sunday liturgy: *mourners* who remained outside the house of worship during liturgy "plead[ing] with the faithful for their prayers and for readmission"; *hearers* who were permitted to stand inside the door in the narthex or foyer so as to hear the first part of the service, and were dismissed with the catechumens before the anaphora; *fallers* "(prostrators) [who] were allowed inside the nave of the church in a posture of self-abasement" and were also dismissed with the catechumens; *bystanders* who were present in the nave for the whole service but did not receive communion; and, finally, complete restoration as *faithful* communicants when the process was complete. Hellwig notes that the "posture of self-abasement" of the fallers or prostrators was "apparently, however, also adopted by catechumens because baptism was also seen in the light of conversion from a life of sin" (ibid., 36).

8. Ibid., 36–43. Irish monastic tradition provided an individual form of tariff penance in which individuals met with the monk, confessed their sins, were given individual penance according to the nature of the sin, and were offered absolution. By the fifth century this system had largely replaced the order of penitents (ibid., 43).

Augustine, John Cassian, and John Chrysostom all mention variations on private confession and penance,[9] including, in Chrysostom, "nine modes of penance available to sinners."[10] Monika Hellwig notes that these early practices point "to a sense of freedom to create the appropriate rites for the circumstances."[11] They arose in response to needs among the (baptized) Christians; some patterns lasted for several centuries, some are with us still, and some did not last beyond the circumstances that gave rise to them. Those that lasted as effective in meeting the pastoral spiritual ritual need have taken their place in the church's sacramental repertoire.

In the same way that ritualizations and practices and rites for reconciliation arose out of a felt need of those seeking to continue and deepen their life in Christ-and-the-Spirit, even though baptism and eucharist were stalwarts and always available, so ritualizations and practices and rites for determinative moments in the human life passage also ought to be offered to persons at the point of their need. Inasmuch as the human situation or life crisis engenders a ritualization, the church enacts a recapitulation on another level of the scandal of particularity. It is in the particular that the universal takes root. With Creation as the original sacrament, and God's *dabar* ("word") spoken in the Torah and in the prophets, and God's *ruach* ("spirit") moving over the waters of creation and animating the patriarchs and judges, still, with all that, God's presence with us, for us, like us, was still necessary for humankind to grasp the message, to see the Spirit. It took the Word becoming flesh and living right in the midst of humankind in a shape they could recognize and relate to, a tangible encounter with the Holy, for people to "see" what God is like, to experience what relationship with God is like, to follow effectively in the way of God. Thus did God enter the world in Christ Jesus, the ultimate scandal in particularity.

In light of this, then, we thus may articulate the first principle for generating ritualizations in the *baptismal process:*

> (1) The starting point for ritualizations in the baptismal process is the focal person(s) for whom the ritual will be designed.

---

9. Ibid., 40–43.
10. Ibid., 42.
11. Ibid., 43.

The motivational and intentional starting point of life passage rites (as well as other ritualizations) should be not only theological principles, but *the experience and/or felt need of the focal person*. We borrow the term "focal person" from the discernment process outlined by *Listening Hearts*,[12] acknowledging that the ritual leader and primary planner must be separate roles from the person who is the focus of the rite. Of the seven sacraments so called by Peter Lombard, six have focal persons. Only the eucharist does not. Yet all the rites, even if they involve only two persons as in reconciliation or anointing, or a handful as in marriage, or hundreds as in marriage or ordination, all the rites are done by the church for the church and on its behalf.

In the same way, we may articulate a second principle of ritualizations concomitant with the first, a principle that may seem obvious but is essential:

> (2) In planning a ritualization for the baptismal process, one must bear responsibility for making manifest the presence of the church.

If a pastor blesses God for fifty years of marriage of a couple in his office, as has been done many times, the church is present. If a minister conducts a private rite of divorce in the sanctuary with two persons and three witnesses, a ritualization the text of which will never be repeated, the church is represented there. How do we know? There are doctrinal signs (which may also be experienced as operational signs) of the presence of the church, usually including (1) location (e.g., conducting the ritualization in a church building or sanctified space); (2) presider (e.g., a person designated by the body); (3) text, either familiar or authorized; (4) repetition of common practice, recognizable by participants; (5) intent of the participants to represent the church, to operate within the ecclesial matrix; (6) the physical embodied presence of church members.

While it may not always be possible or fitting for the congregation to be present, that is the primary way for the church to be there: in the flesh. If the ritualization does not include them, there is a missed opportunity for growth and conversion not only of the focal person but also *of the community as a whole*. As Bell points out, one of the ways in which ritualization "is perceived to be the most effective type

---

12. This helpful term I have borrowed from Farnham, *et.al.*, *Listening Hearts*. They use "focus person" which they attribute to the Quakers (ibid., 78).

of action . . . [is] when the hegemonic order being experienced . . . [is] rendered socially redemptive in order to be personally redemptive."[13] The church is the communal context for theosis. The church is converted as persons are converted; persons grow as the church grows. There is an integral relationship between the person and the *ecclesia*, between the one and the many; and this relationship must be honored in any ritualization conducted by the church on behalf of the maturing process of its baptized members.

The motivation for making and conducting these ritualizations is the love and growth and conversion and care of baptized persons at a turning point and in need of passage. It is important that theological tradition be brought to bear in such ritualizations, even as tradition may be extended through these rites. It is not only ritual competence but theological competence that is required. Two primary requirements, which are the starting principles for engendering a life-passage (or any) ritualization, are focus upon the persons who have arrived at a determinative life moment, and the manifest symbolic presence of the *ecclesia* that is the matrix of their life in Christ.

Ritualizations for Healing

> [T]he relation of entire liturgical orders to what lies outside them [is] . . . that they mend over and over again worlds that are forever breaking apart.[14]

> *For an abused woman, Patricia seemed to have her act together. She had succumbed to the wiles and sexual dominations of a clergyman. The pain showed on her face when she recounted her confession to her husband, and her glad disbelief he had not left her. She had left the clergyman's church and denomination; she had told the synodal authority. She had received funds that she had used for therapy and for attending a retreat for women in her situation.*

> *Now she was attending a church of another denomination, but on the periphery. She worked with the children. She did not come every week. She wanted to be confirmed*

---

13. Bell, *Ritual Theory, Ritual Practice*, 116.
14. Rappaport, "Liturgies and Lies," 82.

but could not bring herself to commit. There was some terrible tension that restrained her from claiming and allowing herself to be claimed by the new parish.

On a women's retreat, her small group's conversation was quite animated. As the women heard her story, something clicked for one of the other participants. "Patricia, do you suppose part of what repels you from returning to church is that church is the Body of Christ—and your body has been—tainted? I wonder if it would be viscerally repugnant, every attempt to bring your defiled body back into the body of Christ, the pure, the holy, the Son of God." Silence. A light seemed to dawn upon Patricia. She nodded, slowly at first. "Yes. Yes—that is some of what I'm feeling." She shuddered. In a small voice: "As I connect with what you've said, I feel a physical revulsion as I imagine myself fully in the midst of parish life, fully in the liturgy." She sounded like a rape victim who had instinctively wanted to "wash out" the intrusive presence, yet in consciously naming that desire, was feeling the icky taint yet again. Her voice got smaller. "My God."

Later, the participant offered Patricia the possibility of a rite of reconciliation and purification. It was agreed that Patricia would select two more people she trusted. She shared her story with the three, and in three weeks of reflection, requested some music, symbols, and stories to be used in the ritualization. In the fourth week, the three planners met together for the final arrangements. The ritualization began in the church, the male pastors of the parish washing Patricia's feet with apology for what the church had done. She then washed their feet and named her pain, her collusion in the violation, and her projection and distancing since. Following this, the men left, and the four women continued with three more parts to the ritualization. When it was completed, the four shared luncheon together.

A different animation was apparent in Patricia following this experience, and she slowly made her way into parish life as a regular participant.

Some life crises are so great that without some kind of mediation, the person gets stuck at that moment and cannot grow beyond it. Healing rites have been endemic to the Christian tradition from the beginning because of the example in memory and in Scripture of Jesus' own profound and widespread ministry of healing. Thus, "the idea of the healing power of Christianity was something that was integral to its central message, and this could not but give rise to a Christian liturgical and pastoral ministry towards the sick."[15] The practice of anointing the sick with prayer became one of the seven rites selected by Lombard as sacramental, especially as it was used in the Middle Ages immediately before death. No argument is needed for the fact that it is fitting for the church to provide liturgies for healing.

Further, the great ground swell in the church for generated rites has focused on rites of healing, and has gained ready acceptance. There is an inherent sense in the church that by whatever terms, *theosis*—becoming into holiness and the likeness of God—cannot happen when persons are riddled with pain or shame,[16] or blocked by illness or alienation. Hospital chaplains have been in a position to generate ritualizations for years, and are beginning now to speak of needs and problems in situations such as miscarriage, stillbirth, and decisions about terminating life-support of those who are brain-dead. Elaine Ramshaw's *Ritual and Pastoral Care* stayed in print over twenty-five years. A recent supplemental liturgical book from the Episcopal Church is a collection of prayers and rites for ministry to the sick.[17]

The primary concern here is the area of ritual competence. If a person is already vulnerable, it is possible in a ritualization to mediate healing, or anomalously to exacerbate the pain, or to mediate that which is partial and therefore untrue, adding to the person's burdens instead of lifting them. What caveat must surely be operative to assure life-giving ritualizations to those who are vulnerable and in need of healing? The next two principles for generating morally integrated and operationally healing ritualizations are:

> (3) The Paschal Mystery in the person's life is identified as it is already present by the grace of the Holy Spirit.

---

15. Bradshaw and Hoffman, "Life Cycle as Theology," 287.
16. See James Fowler's significant treatment of shame in *Faithful Change*.
17. *Enriching Our Worship II: Ministry with the Sick and Dying*.

(4) The full mystery of death and life is incarnated in the ritualization through the juxtaposition of contraries.[18]

In speaking about native American peoples, Steven Charleston has said that not just the Hebrew people but all people have a story, a history, an "Old Testament," within which the love and redemption of Christ may be incarnated and celebrated; and he has claimed the right for First Nations (and, by extrapolation, all peoples) to announce the "New Testament" in their midst.[19] This is no less true in small, subcultural groups than it is in major world cultures.[20] The first implication of this is that no situation is too "far out" to be embraced by the grace of God-in-Christ-and-the-Spirit. There is no situation too dire, no emptiness or death too painful or gruesome, but that the healing grace and love of the Lord can comfort, turn, and redeem it. That is, Christians understand the Paschal mystery—the death and resurrection of Christ—to be the Reality by which the world is understood. This is central to the Christian worldview and is the life-giving way those formed in the Christian faith interpret what happens, whether in a people (like Charleston's native Americans) or an individual (like Patricia). When faced with a vulnerable person facing a life passage or, like Patricia, a situation in need of healing, a Christian ritual-maker, then, would look for signs of both death and resurrection *already extant in the person's life,* in the sure and certain trust that the God known through Christ in the Spirit is already at work in that person's life, turning the dead places to life and creating new redemptive realities for the person. Listening to Patricia's story in preparation for a ritual, then, though difficult to tell and to hear, is the very locus for the always-already (Chauvet's term) work of God-in-Christ-by-the-Spirit toward life and healing.

The second implication of Charleston's claim that all peoples and persons have their own "Old Testament" in relation to which God's new covenant is being created is that a competent ritual-maker would always expect the juxtaposition of contraries. A ritualization that is

---

18. In this notion of juxtaposition of contraries, we draw upon Catherine Bell as noted above, and also upon the liturgical theology of Gordon Lathrop esp. in *Holy Things*.

19. "I am announcing the privilege of my own People to interpret the Christian canon in the light of Israel's experience, but also in the light of their own experience." Charleston, "The Old Testament of Native America," 59.

20. See Susan Marie Smith, "The Scandal of Particularity," 375–96.

true would make real the juxtaposition of death with life. As Gordon Lathrop has said,

> The Christian liturgy . . . embraces contraries: life and death, thanksgiving and beseeching, this community and the wide world, the order expressed here and the disorder and chaos we call by name, the strength of these signs and the insignificance of ritual, one text next to another text that is in a very different voice . . . The mystery of God is the mystery of life conjoined with death for the sake of life. The name of this mystery revealed among us is Jesus Christ. The contraries of the liturgy are for the sake of speaking that mystery. It is by the presence of these contraries in the juxtapositions of the *ordo* that Christians avoid the false alternatives so easily proposed to us today."[21]

One important way that contraries are overlaid with each other is through seeking out the symbols endemic in the situation to reveal and express this reality. In the last chapter, two types of symbols were introduced: *archetypal symbols* of the human family which participate in the very thing they represent (Tillich), similar to what Victor Turner called "dominant" symbols, and also *localized symbols* which are quite particular to their context (similar to what Victor Turner called "instrumental" symbols). Both archetypal and localized symbols can bear opposite meanings at the same time (e.g., water is both life-giving [quenching thirst, first step in birthing] and death-dealing [flood waters, tsunamis]). Thus symbols themselves are both essential and true because they juxtapose opposites, mediating death and resurrection.

In the example opening this section, the woman we have called Patricia had a dream image of a chalice that contained a scream. In the ritualization designed, a chalice was offered to her to carry on a journey that she took through the adjacent woods. A chalice is a potent symbol, signifying both the death of Christ (his blood poured out) and self-giving, life-giving love (eucharistic participation in drinking the cup gives life and eternal life). The particular associations condensed in this action by Patricia were meaningful and healing to her because of the import of that dream, and because of the power of the sym-

---

21. The "major oppositions of the *ordo*" are called to "lively presence in the local assembly." Lathrop is speaking in the more specific context of eucharist and baptism, for which the oppositions are "meeting and week, word and table, thanksgiving and beseeching, teaching and bath, *pascha* and year" (Lathrop, *Holy Things*, 179).

bol's opposite meanings, both archetypal and localized, in her healing process.

Later in the rite, her body was anointed, as a sign of purification, blessing, consecrating. This archetypal (or at least traditional, in Judaism and Christianity) symbol connected her pain and healing to generations and thousands of years of persons who share her story, who had passed from a state of tainting or smudging to one of purity. The juxtaposition of both kinds of symbols connected her story to the Christian mythos while also blessing and claiming the particularity of her individual story as one in which the Holy Spirit could be found to be operating.

Patricia was a good candidate for a healing ritualization. She had been through the psychological processes of therapy, sharing her story with others' stories and therapeutically telling her story over and over. She had identified how and why she may have been seduced; she had taken steps toward justice with the offending pastor and denomination. She had journaled her dreams. She had named her pain, her betrayal at the hand of a trusted minister of God, her loss of a long-time denominational affiliation and the loss of her parish community. All of this was indeed healing. However, together all these things had not effected her freedom to re-enter the Body of Christ. The experience of death/resurrection, with her story *juxtaposed ritually* with The Story, had the possibility of actually carrying her from one reality to another.

In the rite that was developed for her with her guidance and sharing, her victimization was named, as was her vulnerability, and the power of an entrusted other as it was misused to her violation. During a foot-washing ceremony, the two male clergy in her new parish washed her feet, and apologized to her on behalf of the church, at whose hand she had been wronged. Then, she washed their feet; and for the first time, she named her own part in the events that had occurred. The ritual context created a "safe place" with a healing, loving spirit in which the full truth of various "deaths" and "resurrections" could be enacted within finite ritual-time in the palpable presence of Christ-in-the-Spirit. Freedom resulted. There were several examples of such juxtaposition in the course of this several-hour ritualization.

Following this rite, Patricia was able to enter fully into parish life, become confirmed, work again with children, and take her proper place as a full participant in that locus of the Body of Christ.

These two principles, then, are related: the essential inclusion of the whole truth, the embracing of the contraries of the particular situation, by the skill of the liturgist in "seeing" the Paschal mystery already present even in painful circumstances of the situation. These principles allow and enable the incarnation of the fullness of the Paschal Mystery, including both the cross and the resurrection, to be made manifest in any Christian ritualization.

Ritualizations for Vocational Change

My wife realized a call to the ordained Christian ministry. It was not reasonable in the denomination she grew up in; so, over time, she found a denomination in which she could be at home, and in which she would be supported in her Christian vocation. Now she teaches and serves a congregation.

I have always respected her career and her vocation. I have also been a bit envious of the clarity and definition of her calling from God and the concrete way she lives it out, a way which is publicly acknowledged.

I, too, shifted denominations as an adult to a more liturgical tradition that has awakened an avenue of the Spirit in me. I have grown tremendously in my faith and as a Christian. I have a spiritual director; I'm involved deeply in our congregation; I retreat regularly and pray regularly. I try to live my faith in all that I do.

But you know, it's frustrating for me, because I can't seem to find a niche that enables me and everyone around me to know I'm really living my Christian vocation. Oh, I know that my baptism is my primary calling. I'm doing the best I can. But there's something missing. I want to make a public connection between my work and my life of faith. I want to know what it is I'm called to, and I want to clearly live it every day, with a kind of accountability and support from the Body of Christ that will make my vocation tangible and effective.

Actually, I counted the pages in the Prayer Book for liturgies for the ordained. There are fifty-five. And then I counted the pages for liturgies of lay vocations—both of them. If you count confirmation, the number rises from two pages to ten.

My approach to the inequity, after I got over the harumphing, was an attempt to be constructive: I designed a Sunday liturgy in which I would be consecrated as a Christian engineer-manager, which was my work at the time. I elaborated upon the service in the Prayer Book and placed it in the context of a renewal of baptismal vows. I even wrote the sermon. There was a charge to be delivered to me.

But the service was never conducted. After mentioning it quickly to the pastor in the hallway one day, I realized that our church has a busy liturgical calendar, and that we just don't—or, at least, haven't—done services like this on Sunday. Marriages aren't done in the Sunday context, either. My service didn't seem to be an obvious and easy fit. And it would take some work to be sure it was not about promoting me, but about worshipping God. I suppose I could redesign it for a private service, but I wanted both to elicit the support of the body of Christ for my vocation and to affirm that all of us are the body of Christ, not just on Sundays when we gather, but every day in the world. So it just never happened.[22]

Christian theology, in strong, effective, doctrinal language, professes that *all* Christians have a ministry, that *all* the baptized are called to ministry. It is the full engagement of all the baptized in their ministries both as church scattered in the world and as church gathered on Sunday that we refer to as *realized baptismal ecclesiology*. Studies of Christian ministry have been especially strong on this since World War II occupied Europe when Christian clergy were removed from their congregations. The life—the very existence—of the church was dependent upon laity gathering together weekly in secret, and acting like Christians every day in the painful and extremely challenging situations in which they found themselves. Many so-called Christians were unidentifiable as they succumbed to Nazi demands to act cru-

---

22. From several conversations with Jerry Walker of St. Mark's Episcopal Church, Berkeley, California. He has affirmed this paraphrase of his ideas.

elly to fellow humans (e.g., Jews, mentally retarded, gypsies, gays, and lesbians).

> [T]he real resistance against the Nazis had to take place within industry, within community and family life, and, in the end, within politics. This was true for Christians as for others. The Nazis did not object to people gathering for worship, let alone to an individual worshiping on his [or her] own. Preaching could be continued in such a way as to be unobjectionable. What the Nazis could not and would not tolerate was worship and preaching that resulted in action contrary to their wishes . . . One clergyman acting along these lines could accomplish very little and could quickly be removed. A hundred men and women acting in a hundred different places was a different matter entirely.
>
> When the same countries faced the task of rebuilding after the war, some persons in the church had learned their lesson well. They saw that their faith would have little impact except as worship and preaching erupted into action by laymen [sic] in all areas of their lives. They saw, too, that the church itself would have to be reborn. The Nazis had brought out the best in the church; they had also revealed the worst. If laymen [and laywomen] were to share in the ministry, not in some specialized job, but in their everyday lives, the church would have to rethink its nature and its task.[23]

However, in North America, this terrible lesson about lay ministry has hardly taken hold. Experientially, conscious lay Christian ministry hardly occurs except as Christians work within the structure of the church as it gathers together, to prepare coffee and dinners, clean, meet, worship, plan, finance. The primary locus of Christ's ministry, which is the ministry of all the baptized—the world—is assumed and theoretically named, but there are few examples of how this works.[24]

23. Ayres, *The Ministry of the Laity*, 13–14.
24. There is a growing literature on this subject. See, for example, Tom Chappell, *The Soul of a Business*: an Episcopal layman who started a company (Tom's of Maine) and struggled to expand while holding onto his Christian values; Robert K. Greenleaf, *The Servant as Leader* (1972), who worked in servant leadership from his position at AT&T and was a leader in the Servant Society until his death in 1990; C. William Pollard, *The Soul of the Firm*: the story of ServiceMaster Company by its chairman; and David Whyte, *The Heart Aroused*: a poet who coaches businesses to welcome the full humanity of employees into the workplace. Two significant resources are *Greenleaf Center for Servant Leadership* (Indianapolis, IN), and *Shalem Institute for Spiritual Formation* (Bethesda, MD 20814).

The imperative for liturgists *vis-à-vis* the baptismal process, looking for operating effectiveness in addition to theological affirmation, would be to ritualize vocational moments for persons at times of readiness and receptiveness.

We have from Chauvet a quite lucid, pronounced statement, reiterated by M. Aune, that Christian existence is intersubjective, which means that for an actual relationship with God to be effected, Christians, the baptized, must be free to respond in thanks, in ethical living, and in word, thought, and behavior. At baptism we unite ourselves with Christ and give over our lives to Him and the Spirit; then in the baptismal process, as in any ongoing relationship with a friend or family member or mentor—how much more so with God!—we must continue to offer ourselves, our souls and bodies. According to Theodore Jennings, the function of liturgical action "is to give a publicly intelligible account of Christian life, faith and action."[25] Ritualizations for laypersons of any age as they identify their baptismal vocation and place it in the context of their self-offering and thanks-gift to God can render this accounting. This, then, is the fifth principle of post-baptismal ritualization:

> (5) Because baptism is the keystone sacrament and point of departure for post-baptismal theopoetic ritualization, the relationship of the action to baptism, as life thanks-gift in response to baptismal grace, should be clear in the ritual symbolization and enactment (e.g., that it is a renewal of baptismal vows, or a step within those vows, or other response-gift).

The concerns of the person whose story opened this section notwithstanding, there is a reason why fifty-five pages of the *Book of Common Prayer* are given to rites of ordination and commissioning of the ordained: they are the ones designated *to oversee the care of the Body*. Attending to the community, building up the Body, holding unity, modeling love, guiding and catechizing, is essential work done on behalf of the whole community by persons designated to act on the church's behalf. Realizing baptismal ecclesiology is a primary function of the ordained.

Yet the ordained forget. The churches retain Christendom patterns of catechizing less for baptism (or even confirmation) than for ordination: it is those preparing for ordination who spend three to five

---

25. Jennings, "Ritual Studies and Liturgical Theology," 38.

years, study Jesus' teachings, reflect on their lives in light of the Gospel, and change their behavior, work, and primary community of belonging. By the time they are ordained, they have most certainly been converted. But the ordained have now experienced that only the few go through such disciplined sacrifice. They are given congregations and buildings to inspire and maintain. They forget (did they ever learn?) that *forming the laity* to become the body of Christ so as to live Christ's ministry of worship, study and service, teaching, preaching, and healing *is at the top of their job descriptions*. But often, other demands take precedence. Or clergy get distracted by the power. Clericalism is not dead.

Enabling *all the baptized* to lean into Christ's likeness and to take their places in Christ's ministry can renew the church. Clergy—and not only clergy—can enable God's covenanted people to grow in faith and holiness and to offer their lives to God by guiding them across passages, mediating the Spirit's healing, and enabling vocational discernment. Christian ritualization is an essential means.

Yet every ordained person may not have ritual competence; and many lay people do. Ritual competence enacted in situations such as the ones named here would multiply the two *Prayer Book* pages of services for laity to infinite possibilities for the baptized to grow in Christ and the Spirit in a liturgical way of life. Instead of publishing thousands of rites for every individual need, it makes more sense (and is the call of this book) for ritually competent pastoral leaders to develop the skill to offer particular incarnational ritualizations as needed for their own flocks. Those with vision and competent ability and ritual knowledge may be lay or ordained.

However, if these ritualizations are led by the ritually competent, irrespective of their ordained status, the question is raised: can anyone act on the church's behalf? The tension inherent in this question of vocation leads us to the broader issue of the relationship of individuals to the apostolic community. Attention to this central issue is the topic of the final chapter.

12

The One and the Many
Personal Rites for Building the Body

THIS BOOK HAS CALLED CHURCHES IN POST-CHRISTENDOM TO REALize, to make real, the church in the world as the fullness of all those baptized into Christ, living out their gifts for ministry and their call of Christ by the power of the Holy Spirit. And it has proposed a liturgical approach to realized baptismal ecclesiology: namely, the planning and conducting of Christian ritualizations for life-passage, healing, and vocational change, to be offered in a post-baptismal catechetical rhythm to enable the baptized to grow into God, to mature in Christ, and to offer their lives as response- or thanks-gifts to God through the Holy Spirit. Five principles for such ritual-making have been offered for the sake of supporting this pastoral ritual extension of the churches' ritual knowledge through regular weekly worship (what I call "a liturgical way of life"), and for the sake of growing ritual competence among Christian lay and ordained leaders. In this book, examples have been drawn from individual needs for ritualizing passage through a life crisis, the healing of a wound, or the shifting of one's call or vocation. Sometimes ritual competence may be needed for groups: families, communities, or even denominations or nations. Yet this book has focused on individuals. Because I propose two radically different perspectives for the post-Christendom churches to take—making the growth and development of the baptized a central priority of the churches for the sake of the utter fulfillment of their ministries in the world, and supporting this work through intentional creation of ritualizations "custom-made" for particular persons along their Christian journeys—I expect there may be surprise, resistance, or challenge to the book's several theses. Throughout the book, therefore, I have tried to identify some of the arguments that seem likely to arise in challenge to these proposals, and to address them theologically, pastorally, practically, and symbolically.

There are, however, two additional concerns that liturgical theologians may raise about this proposal, which deserve to be addressed. The first is a potential fear that ritualizations for individuals could be too subjective—such as for the trading in of the crib for a "big boy bed" when a child is three,[1] or the calling forward of a parishioner on Sunday morning for a prayer for transition to a new job or to retirement—or could over-emphasize the individual when salvation occurs in the community. Why argue for rites particular to individuals, now, in an age of over-individualism and rising narcissism? There might be a "fear [of] the so-called excesses of our culture that allegedly privilege the subjective at the expense of the objective, and we do not want our worship to take the same turn."[2] Where is the line between faithful mediation of the common worship of God the Unknowable Omniscient Mystery, and the particular, pastoral ritualization of one person's felt need turned as healing, holy thanks-offering? This is the question of the relationship of the *many* to the *one*.

And second, there may be a concern that a plethora of ritualizations in the church may clutter or eclipse the eucharist. As noted in the last chapter, one of the central rites of the church is gathering with other Christians for the weekly eucharist on the Lord's Day, sacrament of our unity, healing, nurturing, and ongoing identity. If we all have the possibility of growing toward the likeness of God, and if participation in liturgy is one important part of this process, then the work of the church has one clear component: conducting liturgy and preparing all the people for participation in it in various roles. But the church is already doing this! Week after week we worship; we have experienced an era of liturgical reform precipitated by Vatican Council II; we train seminarians in liturgy and sacramental theology; and in places, laity are also trained.

The eucharist is the primary sacrament of unity, the "sacrament of the Kingdom of God";[3] it is the continuing component of the sac-

---

1. See Gertrud Mueller Nelson, "The Story of Paul," in *To Dance With God*, 39–41.

2. Michael Aune, "Ritual Practice," 155.

3. For example, Alexander Schmemann writes: In "the divorce between theology and the liturgical experience of the Church . . . theology has come eventually to define

rament of initiation. Through its corporate confession and absolution and the Lord's Prayer, it is the sacrament of reconciliation. It is the central act of identity of the Christian people. It feeds us. In its anamnesis and prolepsis, the present moment is recontextualized to *kairos* eternality. We become who we are.[4] What more, then, do we need? We have the ultimate "pastoral liturgy," and by the grace of God, since the Liturgical Renewal of the 1960s–70s, eucharist has again become the primary action of many Christian people every Sunday, the Lord's Day.

Yet we here argue for a much wider range of liturgical actions for God's people to enable the baptized to become who they are in the likeness of God. We are calling for ritual enactment of moments when the Image and the Likeness show progressive merging. Is this not redundant, a theology of adiaphora, emphasizing the side dishes and ignoring the main meal? What more do we need than the eucharist, and should we put so much energy on anything else?

My own awareness of the tension between operational and doctrinal efficacy was piqued in a conversation about an increasingly common practice in Episcopal parishes: healing prayer offered during the communion portion of the eucharistic service, often at the baptismal font. Persons desirous of prayer for healing, sometimes with anointing, will go to the altar for communion and then go to the font for prayer while communion music is played or sung. My friend and colleague Paul, rector of a small parish, disparaged this practice. "It's redundant!" he exclaimed. "And it confuses people as to the meaning of the eucharist. Eucharist *is* what heals, what forgives, what brings wholeness. To have a second action (and concurrent with commu-

---

the sacraments as no more than 'channels of grace,' and now modern secularised theology has ... turned them into 'channels of help.' But in reality the sacraments are to be seen as the *locus*, the very centre of the Church's eschatological understanding and experience. The whole Liturgy is to be seen as the sacrament of the Kingdom of God, the Church is to be seen as the presence and communication of the Kingdom that is to come. The unique—I repeat, unique—function of worship in the life of the Church and in theology is to convey a sense of this eschatological reality" (Schmemann, "Liturgy and Eschatology," 10).

4. Augustine: "You are the bread on the altar. Be what you see; become who you are" (from sermon 272 [PL 38:1246–48]). "Because you are the body of Christ and his members, it is your own mystery that lies on the altar, it is your own mystery that you receive ... Be what you see, and receive what you are."

nion!) diffuses the focus on what the central action of the community is at that moment."

Certainly, his point has theological currency. His argument is an accepted doctrinal reality: we believe that healing, reconciliation, and wholeness are among the multiple fruits of communion.[5] But shall we, then, deny Christians the personal experienced intimacy of prayer with another because it is in the context of Holy Eucharist? Shall we chastise people for wanting someone to lay hands on them particularly, when we believe that simple participation in Holy Communion could have the same effect? Shall we try to teach people that a longing for such personal prayer in that context is inappropriate and should be abated? Is this practice bound to be ineffective because it is practical, "merely" operating in lives? Must the doctrinal always trump the operational? In a follow-up conversation with Paul, asking his permission to recount our conversation, he replied with a grin, "Healing prayer at the font is indeed theologically redundant. But it's pastorally valid, and we do it every week at my parish."

As we complete our work toward a baptismal theology that will accommodate a realized baptismal ecclesiology—a theology broad enough to allow for both operational efficacies and the carefully-integrated doctrinal efficacies—we find a need here for an excursus on the relationship between the One and the Many. In this example, what is appropriate for the Whole is that everyone attend to, contribute toward, and participate in the central corporate action (Holy Communion). What is helpful for some individuals while others are communicating through the bread and wine is that they be free to connect with fellow parishioners and/or clergy for laying-on-of-hands in prayer. Are these contradictory? Does meeting the need of the individual detract from the strength of the communal, which is so central to Christianity and so marginalized in much post-Christendom North American culture?

This book has argued that in the building up of particular members of the community, the whole community is built up into a stronger whole than when particular members of the community are not built up by the Body. Community celebration of events focused on indi-

---

5. For example, Thomas Cranmer's post-communion prayer for the fruits of communion asks God "so to assist us with thy grace, that we may continue in that holy fellowship" which is the "mystical body" of Jesus Christ. A close paraphrase of Cranmer's prayer may be found in *Book of Common Prayer* 1979, 339. For the original, see Cranmer, ed., *The Two Liturgies, A.D. 1549 and A.D. 1552.*

vidual persons is in this way complementary (and not contradictory) to the whole Body. But just to be sure this proposal for intentionally particular rite-making for one will support the whole community, the many, and not devolve into yet more individualism, we shall bring to bear insights from three fields of study on the question of the one and the many: Scripture, the theology of the Trinity, and process theology.

First, out of innumerable references in Scripture to the building up of members of the Body,[6] we focus upon Paul's first epistle to the Corinthians, 12:12–30. The metaphor of the community of Christ as a Body is foundational in Christian theology. There are many parts; each has different gifts and different needs. Yet all need each other. "If the foot were to say, 'Because I am not a hand, I don't belong to the body,' that would not keep it from being a part of the body" (12:15). Further, it is incumbent upon all the members to take care of the vulnerable parts; for this is what builds up the whole body (12:22–25). "If one part of the body suffers, all the other parts suffer with it; if one part is praised, all the other parts share its happiness" (12:26, TEV). Jesus' actions which privileged the healing of an individual over the keeping of the Sabbath (e.g., John 9) suggest that an action on behalf of a person at the point of need comes closer to the reign of God than the keeping of a routine institutional legalism. In Bell's words, it is "symbolically dominant."

Second, the theology of the Trinity is a theology of God in which God's self is understood to be One, but One-in-relation. The Three of God is as important as the One because, as we noted in our discussion of *theosis*, God is communal in nature, a Divine Community into which human members are invited to have a place (like in the Rublev icon of the three angels around a table). Seen in this way, the very nature of God is to be One-and-Many, "the identity and the diversity,"[7] reiterating John Meyendorff's point about God "the One and the Three."[8] Human encounter with God occurs in encounter with particular Persons of the Trinity who, "although united in a single 'dispensation' (*oikonomia*) to save the world and restore the image of God in the human being, were nevertheless distinct personal encounters."[9]

---

6. *E.g.*, Eph 4:1–16; Col 3:12–17; Rom 12:4–8.
7. Vladimir Lossky, *Orthodox Theology*, 36.
8. Meyendorff, "Theosis," 475.
9. Ibid., 475.

It is true that the East and the West have had somewhat different emphases over the centuries, the West concerned about apparent "tritheism" in the East, and the East with the West's dealing "with the Trinity only as an afterthought"[10] or as either unitarianism or hierarchialism, with God the Father as superior over the Son who is superior over the Spirit.[11] But the personal, relational nature of God is not in dispute. As Meyendorff puts it, "The vision of God as both One and Three is, first of all, a vision of living Persons to whom the human being relates, as a person. It makes the Christian experience distinct from the Neoplatonic communion with the One, or from the Buddhist merger of the human person into an impersonal God. Christianity indeed implies monotheism, but this monotheism is not absolute, because God reveals Godself in *relationships of love*."[12]

The doctrinal theology of the Trinity suggests not only that God *is* three Persons, but that God is not static: God is *in relation*. Humans, made *imago Dei*, male and female, also "be" (have their ontological reality) as distinct persons in relationship. The rhythm of the Athanasian Creed suggests the full interiority[13] of each Person of the Trinity (e.g., "the Father indivisible, the Son indivisible, the Holy Spirit indivisible") as well as their full relationship with one another as One God, and their relationship with human beings as Persons and as One God.

And third, a basic tenet of process theology is the dynamic and complementary relationship between the One and the Many. Process theology is identified originally with Alfred North Whitehead, a mathematician; and endemic to process theology are insights from mathematics and particle physics. Consider this foundational relationship:

> Rutherford discovered the proton and came upon the surprising disclosure that the atom is planetary in character, "a merry-go-round in miniature," as one physicist described it. This

---

10. Ibid.
11. Lossky, *Orthodox Theology*, 36–38.
12. Meyendorff, "Theosis," 475.
13. Thomas Berry, a comparative culturalist, poses a series of movements in nature as well as in culture: differentiation, subjectivity (or interiority), and communion. This movement works from the atomic level, as mass of energy before the Big Bang broke into individuated hydrogen atoms and are now able to recombine into other forms (such as water) as well as the human level where children individuate from their parents, become their own persons, and are then able to enter into honest community with others. *The Dream of the Earth*, 45 *passim*.

was the beginning of the *shift* from an atomistic conception of reality *to the ontological notion of the individual in community*, which is the basic formula in Whitehead's metaphysics. The break in imagery, separating the Newtonian-Cartesian age from that of the new vision of science, occurred as early as 1870. Yet as late as 1920 the new imagery of thought remained relatively unknown in many circles of theology and philosophy.[14]

It is "a central doctrine of Whitehead, that in the creative act which is reality itself 'the many become one and are increased by one' . . . Thus the process or experiencing is a perpetual unification of a pluralistic reality which, as fast as it gets unified, becomes pluralistic again, and so can never be finally unified. Process is creative synthesis, the many into a new one producing a new many—and so on forever. The synthesis is creative."[15]

Another perspective on this is the idea that *becoming* is a more accurate, even normative, way of describing reality than *being*. That which the sciences have taught us about our world have impelled an alteration in our way of "seeing."[16] Even so, the very structure of our language(s) reiterates a "being" orientation in our speech and thereby our thinking.

Bernard Lee points out that the dynamism of an evolving view of the world is more in keeping with the structure of the Hebrew language. In the giving of God's name to Moses, for example (Exod 3:13–15), the name indicates action that is not complete: *Ehyeh asher ehyeh*.[17] "I am who am" does not communicate the vibrant unfolding of the Hebrew. Something like "I am in the process of becoming the one who I will be" begins to approximate the Hebrew meaning. God is revealed, reveals Godself, in history, which is ongoing, changing, and

---

14. Meland. "Faith and the Formative Imagery of our Time," 41 (emphasis added).

15. Hartshorne, "The Development of Process Philosophy," 60–61. He goes on, "Determinism, if carried to the limit, is magic, not rationality. The causal conditions for each free act are previous acts of freedom; creativity feeds upon its own products and upon nothing else! . . . Because the previous products are retained in the new syntheses, there is (in spite of Buddhism) any amount of permanence in this philosophy. The *products of creation are never destroyed by new creation*, but always utilized and preserved forever, at least on the divine level" (Emphasis added.).

16. In the discussion that follows, I am following Lee, *The Becoming of the Church*, 14.

17. Lee, *The Becoming of the Church*, 210.

unfolding. So dynamic also is the relationship between God and God's people; and so dynamic is the way God's people must come to know their God, as this One acts as time unfolds. The Passover "was a continuation of the event by which Yahweh *was still becoming* their God and they *were still becoming* [God's] people, and the yearly Passover executed the continuation.[18]

This continuing-newness animating the Hebrew language contrasts sharply with the subject-object ordering of English. The subject of a sentence *is;* it exists. And it then does something (verb) to something else (object). "The rose is blooming." "The cat is chasing the fly." This structure consists with the philosophy of Aristotle in which "everything that changes is [first] something, and is changed by something into something."[19] In contrast, basic process thought as articulated by Whitehead asserts, "there is not first a subject and then its experiences; rather, 'each actual entity is a throb of experience.' 'The notion of 'substance' is transformed into that of actual entity.' 'Experiencing' is the fundamental unit of reality, not some*thing* which experiences. The very *act-of-becoming is* what is real . . . the event is the subject. The subject is a verb. And the identities that we have called subjects before are the predicates, the functions of event or process."[20]

To say "the event is the real unit of things"[21] is to suggest a dynamic view of liturgy in which reality "happens." For Whitehead, "an actual entity is a process, and is not describable in terms of the morphology of a 'stuff.'"[22] Something's "'being' is constituted by its 'becoming.'"[23] For Whitehead, too, there is an aesthetic aspect to this inherently creative process of reality.[24]

Thus, each "entity" is becoming, and is part of a whole that is greater than the sum of the parts and is also becoming. Each One affects each other One, and each and all affect and are affected by the

---

18. Ibid. Emphasis his. The process of each affects all (chapter 8, n. 12).

19. Aristotle, *Metaphysics*, 1069; in Lee, *The Becoming of the Church*, 53.

20. Lee, *The Becoming of the Church*, 53–54. He quotes Alfred North Whitehead, *Process and Reality*, 290 and 28.

21. Whitehead, *Science and the Modern World*, 152; in Lee, *The Becoming of the Church*, 56.

22. Whitehead, *Process and Reality*, 65.

23. Ibid., 34–35. In Lee, *The Becoming of the Church*, 57.

24. On Whitehead and beauty, see Whitehead, *Science and Philosophy*, 9 *passim*; and *Adventures of Ideas*, esp. chapters 17, 18. In Lee, *The Becoming of the Church*, 59–62, *passim*, and 291 n. 20, n. 24.

Whole, the Many. At "the dawn of Western philosophy, Heraclitus stated that all things are in flux . . . However, he was overshadowed by the mainstream of Greek philosophy, which since the time of Parmenides affirmed the primacy of being over becoming and of absoluteness over relativity. The tension between being and becoming has persisted throughout Western thought. Although the Christian doctrines of the Trinity and Incarnation favor the dynamic and relationship view, they were often interpreted in static terms and subordinated to the notion of God as unmoved mover and timeless absolute."[25]

This short taste of the richness of process thought reflects a perspective wider than theology of complementarity between the one and the many. What happens to the one affects the many. Care for the one, change or transformation for the one, neglect of the one, all affect the nature and the directional vector of the many, of the whole. The foundational sacramental events of the *ecclesia* that focus upon *one*, contribute fundamentally to the upbuilding of the *many*. While we are not able to draw conclusions about the relative value of conducting healing prayer during communion, we are, however, able to accept as premise that a ritual action which is positively experienced by the one should not be eliminated out of hand either on the basis of doctrinal disagreement (without considering operational efficacy) or out of concern that the action of the one (i.e., healing prayer) will necessarily detract from or diminish the action of the many (i.e., the corporate eucharistic action).

The excursus into the One and the Many has yielded a second, unexpected insight. In addition to the complementarity between the personal and the corporate, we find the rhythm of One-and-Many to be not only back and forth, but forward: it is itself directional. We have seen from our discussion of *theosis* the thrust toward growth in Christ by the ongoing activity of the Holy Spirit that the image and likeness may more and more merge. And basic to process thought is that *becoming* is normative over *being*. We conclude that the shifting focus between individuals, leaders, and the community is itself dynamic and thus fitting for the church, the ones "called out." The centrality of eucharist does not obviate the need for particular ritualizations of persons; and their ritualization does not diminish the eucharist.

---

25. Cousins, "Process Models," 8. Thus time, relationship, and novelty are three aspects of process thought (ibid., 19).

Conclusion

> [W]hen pastoral practice does not bear fruit in building up the common life of the Body of Christ, then ritual patterns must be critically revised so that they may more adequately fulfill their role as signs of the abiding action of God in the Church. Liturgical change is the response in the Church to the awareness of God's present imperatives within the community of faith.[26]

As Allchin has pointed out, the personal is corporate. This is certainly manifest in the eucharistic celebration. It is not true that only a few people are communicated as a synechdoche or representation of the fact that "we are one in Christ." Rather *each person there* receives, even if adaptations are required (like taking communion to those indisposed in the back, or those in wheelchairs). In fact, the elements are taken to *persons not there* by reason of illness or house-bounding. In order that all may be in communion with one another and with Christ, *each* partakes of the bread and the cup. The corporate confession expresses both the fact that *each* of us is finite, is a sinner, is incomplete, falls short, and also that as a community we *all* fall short together, parochially, societally, nationally, globally. At the same time, the corporate confession is insufficient for personal confession if no private prayer has taken place in advance, and no amends follow. That is, there is a relationship in the eucharistic rite between the one and the many which points beyond itself. Just as in the eucharist the individuals sharing in the loaf and the cup are what make the many into one body, so as in particular ritualizations of individuals or small groups, the body is built up and made stronger as the community as a whole grows toward Christ.

The point of re-thinking the church's ecclesiology as founded on *all the baptized* presupposes that *at baptism, one IS designated* for a particular mediative role as part of Christ's priestly people to mediate God to the world—namely, to those people and circumstances proximate to one's life; and to mediate the world to God in prayer. The question of baptismal ecclesiology is at its base a question of authority. We put it boldly: one strategy the church has used to hold the solemnity and accountability of its sacramental and ritual life is to keep the

---

26. Weil, "The Gospel in Anglicanism," 63.

ritual authority in the hands of the few (clerical ecclesiology). Now, we find ourselves in a post-Christendom situation when it is increasingly apparent that Christians in the world are already few (and growing proportionally fewer), and that the mediating work of all Christians is necessary for the world's sake and appropriate for the church's sake. As has been reclaimed at various points in the church's history, most dramatically after World War II, we are again in a time which calls for a rearrangement of power and of ritual authority in the church.[27]

If the Christian way of life is a liturgical way of life, then baptized Christians must be enabled to witness to and mediate ritually the ever-always-presence of God in the world. Since the life of the baptized is a process, this book has argued that Christian ritualizing is a way to enable developmental turning points to affirm the unity with Christ forged at baptism. This must be done not by denying laity access to ritual competence and ritualizing support, but by forming them ritually in ongoing conversion, and by providing for those so oriented with the skills of symbolic and ritual competence.

May this argument inspire congregations who have persons with the gifts of ritual competence to begin to offer intentional ritualizing and training in ritualization. May they report their results. May a theopoeisis of persons and of communities be the felicitous result.

---

27. Roland Allen (1869–1947), an Anglican missionary priest, worked throughout the world to empower the laity and to grow the church. His ideas continue to be prophetic and relevant. See his book *Missionary Methods: St. Paul's or Ours? A Study of the Church in the Four Provinces* (London: Robert Scott, 1912). His story was written by his grandson Hubert J. B. Allen, *Roland Allen* (Grand Rapids: Eerdmans, 1995).

Bibliography

Books and Articles

Abbott, Walter M., ed. *The Documents of Vatican II*. New York: American, 1966.

Allchin, A. M. *Participation in God: A Forgotten Strand in Anglican Tradition*. Wilton, CT: Morehouse-Barlow, 1988.

Allen, Hubert J. B. *Roland Allen: Pioneer, Priest, and Prophet*. Cincinnati: Forward Movement Publications, and Grand Rapids: Eerdmans, 1995.

Allen, Roland. *Missionary Methods: St. Paul's or Ours?* Grand Rapids: Eerdmans, 1962.

Allport, Gordon. *Becoming: Basic Considerations for a Psychology of Personality*. New Haven, CT: Yale University Press, 1955.

Ambrose. *On the Sacraments; On the Mysteries*. Translated by T. Thompson. London: SPCK, 1950.

Anderson, Herbert, and Edward Foley. *Mighty Stories, Dangerous Rituals: Weaving Together the Human and the Divine*. San Francisco: Jossey-Bass, 1998.

Andrewes, Lancelot. *Complete Works*. Vol. 3: Library of Anglo-Catholic Theology. London: Parker, 1874.

The Apostolic Fathers. Lightfoot, J. B., and J. R. Harmer, trans. Grand Rapids: Baker, 1989.

Apostolic Tradition. See Cuming, Geoffrey, ed. *Hippolytus, A Text for Students*.

Aquinas, Thomas. *De Principiis Naturae; De Mixtione Elementorum*. Translated by Joseph Bobik. Notre Dame, IN: University of Notre Dame Press, 1998.

———. *Summa Theologiae*. Vol. 56 (IIIa, Questions 60–65). Translated with an introduction and footnotes by David Bourke. Cambridge: Blackfriars, 1964.

———. *Summa Theologiae*. Vol. 57 (IIIa, Q. 66–72). Translated by James J. Cunningham. Cambridge: Blackfriars, 1964.

Augustinus, Aurelius. *The Confessions of St. Augustine*. Translated by John K. Ryan. Garden City, NY: Image, 1960.

———. *St. Augustine: Homilies on the Gospel of John*. A Select Library of the Nicene and Post-Nicene Fathers of the Christian Church, vol. 7, edited by Philip Schaff, 344–45. New York: Scribner, 1888.

———. "On Baptism: Against the Donatists." Translated by J. R. King. In *St. Augustine: The Writings against the Manicheans and against the Donatists*. A Select Library of the Nicene and Post-Nicene Fathers of the Christian Church, vol. 4, edited by Philip Schaff. Buffalo, NY: The Christian Literature Company, 1887.

———. "Sermon 227." In *The Complete Works of Augustine, Bishop of Hippo. Patrologia Latina*, vol. 38, edited by J.-P. Migne, columns 1099–1101. Paris: Migne, 1845.

———. "Treatise on the Gospel of John." In *The Complete Works of Augustine, Bishop of Hippo. Patrologia Latina*, vol. 35, edited by J.-P. Migne, columns 1379–1976. Paris: Migne, 1841.

Aune, Michael B. "'But Only Say the Word': Another Look at Christian Worship as Therapeutic." *Pastoral Psychology* 41.3 (1993) 145–57.

———. "'A Heart Moved': Philip Melanchthon's Forgotten Truth about Worship." *Lutheran Quarterly* 12 (1998) 395–418.

———. "Introductory Essay." In *Religious and Social Ritual: Interdisciplinary Explorations*, edited by Michael B. Aune and Valerie DeMarinis, 139–45. New York: State University of New York Press, 1996.

———. "The Return of the Worshiper to Liturgical Theology: Studies of the Doctrinal and Operational Efficacy of the Church's Worship." Unpublished paper. Berkeley, CA: Pacific Lutheran Theological Seminary, 1992.

———. "Ritual Practice: Into the World, Into Each Human Heart." In *Inside Out: Worship in an Age of Mission*, edited by Thomas H. Schattauer, 151–79. Minneapolis: Fortress, 1999.

———. "The Subject of Ritual: Ideology and Experience in Action." In *Religious and Social Ritual: Interdisciplinary Explorations*, edited by Michael B. Aune and Valerie DeMarinis, 147–73. New York: State University of New York Press, 1996.

———. *"To Move the Heart": Rhetoric and Ritual in the Theology of Philip Melanchthon*. San Francisco: Christian Universities Press, 1994.

———. "Worship in an Age of Subjectivism Revisited." *Worship* 65 (1992) 224–38.

Austin, Gerard. *Anointing with the Spirit: The Rite of Confirmation*. New York: Pueblo, 1985.

Ayres, Francis O. *The Ministry of the Laity: A Biblical Exposition*. Philadelphia: Westminster, 1962.

Baptism, Eucharist and Ministry. Faith and Order Paper No.111. Geneva: World Council of Churches, 1982.

Bateson, Mary Catherine. *Composing a Life*. New York: Atlantic Monthly, 1989.

Battles, Ford Lewis. "God Was Accommodating Himself to Human Capacity." *Interpretation* 31 (1977) 22–38.

Beck, Renee, and Sydney Barbara Metrick. *The Art of Ritual: A Guide to Creating and Performing Your Own Ceremonies for Growth and Change*. Berkeley, CA: Celestial Arts, 1990.

Behr, John. *St. Irenaeus of Lyons on the Apostolic Preaching*. Crestwood, NY: St. Vladimir's Seminary Press, 1997.

Belenky, Mary F., et al. *Women's Ways of Knowing: The Development of Self, Voice, and Mind*. New York: Basic, 1997.

Bell, Catherine. "The Authority of Ritual Experts." *Studia Liturgica* 23 (1993) 98–120.

———. "Discourse and Dichotomies: The Structure of Ritual Theory." *Religion* 17 (1987) 95–118.

———. "The Ritual Body and the Dynamics of Ritual Power." *Journal of Ritual Studies* 4.2 (1990) 299–313.

———. "Ritual, Change, and Changing Rituals." *Worship* 63 (1989) 31–41.

———. *Ritual: Perspectives and Dimensions.* Oxford: Oxford University Press, 1997.

———. *Ritual Theory, Ritual Practice.* New York: Oxford University Press, 1992.

Berling, Judith A. "Orthopraxy." In *The Encyclopedia of Religion*, vol. 10. 2nd ed. Edited by Lindsay Jones et al., 6913–16. Detroit: MacMillan, 2005.

Berry, Thomas. *The Dream of the Earth.* San Francisco: Sierra Club, 1988.

Bettenson, Henry, ed. *Documents of the Christian Church.* London: Oxford University Press, 1963.

Biziou, Barbara. *The Joy of Ritual: Spiritual Recipes to Celebrate Milestones, Ease Transitions, and Make Every Day Sacred.* New York: Golden, 1999.

Bobik, Joseph, trans. *Aquinas on Matter and Form and the Elements: A Translation and Interpretation of the* de Principiis Naturae *and the* De Mixtione Elementorum *of St. Thomas Aquinas.* Notre Dame, IN: University of Notre Dame Press, 1998.

Bobrinskoy, Boris. *Communion du Saint-Esprit.* Spiritualité Orientale 56. Paris: Bellefontaine, 1992.

Book of Common Prayer . . . according to the use of the Episcopal Church. New York: Church Publishing, 1979.

Book of Occasional Services. New York: Church Publishing, 1995.

Bouwsma, William J. "Calvinism as *Theologia Rhetorica*." Protocol of the Colloquy of the Center for Hermeneutical Studies in Hellenistic and Modern Culture. *Colloquy* 54 (1986) 1–21. Berkeley, CA: University of California at Berkeley, 1987.

———. "Christian Adulthood." In *Adulthood*, edited by Erik H. Erikson 81–96. New York: Norton & Company, 1978.

———. *John Calvin: A Sixteenth-Century Portrait.* New York: Oxford University Press, 1988.

———. "Minutes of the Colloquy of 28 September 1986." Protocol of the Colloquy of the Center for Hermeneutical Studies in Hellenistic and Modern Culture. *Colloquy* 54 (1986) 65–82. Berkeley, CA: University of California at Berkeley, 1987.

Boyle, Marjorie O'Rourke. *Erasmus on Language and Method in Theology.* Toronto: University of Toronto Press, 1977.

———. *Rhetoric and Reform: Erasmus' Civil Dispute with Luther.* Cambridge: Harvard University Press, 1983.

———. "Rhetorical Theology: Charity seeking Charity: A Response to William J. Bouwsma." Protocol of the Colloquy of the Center for Hermeneutical Studies in Hellenistic and Modern Culture. *Colloquy* 54 (1986) 22–30. Berkeley, CA: University of California at Berkeley, 1987.

Braaten, Carl, and Robert Jenson, eds. *Union with Christ: The New Finnish Interpretation of Luther.* Grand Rapids: Eerdmans, 1998.

Bradshaw, Paul F. "Difficulties in Doing Liturgical Theology." *Pacifica* 11 (1998) 181–94.

———. *The Search for the Origins of Christian Worship: Sources and Methods for the Study of Early Liturgy.* London: SPCK, 1992.

Bradshaw, Paul F., and Lawrence A. Hoffman. "Life Cycle as Theology." In *Life Cycles in Jewish and Christian Worship*, 286–94. Notre Dame, IN: University of Notre Dame Press, 1996.

―――, eds. *Life Cycles in Jewish and Christian Worship*. Notre Dame, IN: University of Notre Dame Press, 1996.

Bradshaw, Paul, and John Melloh, eds. *Foundations in Ritual Studies: A Reader for Students of Christian Worship*. Grand Rapids: Baker Academic, 2007.

Breck, John. "'The Two Hands of God': Christ and the Spirit in Orthodox Theology." *St. Vladimir's Theological Quarterly* 40 (1996) 231–46.

Breen, Quirinus. "John Calvin and the Rhetorical Tradition." *Church History* 26 (1957) 3–21.

Brown, Peter. "Aspects of the Christianization of the Roman Aristocracy." In *Religion and Society in the Age of St. Augustine*, 161–82. New York: Harper and Row, 1972.

―――. *Augustine of Hippo: A Biography*. Berkeley: University of California Press, 1967.

Browning, Robert L., and Roy A. Reed. *The Sacraments in Religious Education and Liturgy*. Birmingham, AL: Religious Education, 1985.

Buchanan, Colin. *The Renewal of Baptismal Vows*. Grove Worship Series 124. Bramcote, Nottingham: Grove, 1993.

Burke, Kenneth. *A Rhetoric of Motives*. New York: Prentice Hall, 1950.

―――. *The Rhetoric of Religion: Studies in Logology*. Boston: Beacon, 1961.

Burridge, Kenelm. *New Heaven, New Earth: A Study of Millenarian Activity*. New York: Schocken, 1969.

Butterfield, Herbert. *Christianity and History*. New York: Scribner, 1949.

Calvin, John. *Institutes of the Christian Religion*, vols. 20 and 21. Edited by John T. McNeill. Translated and indexed by Ford Lewis Battles. Library of Christian Classics. Philadelphia: Westminster, 1960.

Calvini Opera. Edited by G. Baum, E. Cunitz, and E. Reuss. *Corpus Reformatorum*, vols. 29–87. Brunswick, Germany: Schwetschke, 1863–1900.

Changes: Prayers and Services Honoring Rites of Passage. New York: Church Publishing, 2007.

Chappell, Tom. *The Soul of a Business: Managing for Profit and the Common Good*. New York: Bantam, 1993.

Charleston, Steven. "The Old Testament of Native America." In *Lift Every Voice: Constructing Christian Theologies from the Underside*, edited by Susan Brooks Thistlethwaite and Mary Potter Engel, 49–61. San Francisco: HarperCollins, 1990.

Chastagnol, André. *Les Fastes de la Préfecture de Rome au Bas-Empire*. Etudes Prosopographique 2. Paris: Nouvelles Editions Latines, 1962.

―――. "Le Sénateur Volusien et la conversion d'une famille de l'aristocratie romaine au bas-empire." *Revue des études anciennes* 58 (1956) 241–53.

Chauvet, Louis-Marie. "Sacramentaire et Christologie. La Liturgie, lieu de la christologie." In *Sacraments de Jésus-Christ*, edited by J. Doré, 213–54. Paris: Desclée, 1983.

―――. *Symbol and Sacrament: A Sacramental Reinterpretation of Christian Existence*. Translated by Patrick Madigan and Madeleine Beaumont. Collegeville, MN: Liturgical, 1995.

Cherry, Kittredge, and Zalmon Sherwood, eds. *Equal Rites: Lesbian and Gay Worship, Ceremonies, and Celebrations*. Louisville: Westminster/John Knox, 1995.

Clark, Elizabeth A., ed. *The Life of Melania the Younger.* Studies in Women and Religion 14. Lewiston, NY: Mellen, 1984.
Clarke, Elizabeth. "Silent, Performative Words: The Language of God in Valdesso and George Herbert." *Journal of Literature and Theology* 5 (1991) 355–74.
Coleman-Norton, P. R., ed. *Roman State and Christian Church: A Collection of Legal Documents to A.D. 535,* vol. 1. London: SPCK, 1966.
Collins, Mary. "An Adventuresome Hypothesis: Women as Authors of Liturgical Change." *Proceedings of the North American Academy of Liturgy* (1993) 37–49.
Congar, Yves M.-J. *Lay People in the Church.* Westminster, MD: Newman, 1957.
———. "My Pathfindings in the Theology of Laity and Ministries." *The Jurist* 32 (1972) 169–88.
Cooper, Patricia, and Norma Bradley Allen. *The Quilters: Women and Domestic Art.* New York: Doubleday, 1989.
Corbon, Jean. *The Wellspring of Worship.* Translated by Matthew J. O'Connell. New York: Paulist, 1988.
Corpus Reformatorum. Brunswick, Germany: Schwetschke, 1863–1900.
Countryman, L. William. *Living on the Border of the Holy: Renewing the Priesthood of All.* Harrisburg: Morehouse, 1999.
Cousins, Ewert H. "Process Models in Culture, Philosophy, and Theology." *Process Theology: Basic Writings,* edited by Ewert H. Cousins, 3–20. New York: Newman, 1971.
———, ed. *Process Theology: Basic Writings.* New York: Newman, 1971.
Cram, Ralph Adams. *The Great Thousand Years.* Boston: Marshall Jones Company, 1919.
Cranmer, Thomas. "Questions and Answers concerning the Sacraments and the Appointment and Power of Bishops and Priests," 1540. In *Miscellaneous Writings and Letters of Thomas Cranmer,* edited for the Parker Society by John Edmund Cox, 115–17. Cambridge: Cambridge University Press, 1846.
———, ed. *The Two Liturgies, A.D. 1549 and A.D. 1552: with other Documents set forth by authority in the Reign of King Edward the Sixth.* Edited for The Parker Society by Joseph Ketley. Cambridge: Cambridge University Press, 1844.
Cross, F. L., ed. *St. Cyril of Jerusalem's Lectures on the Christian Sacraments.* Crestwood, NY: St. Vladimir's Seminary Press, 1977.
Cross, F. L., and E. A. Livingstone, eds. *The Oxford Dictionary of the Christian Church.* 2nd ed. Oxford: Oxford University Press, 1983.
Cross, F. L., and P. E. More, eds. *Anglicanism: The Thought and Practice of the Church of England.* London: SPCK, 1951.
Cuming, Geoffrey J. *Hippolytus: A Text for Students.* 2nd ed. Bramcote, Nottingham: Grove, 1987.
Cunningham, David S. "Theology as Rhetoric." *Theological Studies* 52 (1991) 407–30.
Cyril. *St. Cyril of Jerusalem's Lectures on the Christian Sacraments.* Edited by F. L. Cross. Crestwood, NY: St. Vladimir's Seminary Press, 1977.
d'Andrade, Roy G. "Cultural Meaning Systems." In *Culture Theory: Essays on Mind, Self, and Emotion,* edited by Richard A. Shweder and Robert A. LeVine, 88–119. Cambridge: Cambridge University Press, 1984.
Davies, Horton. *Bread of Life and Cup of Joy: Newer Ecumenical Perspectives on the Eucharist.* Grand Rapids: Eerdmans, 1993.

Delattre, Roland A. "Ritual Resourcefulness and Cultural Pluralism." *Soundings* 16 (1978) 281–301.

Diekmann, Godfrey. "Foreward." In *Strong, Loving and Wise: Presiding in Liturgy*, by Robert W. Hovda, v–vi. Collegeville, MN: Liturgical, 1976.

Dix, Gregory. *The Shape of the Liturgy*. San Francisco: Harper and Row, 1982.

Donovan, Mary Ann. *One Right Reading? A Guide to Irenaeus*. Collegeville, MN: Liturgical, 1997.

Doohan, Leonard. "Laity, Theology of the." In *The New Dictionary of Sacramental Worship*, edited by Peter E. Fink, 636–44. Collegeville, MN: Liturgical, 1990.

Douglas, Mary. *Natural Symbols: Explorations in Cosmology*. 2nd ed. New York: Pantheon, 1982.

Douglass, Laurie. "The Divine Timbre of the Word: An Aspect of Augustine's Sense of Meaning in Sacramentality." Unpublished essay. Notre Dame, IN: University of Notre Dame, 1993.

Droege, Thomas A. "The Formation of Faith in Christian Initiation: A Disputation." *The Cresset* XLVI.6 (1983) 16–23.

Duck, Ruth C. *Gender and the Name of God: The Trinitarian Baptismal Formula*. Cleveland, OH: Pilgrim, 1991.

Duffy, Regis. *An American Emmaus: Faith and Sacraments in the American Culture*. New York: Crossroad, 1995.

———. "Sacraments." In *Systematic Theology: Roman Catholic Perspectives, vol. 2*, edited by Francis Schüssler Fiorenza and John P. Galvin, 183–257. Minneapolis: Fortress, 1991.

Dupré, Louis, and Don E. Saliers, eds. *Christian Spirituality III: Post-Reformation and Modern*. New York: Crossroad, 1989.

Eastman, A. Theodore. *The Baptizing Community: Christian Initiation and the Local Congregation*. New York: Seabury, 1982.

Egeria. *Egeria's Travels*. Translated by John Wilkinson. London: SPCK, 1971.

Eliade, Mircea. *The Sacred and the Profane*. Translated by Willard R. Trask. New York: Harcourt Brace Jovanovich, 1959.

Empereur, James L. "Presidential Style." In *The New Dictionary of Sacramental Worship*, edited by Peter E. Fink, 1006–10. Collegeville, MN: Liturgical, 1990.

Engel, Mary Potter. *John Calvin's Perspectival Anthropology*. Atlanta: Scholars, 1988.

Enriching Our Worship II: Ministry with the Sick and Dying; Burial of a Child. New York: Church Publishing, 2000.

Erikson, Erik H., ed. *Adulthood*. New York: Norton, 1978.

———. *Childhood and Society*, 2nd ed. New York: Norton, 1963.

———. "The Development of Ritualization." In *The Religious Situation*, edited by Donald R. Cutler, 711–33. Boston: Beacon, 1968.

———. *Toys and Reasons: Stages in the Ritualization of Experience*. New York: Norton, 1977.

Evans, Abigail Rian. *Healing Liturgies for the Seasons of Life*. Louisville: Westminster/John Knox, 2004.

Evdokimov, Paul. *L'Orthodoxie*. Bibliothèque théologique. Neuchatel: Delachaux et Niestlé, 1959.

Fairless, Caroline. *Children at Worship—Congregation in Bloom*. New York: Church Publishing, 2000.

Farnham, Suzanne G., et al. *Listening Hearts: Discerning Call in Community.* Harrisburg, PA: Morehouse, 1991.
Ferguson, Everett. "Irenaeus' Proof of the Apostolic Preaching and Early Catechetical Tradition." *Studia Patristica* 18 (1989) 119–40.
Fink, Peter. "Towards a Liturgical Theology." *Worship* 47 (1973) 601–9.
Finn, Thomas M. *Early Christian Baptism and the Catechumenate.* 2 vols. Collegeville, MN: Liturgical, 1992.
Fisher, J. D. C. *Christian Initiation: Baptism in the Medieval West.* London: SPCK, 1965.
———. *Christian Initiation: The Reformation Period.* London: SPCK, 1970.
———. *Confirmation Then and Now.* London: Alcuin Club/SPCK, 1978.
Fowler, James W. *Becoming Adult, Becoming Christian: Adult Development and Christian Faith.* San Francisco: Harper and Row, 1984.
———. *Faith Development and Pastoral Care.* Philadelphia: Fortress, 1987.
———. *Faithful Change: The Personal and Public Challenges of Postmodern Life.* Nashville: Abingdon, 1996.
———. "Perspectives on the Family from the Standpoint of Faith Development Theory." *Perkins Journal* 33 (1979) 1–19.
———. *Stages of Faith: The Psychology of Human Development and the Quest for Meaning.* San Francisco: Harper and Row, 1981.
———. *To See the Kingdom: The Theological Vision of H. Richard Niebuhr.* Nashville: Abingdon, 1974.
———. *Weaving the New Creation: Stages of Faith and the Public Church.* San Francisco: Harper, 1991.
Frend, W. H. C. *The Donatist Church.* Oxford: Clarendon, 1952.
Fuller, Reginald H. "Confirmation in the Episcopal Church and in the Church of England." In *Confirmation Re-Examined*, edited by Kendig Cully, 11–22. Wilton, CT: Morehouse-Barlow, 1982.
Ganoczy, Alexandre. *The Young Calvin.* Philadelphia: Westminster, 1987.
Garcia-Rivera, Alejandro. *The Community of the Beautiful: A Theological Aesthetics.* Collegeville, MN: Liturgical, 1999.
Geertz, Clifford. "Ethos, World View, and the Analysis of Sacred Symbols." In *The Interpretation of Cultures*, 126–41. New York: HarperCollins, 1973.
———. "Religion as a Cultural System." In *The Interpretation of Cultures*, 87–125. New York: HarperCollins, 1973.
———. "Ritual and Social Change: A Javanese Example." In *The Interpretation of Cultures*, 142–69. New York: HarperCollins, 1973.
Gelpi, Donald L. *The Conversion Experience: A Reflective Process for RCIA Participants and Others.* New York: Paulist, 1998.
Gerrish, B. A. "'To the Unknown God': Luther and Calvin on the Hiddenness of God." *The Old Protestantism and the New: Essays on the Reformation Heritage.* Chicago: University of Chicago Press, 1982.
Gilligan, Carol. "Adolescent Development Reconsidered." In *Mapping the Moral Domain: A Contribution of Women's Thinking to Psychological Theory and Education*, edited by Carol Gilligan et al., vii–xxxix. Cambridge: Harvard University Press, 1988.
———. *In a Different Voice: Psychological Theory and Women's Development.* Cambridge: Harvard University Press, 1982.

———, et al., eds. *Mapping the Moral Domain: A Contribution of Women's Thinking to Psychological Theory and Education*. Cambridge: Harvard University Press, 1988.

Gilligan, Carol, and Lyn Mikel Brown. *Meeting at the Crossroads: Women's Psychology and Girls' Development*. Cambridge: Harvard University Press, 1992.

Gobbel, A. Roger, and Phillip C. Huber. *Creative Designs with Children at Worship*. Atlanta: John Knox, 1981.

Gooden, Winston. "The Adult Development of Black Men." PhD diss. Yale University, 1980.

Gramsci, Antonio. *The Modern Prince and Other Writings*. Translated by Louis Marks. New York: International, 1957.

Grant, R. M. *A Short History of the Interpretation of the Bible*. 2nd ed. Philadelphia: Fortress, 1984.

Greenleaf, Robert K. *Servant Leadership: A Journey into the Nature of Legitimate Power and Greatness*. Mahwah, NJ: Paulist, 2002.

Grimes, Ronald L. *Beginnings in Ritual Studies*. Lanham, MD: University Press of America, 1982.

———. "Breaking the Glass Barrier: the Power of Display. *Journal of Ritual Studies* 4 (1990) 239–61.

———. *Deeply Into the Bone: Re-Inventing Rites of Passage*. Berkeley, CA: University of California Press, 2000.

———. "Defining Nascent Ritual." In *Beginnings in Ritual Studies*, 53–69. Lanham, MD: University Press of America, 1982.

———. "Emerging Ritual." In *Reading, Writing, and Ritualizing: Ritual in Fictive, Liturgical and Public Places*, 23–37. Washington, DC: Pastoral, 1993.

———. "Modes of Ritual Necessity." *Worship* 53 (1979) 126–41.

———, ed. *Readings in Ritual Studies*. Upper Saddle River, NJ: Prentice Hall, 1996.

———. "Ritual." In *A New Handbook of Christian Theology*, edited by Donald W. Musser and Joseph L. Price, 413–15. Nashville: Abingdon, 1992.

———. "Ritual Criticism and Reflexivity in Fieldwork." *Journal of Ritual Studies* 2 (1988) 217–39.

———. *Ritual Criticism: Case Studies in its Practice, Essays on its Theory*. Columbia, SC: University of South Carolina Press, 1990.

———. "Ritual Studies." In *The Encyclopedia of Religion*, vol. 12, edited by Mircea Eliade *et al.*, 422–25. New York: MacMillan, 1987.

Guilbert, Charles Mortimer. *Words of our Worship: A Practical Liturgical Dictionary*. New York: Church Hymnal, 1988.

Guzie, Tad. *The Book of Sacramental Basics*. New York: Paulist, 1981.

Hamman, Adalbert. "Catechumen, Catechumenate." In *Encyclopedia of the Early Church*, edited by A. De Berardino, 151–52. Cambridge: James Clarke, 1992.

Hapgood, Isabel Florence, ed. and trans. *Service Book of the Holy Orthodox-Catholic Apostolic Church, arranged from the Old Church-Slavonic Service Books of the Russian Church and Collated with the Service Books of the Greek Church*. 6th ed. Englewood, NY: Antiochian Orthodox Christian Archdiocese, 1983.

Harris, George Clinton. "Ministry and Work: Problems of Identity, Acceptance and Status in the Non-Stipendiary Ministry." DD diss. New York: General Theological Seminary, 1970.

Harrison, Nonna Verna. *God's Many-Splendored Image: Theological Anthropology for Christian Formation*. Grand Rapids: Baker Academic, 2010.

Hartranft, Chester D. "Analysis of Augustin's Writings Against the Donatists." In *St. Augustin: The Writings against the Manicheans and against the Donatists. A Select Library of the Nicene and Post-Nicene Fathers of the Christian Church*, vol. 4, edited by Philip Schaff, 372–404. Buffalo, NY: The Christian Literature Company, 1887.

Hartshorne, Charles. "The Development of Process Philosophy." In *Process Theology: Basic Writings*, edited by Ewert H. Cousins, 47–66. New York: Newman, 1971.

Hatchett, Marion. *Commentary on the American Prayer Book*. Minneapolis, MN: Seabury, 1980.

Hellwig, Monika K. *Sign of Reconciliation and Conversion: The Sacrament of Penance for Our Times*. Wilmington, DE: Glazier, 1982.

Hick, John H. *Philosophy of Religion*. 3rd ed. Englewood Cliffs, NJ: Prentice Hall, 1983.

Hoffman, Lawrence A. *Beyond the Text: A Holistic Approach to Liturgy*. Bloomington, IN: Indiana University Press, 1987.

———. "How Ritual Means: Ritual Circumcision in Rabbinic Culture and Today." *Studia Liturgica* 23 (1993) 78–97.

———. "Life Cycle as Religious Metaphor." In *Life Cycles in Jewish and Christian Worship*, edited by Paul F. Bradshaw and Lawrence A. Hoffman, 1–12. Notre Dame, IN: University of Notre Dame Press, 1996.

Hoffmann, Lawrence, A., and Yoel Kahn. "Contemporary Challenges to Jewish Life-Cycle Ritual." In *Life Cycles in Jewish and Christian Worship*, edited by Paul F. Bradshaw and Lawrence A. Hoffman, 262–85. Notre Dame, IN: University of Notre Dame Press, 1996.

Hoffmann, Lawrence, A., and Paul F. Bradshaw, eds. *Life Cycles in Jewish and Christian Worship*. Notre Dame, IN: University of Notre Dame Press, 1996.

Holeton, David R., ed. *Anglican Orders and Ordinations: Essays and Reports from the Interim Conference at Jarvenpää, Finland, of the International Anglican Liturgical Consultation, 4–9 August, 1997*. Cambridge, UK: Grove, 1997.

Hooker, Richard. *Ecclesiastical Polity*. Oxford: Clarendon, 1888.

Hovda, Robert. *Strong, Loving, and Wise: Presiding in Liturgy*. Collegeville, MN: Liturgical, 1976.

Huck, Gabe. "How Would They Know What to Do?" *Proceedings of the North American Academy of Liturgy* (2001) 3–20.

Hugh of St. Victor. *On the Sacraments of the Christian Faith (De sacramentis Christianae fidei)*. Translated by Roy J. Deferrari. Cambridge, MT: The Mediaeval Academy of America, 1951.

Hughes, Kathleen. *Saying Amen: A Mystagogy of Sacrament*. Chicago: Liturgy Training, 1999.

Hyde, Lewis. *The Gift: Imagination and the Erotic Life of Property*. New York: Random House, 1983.

Hymnal 1982. New York: Church Hymnal, 1985.

Irenaeus. *Adversus haereses*. Translated by F. Sagnard. *Sources Chrétiennes* 34. Paris: Cerf, 1952.

———. *Five Books of St. Irenaeus Against Heresies*. Translated by John Keble. London: Parker, 1872.

———. *St. Irenaeus of Lyons on the Apostolic Preaching*. Translated by John Behr. Crestwood, NY: St. Vladimir's Seminary Press, 1997.

———. *The Scandal of the Incarnation: Irenaeus Against the Heresies*. Translated by John Saward. San Francisco: Ignatius, 1990.

Irwin, Kevin. *Liturgical Theology: A Primer*. Collegeville, MN: Liturgical, 1990.

James, William. *The Varieties of Religious Experience*. New York: Penguin Books, 1982.

Jeanrond, Werner G. *Theological Hermeneutics: Development and Significance*. New York: Crossroad, 1991.

Jennings, Theodore W. "On Ritual Knowledge." *Journal of Religion* 62 (1982) 111–27.

———. "Ritual Studies and Liturgical Theology: An Invitation to Dialogue." *Journal of Ritual Studies* 1 (1987) 35–56.

Johnson, Maxwell E. *The Rites of Christian Initiation: Their Evolution and Interpretation*. Collegeville, MN: Liturgical, 1999.

Jones, Paul H. "We are *How* we Worship: Corporate Worship as a Matrix for Christian Identity Formation." *Worship* 69.4 (1995) 346–60.

Jourjon, M. "Les Pères de l'Eglise ou le dialogue de l'identité chrétienne." In *Sacraments de Jésus-Christ*, edited by J. Doré, 47–68. Paris: Desclée, 1983.

Kahn, Yoel, and Lawrence A. Hoffman. "Contemporary Challenges to Jewish Life-Cycle Ritual." In *Life Cycles in Jewish and Christian Worship*, edited by Paul Bradshaw and Lawrence Hoffman, 262–85. Notre Dame, IN: University of Notre Dame Press, 1996.

Kavanagh, Aidan. "The Role of Ritual in Personal Development." In *The Roots of Ritual*, edited by James D. Shaughnessy, 145–60. Grand Rapids: Eerdmans, 1973.

Keble, John, trans. *Five Books of Irenaeus Against Heresies*. London: Parker, 1872.

Kee, Howard Clark. *Understanding the New Testament*. 5th ed. Englewood Cliffs, NJ: Prentice Hall, 1993.

Keen, Sam. *The Passionate Life: Stages of Loving*. San Francisco: Harper, 1998.

Kegan, Robert. *The Evolving Self: Problem and Process in Human Development*. Cambridge: Harvard University Press, 1982.

Kelleher, Margaret Mary. "Baptism, Ecclesial Nature of." In *The New Dictionary of Sacramental Worship*, edited by Peter E. Fink, 87–90. Collegeville, MN: Liturgical, 1990.

Kelly, J. N. D. *Early Christian Creeds*. 3rd. ed. New York: Longman, 1972.

Kennedy, George A. *New Testament Interpretation through Rhetorical Criticism*. Chapel Hill, NC: University of North Carolina, 1984.

Kertzer, David I. *Ritual, Politics, and Power*. New Haven, CT: Yale University Press, 1988.

Kilmartin, Edward J. *Christian Liturgy: Theology and Practice*. Vol. I: *Systematic Theology of Liturgy*. Kansas City, MO: Sheed & Ward, 1988.

———. "A Modern Approach to the Word of God and Sacraments of Christ: Perspectives and Principles." In *The Sacraments: God's Love and Mercy Actualized*, edited by Francis Eigo, 59–109. Villanova, PA: The Villanova University Press, 1979.

———. "Theology of the Sacraments: Toward a New Understanding of the Chief Rites of the Church of Jesus Christ." In *General Introduction*, edited by Regis A. Duffy, 123–75. Alternative Futures of Worship, vol. 1. Collegeville, MN: Liturgical, 1987.

Kinast, Robert L. *Caring for Society: A Theological Interpretation of Lay Ministry*. Chicago: Thomas More, 1985.

Kinneavy, James L. *Greek Rhetorical Origins of Christian Faith*. New York: Oxford University Press, 1987.

Klingbeil, Gerald A. "Between Law and Grace: Ritual and Ritual Studies in Recent Evangelical Thought." *Journal of the Adventist Theological Society* 13 (2002) 46–63.

———. *Bridging the Gap: Ritual and Ritual Texts in the Bible*. Winona Lake, IN: Eisenbrauns, 2007.

Kohlberg, Lawrence. *The Philosophy of Moral Development*. San Francisco: Harper & Row, 1981.

Kreider, Alan. *The Change of Conversion and the Origin of Christendom*. Harrisburg, PA: Trinity, 1999.

———. *Worship and Evangelism in Pre-Christendom*. Cambridge, UK: Grove, 1995.

LaCugna, Catherine Mowry. *God For Us: The Trinity and Christian Life*. New York: HarperSanFrancisco, 1991.

———. "The Trinitarian Mystery of God." In *Systematic Theology*, vol. 1, edited by Francis Schüssler Fiorenza and John P. Galvin, 151–92. Minneapolis: Fortress, 1991.

LaFontaine, Mary J. "Melanchthon's 'Elementorum Rhetorices Libri Duo.'" PhD diss., University of Michigan, 1968.

Laitin, David. *Hegemony and Cultures*. Chicago: University of Chicago Press, 1986.

Lakoff, George, and Mark Johnson. *Metaphors We Live By*. Chicago: University of Chicago Press, 1980.

Langer, Susanne K. *Philosophy in a New Key*. 3rd ed. Cambridge: Harvard University Press, 1957.

Langhauser, Susan. *Blessings and Rituals for the Journey of Life*. Nashville: Abingdon, 2000.

Lathrop, Gordon. *Holy People: A Liturgical Ecclesiology*. Minneapolis: Augsburg Fortress, 1999.

———. *Holy Things: A Liturgical Theology*. Minneapolis: Fortress, 1993.

Lea, Henry Charles. *A History of Auricular Confession and Indulgences in the Latin Church*. Philadelphia, PA: Lea, 1896.

Leach, Edmund R. "Ritual." In *International Encyclopedia of the Social Sciences*, vol. 13, edited by David Sills, 520–26. New York: MacMillan, 1968.

Leckey, Dolores R. *Laity Stirring the Church: Prophetic Questions*. Philadelphia: Fortress, 1987.

Lee, Bernard. *The Becoming of the Church: A Process Theology of the Structure of Christian Experience*. New York: Paulist, 1974.

Lee, Bernard, and Harry James Cargas, eds. *Religious Experience and Process Theology: The Pastoral Implications of a Major Modern Movement*. New York: Paulist, 1976.

Leith, John H. "Calvin Study for Today" (editorial). *Interpretation* 31 (1977) 3–7.

Levinson, Daniel J., et al. *The Seasons of a Man's Life*. New York: Knopf, 1978.

Liégé, Pierre André. *Adultes Dans le Christ*. Liège, Belgium: L'Imprimerie Soledi, 1965.

———. *What is Christian Life?* New York: Hawthorn, 1961.

Loevinger, Jane. *Ego Development*. San Francisco: Jossey-Bass, 1976.

Lossky, Nicholas. *Lancelot Andrewes: Le Prédicateur*. Paris, 1986.

Lossky, Vladimir. *Orthodox Theology: An Introduction*. Translated by Ian and Ihita Kesarcodi-Watson. Crestwood, NY: St. Vladimir's Seminary Press, 1978.

MacMullen, Ramsay. "Judicial Savagery in the Roman Empire." In *Changes in the Roman Empire: Essays in the Ordinary*, 204–17. Princeton: Princeton University Press, 1990.

Made, Not Born: New Perspectives on Christian Initiation and the Catechumenate. Notre Dame, IN: University of Notre Dame Press, 1976.

Mannermaa, Tuomo. "Theosis as a Subject of Finnish Luther Research." *Pro Ecclesia* 4 (1995) 37–48.

Markus, R. A. *Saeculum: History and Society in the Theology of St. Augustine*. Cambridge: Cambridge University Press, 1970.

Mauss, Marcel. *The Gift: The Form and Reason for Exchange in Archaic Societies*. Translated by W. D. Halls. New York: Norton, 1990.

McEwan, Dorothea, Pat Pinsent, Ianthe Pratt, and Veronica Seddon. *Making Liturgy: Creating Rituals for Worship and Life*. Cleveland: Pilgrim, 2001.

McGann, Mary E. *Exploring Music as Worship and Theology: Research in Liturgical Practice*. American Essays in Liturgy series. Collegeville, MN: Liturgical, 2002.

———. *A Precious Fountain: Music in the Worship of an African American Catholic Community*. Collegeville, MN: Liturgical, 2004.

Meeks, Wayne A. *The First Urban Christians: The Social World of the Apostle Paul*. New Haven, CT: Yale University Press, 1983.

———. *The Origins of Christian Morality: The First Two Centuries*. New Haven, CT: Yale University Press, 1993.

Meland, Bernard E. "Faith and the Formative Imagery of our Time." In *Process Theology: Basic Writings*, edited by Ewert H. Cousins, 37–45. New York: Newman, 1971.

Meyendorff, John. *Christ in Eastern Christian Thought*. Crestwood, NY: St. Vladimir's Seminary Press, 1975.

———. "Theosis in the Eastern Christian Tradition." In *Christian Spirituality III: Post-Reformation and Modern*, edited by Louis Dupré and Don E. Saliers, 470–76. New York: Crossroad, 1996.

Millar, Sandra. "'It's Such a Struggle': Women Learning Faith." PhD diss. University of Warwick, England, 1998.

Mitchell, Nathan. *Cult and Controversy: The Worship of the Eucharist Outside Mass*. Collegeville, MN: Liturgical, 1990.

———. *Liturgy Digest* 1 (1993) 2–151.

Moore, Sally F., and Barbara G. Myerhoff. "Secular Ritual: Forms and Meanings." In *Secular Ritual*, 3–24. Amsterdam: Van Gorcum, 1977.

———, eds. *Secular Ritual*. Amsterdam: Van Gorcum, 1977.

Moran, Gabriel. *Education Towards Adulthood*. Dublin: Gill and MacMillan, 1980.

Morrill, Bruce T. *Anamnesis as Dangerous Memory: Political and Liturgical Theology in Dialogue*. Collegeville, MN: Liturgical, 2000.

———. *Divine Worship and Human Healing: Liturgical Theology at the Margins of Life and Death*. Collegeville, MN: Liturgical, 2009.
Morris, Clayton L. "Prayer Book Revision or Liturgical Renewal? The Future of Liturgical Text." In *A Prayer Book for the 21st Century*. Liturgical Studies 3, edited by Ruth A. Meyers, 241–55. New York: Church Hymnal, 1996.
Muto, Susan, and Adrian van Kaam. *Commitment: Key to Christian Maturity*. New York: Paulist, 1989.
Myerhoff, Barbara. "Rites of Passage: Process and Paradox." In *Celebration: Studies in Festivity and Ritual*, edited by Victor Turner, 109–35. Washington, DC: Smithsonian Institution, 1982.
Nelson, Gertrud Mueller. *To Dance With God: Family Ritual and Community Celebration*. New York: Paulist, 1986.
Neville, Robert C. *The Truth of Broken Symbols*. Albany, NY: State University of New York, 1996.
Newman, John Henry. *An Essay in Aid of a Grammar of Assent*. New York: Catholic Publication Society, 1870.
Niebuhr, H. Richard. *Radical Monotheism and Western Culture*. New York: Harper & Row, 1960.
Niesel, Wilhelm. *The Theology of Calvin*. Translated by Harold Knight. Philadelphia: Westminster, 1956.
O'Malley, William J. *Sacraments, Rites of Passage*. Allen, TX: Thomas More, 1995.
Osborne, Kenan B. *Christian Sacraments in a Postmodern World: A Theology for the Third Millennium*. New York: Paulist, 1999.
Ostdiek, Gilbert. "Human Situations in Need of Ritualization." *New Theology Review* 3:2 (May, 1990), 36–50.
———. "Ritual and Transformation: Reflections on Liturgy and the Social Sciences." *Liturgical Ministry* 2 (1993) 38–48.
Oswald, Roy M., and Jean Morris Trumbauer. *Transforming Rituals: Daily Practices for Changing Lives*. Alban Institute: 1999.
Oxford Dictionary of the Christian Church, 2nd ed. Edited by F. L. Cross and E. A. Livingstone. Oxford: Oxford University Press, 1974.
Palmer, Paul F., trans. *Sacraments and Worship*. London: Darton, Longman & Todd, 1957.
Parks, Sharon. "Faith Development and Imagination in the Context of Higher Education." PhD diss., Harvard Divinity School, 1980.
Patrologiae Latina. Edited by J.-P. Migne. Paris: Migne, 1845.
Pauson, John J. *Saint Thomas Aquinas, De Principiis Naturae*, vol. 2: Textus Philosophici Friburgenses. Fribourg: Société Philosophique, 1950.
Peterman, Janet S. *Speaking to Silence: New Rites for Christian Worship and Healing*. Louisville: Westminster/John Knox, 2007.
Pharr, Clyde, ed. *The Theodosian Code and Novels and the Sirmondian Constitutions*. Princeton: Princeton University Press, 1952.
Piaget, Jean. "Piaget's Theory." In *Carmichael's Manual of Child Psychology*, vol. 1. 3rd ed., edited by Paul Mussen, 703–32. New York: Wiley, 1970.
Pollard, C. William. *The Soul of the Firm*. Grand Rapids: Zondervan, 1996.
Rahner, Karl. *Theological Investigations*. Vol. 5. Baltimore: Helicon, 1966.
Raitt, Jill. "'Three Inter-Related Principles in Calvin's unique Doctrine of Infant Baptism." *The Sixteenth Century Journal* 11 (1980) 51–62.

Rambo, Lewis R. *Understanding Religious Conversion.* New Haven, CT: Yale University Press, 1993.

Ramshaw, Elaine J. *Ambivalence and Faith: A Psychoanalytically informed Approach to the Theological Anthropology of the Sacraments.* PhD diss., University of Chicago, 1989.

———. *Ritual and Pastoral Care.* Philadelphia: Fortress, 1987.

Rappaport, Roy A. "Liturgies and Lies." *International Yearbook for the Sociology of Knowledge and Religion* 10 (1976) 75–104.

———. "The Obvious Aspects of Ritual." *Cambridge Anthropology* 2 (1974) 3–69.

———. *Ritual and Religion in the Making of Humanity.* Cambridge: Cambridge University Press, 1999.

RCIA. See *Rite of Christian Initiation of Adults.*

Ricoeur, Paul. *Freud and Philosophy: An Essay on Interpretation.* New Haven, CT: Yale University Press, 1970.

———. *Hermeneutics and the Human Sciences: Essays on Language, Action, and Interpretation.* Edited and translated by John B. Thompson. Cambridge: Cambridge University Press, 1981.

———. "The Hermeneutical Function of Distanciation," in *Hermeneutics and the Human Sciences*, edited and translated by John B. Thompson, 131–44. Cambridge: Cambridge University Press, 1981.

———. *Interpretation Theory: Discourse and the Surplus of Meaning.* Fort Worth, TX: Texas Christian University Press, 1976.

———. "The Model of the Text: Meaningful Action Considered as a Text." In *Hermeneutics and the Human Sciences*, edited and translated by John B. Thompson, 197–221. Cambridge: Cambridge University Press, 1981.

———. "Phenomenology and Hermeneutics." In *Hermeneutics and the Human Sciences*, edited and translated by John B. Thompson, 101–28. Cambridge: Cambridge University Press, 1981.

Riggs, John W. *The Development of Calvin's Baptismal Theology, 1536–1560.* PhD diss. University of Notre Dame, 1985.

Rite of Christian Initiation of Adults (RCIA). Chicago: Liturgy Training, 1988.

Roberge, R.-Michel. "Un Tournant Dans la Pastorale du Baptême: I. Problématique." *Laval Théologique et Philosophique* 31 (1975) 227–38.

Rosaldo, Renato. *Culture and Truth: The Remaking of Social Analysis.* Boston: Beacon, 1993.

Ruether, Rosemary Radford. *Gregory of Nazianzus: Rhetor and Philosopher.* Oxford: Clarendon, 1969.

Runyon, Theodore. "The World as the Original Sacrament." *Worship* 54 (1980) 495–511.

Ruth, Lester. "Lex Agendi, Lex Orandi: Toward an Understanding of Seeker Services as a New Kind of Liturgy." *Worship* 71 (1996) 386–405.

Saliers, Don E. *The Soul in Paraphrase.* New York: Seabury, 1980.

———. *Worship as Theology: Foretaste of Glory Divine.* Nashville: Abingdon, 1994.

———. *Worship Come to Its Senses.* Nashville: Abingdon, 1996.

Saliers, Don E., and Louis Dupré, eds. *Christian Spirituality III: Post-Reformation and Modern.* New York: Crossroad, 1989.

Saward, John, trans. *The Scandal of the Incarnation: Irenaeus Against the Heresies*. Selected and with an introduction by Hans Urs von Balthasar. San Francisco: Ignatius Press, 1990.
Schaff, Philip. *The Creeds of Christendom, with a History and Critical Notes*. Vol. 2: *The Greek and Latin Creeds with Translations*. New York: Harper, 1877.
———, ed. *A Select Library of the Nicene and Post-Nicene Fathers of the Christian Church*. Vol. 4: *St. Augustin: The Writings against the Manicheans and against the Donatists*. Translated by J. R. King. Buffalo, NY: Christian Literature Company, 1887.
Schaffran, Janet, and Pat Kozak. *More than Words: Prayer and Ritual for Inclusive Communities*. New York: Crossroad, 1992.
Scharen, Christian B. "Baptismal Practices and the Formation of Christians: A Critical Liturgical Ethics." *Worship* 76 (2002) 43–66.
Schillebeeckx, Edward. *Christ the Sacrament of the Encounter with God*. New York: Sheed and Ward, 1963.
———. "The Typological Definition of Christian Layman according to Vatican II." In *The Mission of the Church*, 90–116. New York: Seabury, 1973.
Schmemann, Alexander. *Introduction to Liturgical Theology*. Translated by Asheleigh E. Moorhouse. Crestwood, New York: St. Vladimir's Seminary Press, 1986.
———. "Liturgy and Eschatology." *Sobornost* 7 (1985) 6–14.
Searle, Mark. "Culture." In *Liturgy: Active Participation in the Divine Life*, edited by James P. Moroney, 26–51. Collegeville, MN: Liturgical, 1990.
———. "*Fons Vitae*: A Case Study in the Use of Liturgy as a Theological Source." In *Fountain of Life: Essays in Memory of Niels K. Rasmussen*, edited by Gerard Austin, 217–42. Washington, DC: Pastoral, 1991.
———. "Infant Baptism Reconsidered." *Baptism and Confirmation*, Vol. 2: *Alternative Futures for Worship*, edited by Bernard Lee, 15–54. Collegeville, MN: Liturgical, 1987.
———. "New Tasks, New Methods: The Emergence of Pastoral Liturgical Studies." *Worship* (1983) 291–308.
———. "The Pedagogical Function of the Liturgy." *Worship* 55 (1981) 332–59.
———. "Ritual." In *The Study of Liturgy*, rev. ed., 51–58. London: SPCK, 1992.
Selman, Robert L. "The Development of Conceptions of Interpersonal Relations: A Structural Analysis and Procedures for the Assessment of Levels of Interpersonal Reasoning Based on Levels of Social Perspective Taking." Unpublished scoring manual, vols. 1 and 2. Boston: Harvard–Judge Baker Social Reasoning Project, 1974.
———. "Social Cognitive Understanding: A Guide to Educational and Clinical Practice." In *Moral Development and Behavior*, edited by Thomas Lickona, 299–316. New York: Holt, Rinehart & Winston, 1976.
A Short Catechism or Plain Instruction containing the sum of Christian Learning, set forth by the King's Majesty's Authority, for all Schoolmasters to Teach (1553). In *The Two Liturgies with Other Documents Set Forth by Authority in the Reign of King Edward VI*, 485–540. Cambridge: Cambridge University Press, 1844.
Sider, Robert Dick. *Ancient Rhetoric and the Art of Tertullian*, Oxford Theological Monographs. Oxford: Oxford University Press, 1971.
Singh, Nikky-Guninder Kaur. "Why did I Not Light the Fire? The Refeminization of Ritual in Sikhism." *Journal of Feminist Studies in Religion* 16 (2000) 63–85.

Slocum, Robert Boak, ed. *A New Conversation: Essays on the Future of Theology and the Episcopal Church*. New York: Church Publishing, 1999.

———. "A Story to Tell: Personal Narrative in the Synthesis of Pastoral Experience and Theological Reflection." In *A New Conversation: Essays on the Future of Theology and the Episcopal Church*, edited by Robert Boak Slocum, 20–35. New York: Church, 1999.

Smith, Jonathan Z. "The Bare Facts of Ritual." *History of Religions* 20 (1980) 112–27.

Smith, Susan Marie. *Caring Liturgies: The Pastoral Power of Christian Rituals*. Minneapolis: Fortress, forthcoming, 2013.

———. "Confirmation as Perlocutionary Response to Infant Baptism in the Episcopal Church: A Suggestion from Liturgical Hermeneutics." *Liturgical Ministry* 9 (2000) 72–83.

———. "Confirmation: A Suggestion from Liturgical Hermeneutics." Unpublished PhD comprehensive examination question, Graduate Theological Union, 1998.

———. "Receiving: The Act of Creating a Gift." *Sisters Today* 65 (1993) 345–51.

———. "Rites of Healing Along the Baptismal Journey: An Example and Several Principles." *Liturgy* 22.3 (2007) 49–56.

———. "The Scandal of Particularity Writ Small: Principles for Indigenizing Liturgy in the Local Context." *Anglican Theological Review* 88 (2006) 375–96.

——— [Susan M. S. Shutt]. "Spiritual Guidance: An Exploration of its Practice in the Roman Catholic Church in Anchorage and Implications for the Episcopal Church in Anchorage, Alaska." MTS thesis. Atlanta: Emory University, 1985.

Smith, Wilfred Cantwell. *Faith and Belief*. Princeton, NJ: Princeton University Press, 1979.

Stauffer, S. Anita. *Re-Imagining Baptismal Fonts: Baptismal Space for the Contemporary Church*. Videotape. 36 min. Collegeville, MN: Liturgical, 1991.

Stern, Daniel N. *The Interpersonal World of the Infant: A View from Psychoanalysis and Developmental Psychology*. New York: Basic, 1985.

Stevick, Daniel B. *Baptismal Moments; Baptismal Meanings*. New York: Church Hymnal, 1987.

———. "Supplement." *Holy Baptism*. Prayer Book Studies 26. New York: Church Hymnal, 1973.

Stringer, Martin. "Liturgy and Anthropology: The History of a Relationship." *Worship* 63 (1989) 503–21.

Talley, Thomas J. *The Origins of the Liturgical Year*. Collegeville, MN: Liturgical, 1986.

Tambiah, Stanley J. "A Performative Approach to Ritual." In *Readings in Ritual Studies*, edited by Ronald L. Grimes, 495–511. Upper Saddle River, NJ: Prentice Hall, 1996.

Taylor, Jeremy. *Holy Living and Dying, with Prayers: Containing the Complete Duty of a Christian*. New York: D. Appleton, 1851.

Tertullian. *Tertullian's Homily on Baptism*. Translated by Ernest Evans. London: SPCK, 1964.

This is the Night. Videotape. 30 min. Produced by Eileen Crowley-Horack. Chicago: Liturgy Training, 1992.

Thompson, Andrew D. "Infant Baptism in the Light of the Human Sciences." In *Baptism and Confirmation*, edited by Mark Searle, 55–102. Alternative Futures of Worship 2. Collegeville, MN: Liturgical, 1987.

Thompson, Virgil. "The Promise of Catechesis." *Lutheran Quarterly* 4 (1990) 259–70.
Thornton, Edward E. *Professional Education for Ministry: A History of Clinical Pastoral Education.* Nashville: Abingdon, 1970.
Tickle, Phyllis. *The Great Emergence: How Christianity Is Changing and Why.* Grand Rapids: Baker, 2008.
Tillich, Paul. *Dynamics of Faith.* New York: Harper & Row, 1957.
Titmuss, Richard. *The Gift Relationship: From Human Blood to Social Policy.* New York: New, 1997.
Trinkaus, Charles. *In Our Image and Likeness: Humanity and Divinity in Italian Humanist Thought.* Chicago: University of Chicago Press, 1970.
Turner, Paul. *The Hallelujah Highway: A History of the Catechumenate.* Chicago: Liturgy Training, 2000.
Turner, Victor. *The Forest of Symbols: Aspects of Ndembu Ritual.* Ithaca, NY: Cornell University Press, 1967.
———. "Symbols in Ndembu Ritual." In *The Forest of Symbols*, 19–47. Ithaca, NY: Cornell University Press, 1967.
The Two Liturgies, A.D. 1549 and A.D. 1552: With Other Documents Set Forth by Authority in the Reign of King Edward the Sixth. Edited for The Parker Society by Joseph Ketley. Cambridge: Cambridge University Press, 1844.
The United Methodist Hymnal. Nashville: United Methodist, 1989.
Vaughan, Genevieve. *For-Giving: A Feminist Criticism of Exchange.* Austin, TX: Plain View, 1997.
———. "The Gift Economy." *Ms.* (1991) 84–85.
Vincie, Catherine. "Gender Analysis and Christian Initiation." *Worship* 69 (1995) 505–30.
Visser, Margaret. *The Rituals of Dinner: The Origins, Evolution, Eccentricities, and Meaning of Table Manners.* New York: Penguin, 1991.
Vorgrimler, Herbert. *Sacramental Theology.* 3rd ed. Translated by Linda M. Maloney. Collegeville, MN: Liturgical, 1992.
Wakefield, Gordon S. "Anglican Spirituality." *Christian Spirituality III: Post-Reformation and Modern*, edited by Louis Dupré and Don E. Saliers, 257–93. New York: Crossroad, 1989.
Walker, Williston. *A History of the Christian Church.* 3rd ed. New York: Scribner, 1970.
Wallace, Ronald S. *Calvin's Doctrine of the Word and Sacrament.* Edinburgh: Oliver and Boyd, 1953.
Weber, Hans-Ruedi. *Salty Christians.* New York: Seabury, 1963.
Weil, Louis. "Children and the Liturgy: A Perspective." Introduction to *Children at Worship: Congregation in Bloom*, by Caroline Fairless, i–v. New York: Church, 2000.
———. "The Gospel in Anglicanism." In *The Study of Anglicanism*, edited by Stephen Sykes and John Booty, 51–76. London: SPCK, 1988.
———. "Liturgy in a Disintegrating World." *Worship* 54 (1980) 291–302.
———. "A Perspective on the Relation of the Prayer Book to Anglican Unity." In *With Ever Joyful Hearts: Essays on Liturgy and Music Honoring Marion J. Hatchett*, edited by J. Neil Alexander, 321–32. New York: Church, 1999.

———. "The Practice of Infant Communion." *Liturgy: Putting on Christ* 4 (1983) 69–73.

———. "Prayer, Liturgical." In *The New Dictionary of Sacramental Worship*, edited by Peter E. Fink, 949–59. Collegeville, MN: Liturgical, 1990.

———. "The Structure of Christian Community." In *Theology in Anglicanism*, edited by Arthur A. Vogel, 115–41. Wilton, CT: Morehouse-Barlow, 1984.

———. *A Theology of Worship*. Cambridge, MA: Cowley, 2002.

———. "Worship and Pastoral Care." In *Anglican Theology and Pastoral Care*, edited by James E. Griffiss, 115–31. Harrisburg: Morehouse, 1985.

Weil, Louis, and Charles P. Price. *Liturgy for Living*. Rev. ed. Harrisburg, PA: Morehouse, 2000.

Weiner, Annette B. *Inalienable Possessions: The Paradox of Keeping-While-Giving*. Berkeley, CA: University of California Press, 1992.

Weldon, Michael. *A Struggle for Holy Ground: Reconciliation and the Rites of Parish Closure*. Collegeville, MN: Liturgical, 2004.

Wesley, Charles, and John Wesley. *A Rapture of Praise: Hymns of John and Charles Wesley*. Edited by H. A. Hodges and A. M. Allchin. London: Hodder & Stoughton, 1968.

Wesley, John. *A Plain Account of Christian Perfection*. 1759–1761. Peterborough, UK: Epworth, 1997.

Whitaker, E. C. *Documents of the Baptismal Liturgy*. Alcuin Club 42. 2nd ed. London: SPCK, 1970.

———. *Sacramental Initiation Complete in Baptism*. Bramcote, Nottingham: Grove, 1975.

White, James F. *Documents of Christian Worship: Descriptive and Interpretive Sources*. Louisville, KY: Westminster/John Knox, 1992.

———. *Protestant Worship: Traditions in Transition*. Louisville: Westminster/John Knox, 1989.

Whitehead, Alfred North. *Adventures of Ideas*. New York: Mentor, 1933.

———. *Process and Reality*. New York: Harper, 1960.

———. *Science and the Modern World*. New York: Free, 1967.

———. *Science and Philosophy*. Paterson, NJ: Littfield, Adams, 1964.

Whyte, David. *The Heart Aroused: Poetry and the Preservation of the Soul in Corporate America*. New York: Doubleday, 1994.

Wilkinson, John, ed. and trans. *Egeria's Travels*. London: SPCK, 1971.

———. "Introduction: The Orient in the Fourth Century." In *Egeria's Travels*, 12–13. London: SPCK, 1971.

Williams, A. N. *The Ground of Union: Deification in Aquinas and Palamas*. New York: Oxford University Press, 1999.

Willis, E. David. "Rhetoric and Responsibility in Calvin's Theology." In *The Context of Contemporary Theology*, edited by A. McKelway and E. David Willis, 43–63. Atlanta: John Knox, 1974.

Winkler, Gabriele. "Confirmation or Chrismation? A Study in Comparative Liturgy." *Worship* 58 (1984) 2–17.

Witvliet, John D. "For Our Own Purposes: The Appropriation of the Social Sciences in Liturgical Studies." In *Foundations in Ritual Studies*, edited by Paul Bradshaw and John Melloh, 18–40. Grand Rapids: Baker Academic, 2007.

Yarnold, Edward. *The Awe-Inspiring Rites of Initiation: The Origins of the R.C.I.A.* 2nd ed. Collegeville, MN: Liturgical, 1994.
Yeago, David. "The Bread of Life: Patristic Christology and Evangelical Soteriology in Martin Luther's Sermons on John 6." *St. Vladimir's Theological Quarterly* 3 (1995) 257–79.
Zuesse, Evan M. "Ritual." In *The Encyclopedia of Religion, vol. 12*, edited by Mircea Eliade *et al.*, 405–22. New York: MacMillan, 1987.
Zimmerman, Joyce Ann. "Liturgical Assembly: Who is the Subject of Liturgy?" *Liturgical Ministry* 3 (1994) 41–51.
Zimmerman, Martha. *Celebrate the Feasts of the Old Testament in your Own Home or Church*. Minneapolis: Bethany House, 1981.

Other Resources

Associated Parishes for Liturgy and Mission, an association of people in the Episcopal Church USA and the Anglican Church in Canada, www.associatedparishes.org.
Greenleaf Center for Servant Leadership (Indianapolis, IN) http://www.greenleaf.org
North American Association for the Catechumenate, 811A Indian Trails, Carmel, IN 46032, webmaster@catechumenate.org.
The North American Forum on the Catechumenate, 125 Michigan Ave. NE, Washington, DC 20017; Phone: (202) 884-9758; Facsimile: (202) 884-9747; www.naforum.org.
Re-Examining Baptismal Fonts: Baptismal Space for the Contemporary Church. VHS Videotape, 36 minutes. Presented by S. Anita Stauffer. Collegeville: Liturgical, 1991.
Shalem Institute for Spiritual Formation (Bethesda, MD 20814) info@shalem.org.
This is the Night: A Parish Welcomes New Catholics. VHS Videotape, 30 minutes. Created by Eileen Crowley-Horack. Chicago: Liturgy Training Publications, 1992.

Index

Adulting in Christ, 59, 191, 192.
    See also Maturing in Christ
Allchin, A. M., 120–21, 123n58
Allport, Gordon, 139–41
Andrewes, Lancelot, 120–22
Aquinas, Thomas, 12, 35–37, 42, 58
    on baptism, 21–34, 108, 132, 176
    on deiformity (theosis), 58, 113n20, 119–20, 126n65, 131
    on intention in ministers, 30–31 (text-box), 31n24
    on sacramental ministers as instruments, 27–31
    See also Sacraments, as causes of grace
Aristotle, 21, 23–24, 24 (text-box), 27n16, 36, 43, 134, 141, 240
    See also Aquinas, Thomas
Athanasius, 113–14, 118, 120
Augustine, 4, 12, 14–20, 22, 35, 36, 42, 57, 75, 84, 201, 220
    on baptism, 14–20
    on catechizing, 77–78, 96–97
    Definition of sacrament by, 18, 22n4, 27, 29, 36n2, 136, 201
    Sermon excerpts from, 3, 235n4
    Struggle against concupiscence of, 68
Aune, Michael, 8, 42n23, 47n45, 178, 190–91, 206, 231, 234

Baptism
    Metaphors for, 3, 9, 17, 18, 20, 22–23, 35–36, 40, 46, 50–51, 115–16, 128–29
    Re-baptism, 15, 17
    Role of ministers in, 18–19, 27–29, 30–31 (text-box), 31
    as "taking," 9–10, 15, 18, 33, 115, 193, 213
    See also Augustine, Aquinas, *and* Calvin
Baptism, Eucharist, Ministry, 175, 193n1
Baptismal ecclesiology, 11, 21, 50, 86
Baptismal ecclesiology, realized, 61, 82, 105, 111, 119, 147, 177, 193–95, 212, 229, 231, 233
    as ethical, 125, 132.
    explained, 11, 109, 229, 236, 242
    Role of Christian ritual in, 62, 103, 105, 172, 176–77, 188, 195, 212–13, 232
    Role of ongoing conversion in, 61
    Role of ministers in, 231, 243
Baptismal ingemination. *See* Ingemination, baptismal
Baptismal process
    Catechumenal rhythm after baptism as, 87, 132n74, 177, 194, 205–6
    Christian existence as, 11, 132, 194, 206
    Flexibility in history of, 201–210.

265

Baptismal process (*cont.*)
    Principles for
        Focal person is starting point, 214, 220–21
        Church is present, 214, 221–22
        Contraries of death and life exist together, 214, 225–28.
        Paschal Mystery is existing pattern, 214, 224–28
    as thanks-gift, 195–96
    Baptism as referent is made manifest, 211, 214–15, 231–32
    Role of liturgy and ritual in, 6, 62, 103, 105, 111, 176, 188, 195, 212–13, 216, 232
    See also Catechumenal process
Baptized, the, 6, 11
    as called into the Christian mystery, 122, 130, 132, 192, 210, 229, 235, 242
    Church as, 11, 19n9, 59, 82, 94, 103, 114, 126, 177, 216, 218
    Experience of Christ in sacrament by, 6, 8, 12, 13, 20, 57–58, 108, 127, 147, 175–76, 210
    as having particular identity, 6n8
    in maturing process for ministry, 11, 58, 61, 104, 109, 171, 192–95, 200, 213, 229–30, 243
    Role of, in Aquinas, 31–33
    Role of ritual in, 177, 188, 190, 201, 210–12, 216, 232–33
    as taken seriously, 109, 111, 132, 176, 233
Becoming, 59, 102, 112–15, 122, 125, 133–34, 139–41, 146, 171, 194, 240
    God as, 239–40
    like God, 128, 212, 224. *See also* deiformity *and* theosis
    a particular kind of person or community, 58, 190, 190n59, 206
    Practice of (praxological), 193–94, 206
    Theology of human, 121, 133–34, 141n8, 142, 143n12, 143n13
    vs. being, 58, 108, 134, 135n91, 139, 141–42, 146, 206, 239, 240–41
    See also Stages of faith
Behavior, belief, and belonging. *See* Conversion, in early church
Bell, Catherine, 178, 179–85, 185n27, 190, 198–200, 210, 221–22
    Aspects of ritual as human practice, 179–84
    Misrecognized, 183, 186
    Redemptively hegemonic, 183–84, 190
    Situational, 183
    Strategic, 180–83
Bouwsma, William
    on Calvin, 39, 40, 43–47
    on maturing in Christ, 142–43
    on theologia rhetorica, 39, 40–41, 43, 44

Calvin, John, 12, 34, 35–54, 57, 108, 132–33, 134, 176
    on the church, 52–54
    Two-perspective approach to sacraments of, 37–54, 57
    Nature *vs.* right use, 44–45
    See also Bouwsma, W.; Riggs, J.; *Theologia rhetorica*
Catechumenal process, 83, 84–104
    as conversionary process, 58, 86, 176, 194
    in early church, explained, 87–95, 206
    Historic role of ritual in, 92–95

Catechumenal process (*cont.*)
   OCIA as, 101
   Reclaiming today after baptism,
      86, 96–101, 101–3
   See also Conversion
Chauvet, Louis-Marie, 5n4, 21,
      57–58, 104, 131, 196, 225
   against Aquinas, 21n2, 25n12,
      58n1, 132, 134n80
   on Christian existence, identity,
      103n50, 106, 125, 132, 134,
      196, 231
   on response-giving, 57–58, 110,
      131, 132–37, 211, 231
Christendom, 58, 59, 61–83, 72,
      85, 86, 105, 109, 117, 195,
      203, 231
   Before, 86, 87, 92, 112
   End of, 60, 61, 62, 85, 87
   explained, 58, 61, 62, 81–82
      (text-box), 85, 109
   See also Post–Christendom
Christian ritualizing. *See*
      Ritualizing, Christian
Collins, Mary, 178, 189–90,
      210n36
Constantine, the emperor, 61, 62,
      72n40, 73–74, 77, 77n59,
      79, 97
   Peace of, 61–63, 72, 96
Conversion, 19, 20, 58, 63–70, 131,
      193n1
   Change in meaning of, 62–63,
      65, 67n17, 72–79, 79–82, 83
   in Early Church, 63–72
      in behavior, 64–71
      in belief, 72
      in belonging, 70–71
   as necessary for baptismal
      ecclesiology, 85–86, 103,
      176
   Ongoing, 20, 61–62, 103–4,
      105, 109, 176, 192, 194, 210,
      243

   as radical transformation, 63,
      109
   See also Ecclesiology,
      Baptismal, realized
Conversionary process, 62, 86,
      101, 105, 111
   Conversionary rhythm, 84, 87,
      103, 130
   Half-converts, 73–78, 79
   See also Baptismal process;
      Catechumenal process
Corpus permixtum, 19, 76, 84–85,
      97n34
Cyprian of North Africa, 15, 19n9,
      64–65, 67, 71, 75, 127
Cyril of Jerusalem, 64, 87, 88–89,
      91, 100, 102, 126, 204, 205

Decorum, 40, 44–46, 47, 49, 50–53
Delattre, Roland, 178, 184n26,
      188–89, 212
Deiformity, 58, 119, 126n65, 131.
      See also Aquinas, Thomas,
      and Theosis
Doctrinal efficacy, 7–8, 10–12, 19,
      20, 22, 40, 61, 105–9, 113
   Distinction with operational
      efficacy, 191, 191n63, 216,
      235
   Reasons for historic priority of,
      105–9
   of theosis, 124
Donatism, 14–15, 17, 19n9, 31n22,
      136, 137n93
   Persecution of, 78

Ecclesiology, baptismal. *See*
      Baptismal ecclesiology
Ecclesiology, baptismal, realized.
      See Baptismal ecclesiology,
      realized
Egeria, 97–98, 204n22, 205
Engel, Mary Potter, 38n6, 38n9, 39

Eucharist
  Argument that other ritualizations are precluded by, 217–18, 235
  Argument that ritualizations may eclipse the, 234, 235, 241
  Doctrinal theology of, 202–3
  as ground of thanks-(response-)giving, 104
  Other ritualizations as grounded by communal rite of, 219–20, 221, 235n6, 241
  as part of initiation, 92, 208, 209n32
  in relationship to baptism, 125
  as ritual, 180–81
  as sacrament of unity, 234, 242
  Experience of the worshipper, 5–6, 8, 32–34, 36, 57, 61, 111, 113, 126–27, 126n62, 176, 227
    as attractive, 13, 72
    of church community, 61, 126
    in ethical living, 125, 196
    of meaning-making, 145
    Metaphors of, 46
    See also Operational efficacy and Post-Christendom

Fowler, James, 144–51, 169–72, 215. See also Stages of faith

Ganoczy, Alexander, 40
Gerrish, B. A., 47, 49
Gift paradigm, 135, 136n91
Grimes, Ronald, 5, 178, 185–87, 190, 194
Growing in Christ. See Maturing in Christ
Guzie, Tad, 132n74, 196

Hoffman, Lawrence, 5, 6n7, 107, 180, 182, 188n50, 215–16, 224

Incarnation of God, 40n12, 111, 114, 116–17, 119–21, 128, 141, 145, 211–12, 228, 241
Ingemination, baptismal, 193, 210–11
Irenaeus, 91, 105, 113, 116–17, 123–26, 127n65, 128
  on children of God maturing, 124–25, 128–29, 195
  Two hands of God in, 117, 122, 125, 127, 130, 131

Jennings, Theodore, 178, 187–88, 190, 206, 231

Liturgical theology, 5, 5n3, 6, 111, 134n84, 186n38, 189, 225n18
Liturgical way of life, 198, 200, 212, 232, 233, 243
Lombard, Peter, 22, 29n20, 106, 108n5, 190, 203n17, 221
Lossky, Nicholas, 120, 122
Lossky, Vladimir, 114n24, 122, 237, 238

Maturing in Christ, 52, 58, 59, 109, 128–29, 144–48, 169–72, 190, 192, 194, 195
  As process, 109, 116, 139–43, 185, 213
  of faith development, 148–69. See also Stages of faith
  of response-giving, 210. See also Response-giving
  of sanctification and self-offering, 194
  of theosis, 124. See also Theosis
  See also Baptismal process, Becoming, Catechumenal process, and Reconciliation process after sin
McGann, Mary, 6n7, 109n8
Moore, Sally F., 7, 105

Myerhoff, Barbara G., 7, 105
Mystagogical catecheses, 87–89, 88n12, 91, 204
Mystagogy, 63n8, 100–101, 128, 130, 204, 219n7

Nascent ritual, 185n30, 185–86, 190
Nominalism, philosophy of, 24 (text-box)
Normative meaning in ritual, 6n7, 107, 107n3, 188, 188n50, 189

OCIA. *See* Order of Christian Initiation of Adults
Operational Efficacy, 12, 193, 216, 218, 231
    in Aquinas, 21–22, 31–34
    in Augustine, 19–20
    in Calvin, 38, 39–40, 45, 157
    in Christian ritualizing, 211, 216
    as contrasted with doctrinal efficacy, 7, 11, 105–9, 124, 218, 235, 241
    described, 7–8, 61, 191
    in theology of sacrament, 57, 108, 113, 175–76
Order of Christian Initiation of Adults, 86, 98, 101, 102

Pachomius, 66–67, 81, 88.
Participation in God, 109, 113–15, 120. *See also* Theosis
Pastoral liturgical studies, 5
Post-Christendom, 59, 60–62, 82, 83, 85, 87, 103 196, 214, 236, 243
    Church in, 103, 105, 109, 119, 126–31, 176–77, 195–96, 233
Praxological becoming. *See* Becoming, practice of (praxological)

Process theology, 111n17, 141n8, 237, 238–41
Progressing into Christ. *See* Maturing in Christ

Radbertus, 202–3
Ratramnus, 202–3
RCIA. *See* Order of Christian Initiation of Adults
Realism, philosophy of, 24 (text-box)
Realized baptismal ecclesiology. *See* Ecclesiology, baptismal, realized
Receiving, 135, 135n89, 242
    as active, 45, 51, 53, 98
    as creating gift, 110, 133n77
    as creating identity, 135, 211, 242
    as creating relationship, 132, 134–35, 135–36n91, 137, 242
    as different role from giving
    in Aquinas, 28, 31n24
    in Augustine, 19
    in Calvin, 37, 45, 51, 53–54, 57, 133
    as passive, 28, 32n26
    for the baptized, in Aquinas, 32
    as submission, 125 (Irenaeus), 167 (Ricoeur)
    as tradition, 196, 200–201
Receptivity of sacramental grace, active, 37, 57, 133, 235n4
    Inner state needed for
    in Aquinas, 30 (text-box), 32–33
    in Augustine, 16, 19
    in Calvin, 37
    as responding, thanking, or offering, 111, 133, 135–36, 211
    in Chauvet, 58–59, 132, 134–35, 137
    in early catechumenate, 102

Receptivity of sacramental grace (*cont.*)
 as sign of readiness, healing, or completed penitence, 94–95, 96n32, 211, 219n7
Reconciliation process after sin, 96n32, 219–20, 219n7
Response-gift. *See* Response-giving
Response-giving, 58, 104–6, 131–38, 134n83, 176, 179, 190, 194, 213, 231
Return-gift, 110, 133, 135, 137. *See also* Response-giving
Rhetoric, 39, 41–43, 43n26, 44–47, esp.47, 191. *See also* Calvin, Two-perspective approach
Riggs, John, 37n4, 39, 40, 43, 44–45, 50–51
Rites of Christian Initiation of Adults, 86, 98. *See also* Order of Christian Initiation of Adults
Ritual competence, 188, 189, 193–213, 200, 211, 216, 224, 233, 243. *See also* Delattre, Roland
Ritual criticism, 185, 186, 190, 194, 194n2. *See also* Grimes, R., and Aune, M.
Ritual knowledge, 178, 187–88, 198, 200, 212, 232, 233. *See also* Jennings, T.
Ritual meaning, normative, 6n7, 107, 107n3, 188, 188n50, 189
Ritual, nascent, 185n30, 185–86, 190
Ritualism, 185, 196–97
Ritualization, Christian, 11, 103, 105, 178, 179, 184–85, 192, 193, 195, 205, 212–13.
 See also Bell, C., esp. Aspects of ritual as human practice
 Five principles for the creating of, 214–15 (summary), 214–32
 See also Baptismal process, principles for
 for healing, 194, 213, 222–28
 for life passage, 194, 213, 215–22
 for vocational change, 194, 213, 228–32
 in received baptismal tradition, 201–6, 209
 See also Ecclesiology, baptismal, realized, Role of Christian ritual in
Ritualizing, 11, 151–53, 179, 185–86, 187–88, 189. *See also* Ritualization, Christian
 as response-giving, 137–38, 198, 210–11
 Generative, 130, 185, 190, 200, 233–34

Sacramental principle, 106–11, 132
Sacraments. *See also* Baptism, Eucharist
 in Aquinas, 21n1, 22, 25–29
 in Augustine, 18, 20. *See also* Augustine, definition of sacrament by
 in Calvin, 35n1, 35, 38, 39–40n12, 52–53
 Function, 37–38, 37n5
 Nature *vs.* right use, 44
 Word as, 53n55, 53n57
 as causes of grace, 22–23, 25–27, 29, 37, 132
 Aristotle as source of, 23–25
 through instruments, in Aquinas, 21, 23, 27–31
 in Chauvet, 196
 defined, 22n4, 198n6. *See also* Augustine, definition of sacrament by

Sacraments (*cont.*)
  Number of, 106, 108n5, 190, 203
Schmemann, Alexander, 5, 123, 234n3
Searle, Mark, 5, 5n4, 187
Stages of faith, 150–69
  Primal, 151–53
  Intuitive-projective, 153–56
  Mythic-literal, 156–58
  Synthetic-conventional, 158–61
  Individuative-reflective, 162–66
  Conjunctive, 166–68
  Universalizing, 168–69
Stories, illustrative
  of Jerry (vocational change), 228–29
  of Margaret and John (baptism "taking"), 8–9, 48, 115
  of Patricia (healing), 222–23, 226
Symbol, 22, 22n3, 93, 102, 144, 152, 156, 189, 196, 198–99, 198n6, 226, 237
  Broken, 164, 183
  as catechesis, 102, 205
  Clergy and monastics as, 107
  Ecclesia (the baptized) as, 222
  Maturing relationship to, 148, 150, 152, 153–55, 157, 160, 163, 165–66, 171, 215
  as mediating the numinous, 133
  in ritualizing, 180, 183, 186, 186n32, 195, 196, 198, 231, 234
  Sacrament as, 50, 52, 91, 107. See also Chauvet, L–M.
Symbolization, 62, 92, 93, 152, 160, 198n5, 215
Types of
  Archetypal or dominant, 198, 226
  Local or instrumental, 198n5, 199, 226
  See also Stages of Faith
Symbolic competence, 199, 200, 212, 243
Symbolic exchange, 135. See also Receiving, as creating identity, relationship

Theologia rhetorica, 40n14, 41, 41n16
  Calvin's theology of sacrament as, 40–47
Theopoeisis, 58, 112, 114, 131, 210, 243. See also Athanasius *and* Theosis
Theopoetic rhythm, 195
Theosis, 58, 112–26, 126n65, 106, 131, 224, 241
  explained, 104, 112, 125, 191
  as process of spiritual maturing, 105, 112, 124–25, 130–31, 176, 194–95, 241
  as related to baptism, 106, 125, 128, 131, 205, 210, 222
  Role in contemporary conversion of, 126, 210, 222, 224
  Theology of, 111–26, 119n.46, 131
  See also Andrewes, L., Ingemination, *and* Irenaeus
Thomas Aquinas. See Aquinas, Thomas
Tickle, Phyllis, 60
Traditores, 14–15, 17
Two hands of God. See Irenaeus, Two hands of God

Vatican Council II, 3, 5n4, 12, 86, 189, 234

www.ingramcontent.com/pod-product-compliance
Lightning Source LLC
Chambersburg PA
CBHW071242230426
43668CB00011B/1554